Turtle Mountain Chippewa Pembina Band 1865-1892

**Annuity Payments 1865, 1868, 1869, 1870, 1871, 1872, 1873, 1874
Turtle Mountain Agency Census 1884, 1885, 1886, 1887, 1888, 1889,
1890, 1892**

Gail Morin

© 1999
© 2016 Revised

Sources used:

National Archives and Records Administration; Item 263 Pembina; Item 294, 2 volumes; Pembina Indians Pay Roll and Annuity Payments, 1865, 1868, 1869, 1870, 1871, 1872, 1873, 1874

National Archives Microfilm Publications; Microcopy No. 599; Indian Census Rolls, 1885-1890; Roll 94; Devils Lake (Sioux and Chippewa Indians); Census of the Half-breeds, Turtle Mountain Band of Chippewas 1885, 1886, 1887, 1888, 1889, 1890

National Archives Records, Turtle Mountain Band of Chippewa Census, 1884-1886.

National Archives and Records; Turtle Mountain Indian and Mixed Blood (McCumber) Census, 1 October 1892

The above records were located and copies obtained by Francis Morin (1987), Mary McClammy (1993), and Al Yerbury (1998). David Courchane assisted with reading the difficult, but not impossible handwriting. Their meticulous record gathering, generosity, and assistance to this Metis researcher is greatly appreciated.

Goods and provisions 1 Oct 1868
142 pairs Blankets
918 yards Blue Drilling
132 ½ yards Blue List Cloth
1777 1/4 yards Calico
548 3/4 yards Linsey
86 Barrels Flour
22-12 Barrels Pork
300 Hanks Tobacco
25 Tea

Goods and provisions 25 Sep 1869
130 pairs 3 point Blankets
60 pairs 2 ½ point Blankets
185 yards Blue Cloth
2788 ½ yards Calico
1052 ½ yardss Blue Drill
788 ½ yardss Linsey
1 Yoke Beef Cattle
176 barrels Flour
12 barrels Mess Pork
500 Hanks Tobacco

Goods and provisions 5 Dec 1870
200 pairs 3 point Blankets
50 pairs 2 ½ point Blankets
1700 yards Drill
31 barrels Flour
80 dozen pairs Hose and Socks
807 yards Linsey
194 yards List Cloth
2 Oxen (killed at payment)
6 barrels Pork
3016 yards Prints
11 lbs. Tobacco
209 lbs. Gilling Twine
200 lbs. Cotton [...]
5 pairs Wrappers

Good and provisions 14 Sep 1872
300 3 pt. Blankets
50 2 ½ pt. Blankets

4 Wrappers
199 3/4 yards List Cloth
204 Scarfs
20 Coats
240 Shawls
1498 yards Linsey
4045 3/4 yards Print
20 Pants
2/3 dozen axes
1 Chain
1 Cow
1 Sack Flour
10 Barrels Flour
1 Single Harness
1 Mule
1 ½ Yoke Oxen
203 ½ # Tobacco
8 Barrels Pork

Goods and provisions 26 Nov 1873
100 Pairs 2 ½ Point Blankets
50 Pairs 3 Point Blankets
93 yards Scarlet Cloth
49 yards Blue Cloth
1497 yards Linsey
2000 yards Denim
4000 yards Print
25 Grey Coats
40 Grey Pants
8 Overcoats
15 Dozen Coarse Combs
10 Dozen Butcher Knives
15 Dozen Fine Tooth Combs
20 Dozen Zinc Mirrors
10 Dozen Pocket Knives
20 Dozen Wool Scarfs
916 Lbs. Pork
80 Sacks Flour
1515 Lbs. Beef
98 Lbs. Tobacco
212 Lbs. Corn Meal
37   Sacks

Turtle Mountain Chippewa Pembina Band 1865-1892

Akins, Archibald

Archibald Aitkins (x), 1 man, 1 child, 2 total, $3.00 a share, $6.00 paid. (1868 TM annuity)

Archibald Atkins (x), 1 man, 1 boy, 2 total, $5.00 a share, $10.00 paid. (1869 TM annuity)

Archibald [Atkins] (x), 1 man, 3 women, 1 child, 5 total, $5.00 a share, $25.00 paid. (1870 TM annuity)

Archibald Aikins (x), 1 man, 1 woman, 2 total, $8.50 a share, $17.00 paid. (1871 TM annuity)

Archabel Akins, father, 42; Marie, wife, 42; Madeline, daughter, 17; Larose, daughter, 12; John, son, 10; Josephine, daughter, 8; Antoine, son, 6; Margurete, 3; (June 1885), Marie, daughter, 6 months; one DB shot gun. (1884-TMC)

#167-175; Archibald Akins, father, male, 43; Marie, wife, female, 38; Madeleine, daughter, female, 18; Larose, daughter, female, 13; John, son, male, 11; Josephine, daughter, female, 9; Antoine, male, 7; Marguerite, daughter, female, 4; Marie, daughter, female, 6 months. (1885-TMC)

#132-141; Archibel Akins, father, male, 44; Marie, wife, female, 44; Alexandre, son, male, 24; Madelina, daughter, female, 19; La Rose, daughter, female, 14; John, son, male, 12; Josephine, daughter, female, 10; Antoine, son, male, 8; Marguerite, daughter, female, 5; Marie, daughter, female, 2. (1886-TMC)

#10-18; Archibald Aiken, father, 45; Marie, wife, 45; Madaleine, daughter, 19; Larose, daughter, 15; John, son, 13; Josephine, daughter, 11; Antoine, son, 9; Marguerite, daughter, 6; Marie, daughter, 9. (1887-TMC)

#11-18; Archibault Aiken, father, 46; Marie, wife, 45; Larose, daughter, 17; John, son, 14; Josephine, daughter, 11; Antoine, son, 9; Margaret, daughter, 7; Juliene, daughter, 5. (1888-TMC)

#21-29; Archibault Aiken, male, father, 47; Marie, female, wife, 46; Alexander, male, son, 26; John, male, son, 14; Antoine, male, son, 10; Marie Rose, female, daughter, 17; Josephine, female, daughter, 12; Marguerite, female, daughter, 8; Julia, female, daughter, 5. (1889-TMC)

#21-27; Archibauld Aiken, male, father, 49; Marie, female, mother, 48; Alexander, male, son, 28; John, male, son, 14; Josephine, female, daughter, 12; Margaret, female, daughter, 9; Julia, female, daughter, 7. (1890-TMC)

Family 1; #1-7; Archibalt Aikin, male, father, 50, mixed bloods on reservation; Marie, female, wife, 50; John, male, son, 18; Josephine, female, daughter, 16; Margaret, female, daughter, 12; Julien, female, daughter, 10; Alexander, male, son, 30. (1892-TMC)

Allard, Michael

#47-54; Michael Alard, male, father, 47; Betsy, female, wife, 45; Joseph, male, son, 15; Alexis, male, son, 13; Mary Jane, female, daughter, 11; John, male, son, 9; Ambroise, male, son, 4; Alexander, male, son, 2. (1889-TMC)

#44-51; Michael Allard, male, father, 53; Betsy, female, mother, 46; Joseph, male, son, 17; Ezear, male, son, 13; Marie Virginie, female, daughter, 11; John, male, son, 10; Ambroise, male, son, 5; Alexander, male, son, 4. (1890-TMC)

Allery/Allary

Allery, Abraham

#851-853; Abraham Allery, father, male, 30; Mary, wife, female, 27; Joseph, son, male, 3. (1886-TMC)

Family 25; #93-97; Abraham Allery, male, father, 35, mixed bloods on reservation; Margarett (Mary), female, wife, 42; Louis Phillip, male, son, 9; Marie Rose, female, daughter, 6; Margarett, female, daughter, 4. (1892-TMC)

Allery, Andrew

Family 7; #34-37; Andrew Allery, sr., male, father, 66, mixed bloods in vicinity of reservation; Marie, female, wife, 63; Louise, female, daughter, 22; Josephine, female, daughter, 20. (1892-TMC)

Allery, Andrew J.

Family 6; 25-33; Andrew J. Allery, male, father, 49, mixed bloods in vicinity of reservation; Jossett, female, wife, 39; Batrice, male, son, 19; Alphonsin, female, daughter, 16; William, male, son, 14; Jean Marie, male, son, 11; Margaret, female, daughter, 8; Viriginie, female, daughter, 7; Elizabeth, female, daughter, 3. (1892-TMC)

Allery, Antoine

#94-99; Antoine Allery, male, father, 50; Julia, female, wife, 50; Olivier, male, son, 19; Pierre, male, son, 16; John, male, son, 14; Joseph, male, son, 4. (1889-TMC)

#86-92; Antoine Allery, male, father, 53; Julia, female, mother, 55; Olivier, male, son, 21; Pierre, male, son, 18; John, male, son, 15; Joseph, male, son, 7; Emerize, female, daughter, 3. (1890-TMC)

Allery, Baptist

Family 2; #8-11; Baptist Allery, male, father, 38, mixed bloods in vicinity of reservation; Mary, female, wife, 31; Gabriel, male, son, 6; Julia, female, daughter, 2. (1892-TMC)

Allery, Baptiste

#120-121; Baptiste Allery, male, father, 28; Judy, female, mother, 18. (1890-TMC)

Allery, Francois

#85-93; Francois Allery, male, father, 64; Charlotte, female, wife, 59; Madalain, female, daughter, 37; Adele, female, daughter, 15; Michael, male, son, 13; Marie, female, daughter, 9; Clemence, female, granddaughter, 17; Marie, female, granddaughter, 11; Moses, male, grandson, 4. (1889-TMC)

#78-85; F. H. Allery, male, father, 65; Charlotte, female, mother, 62; Madelaine, female, daughter, 37; Adele, female, daughter, 15; Michael, male, son, 18; Marie Emily, female, daughter, 7; Marie, female, daughter, 11; Moses, male, son, 5. (1890-TMC)

Allery, Francois

#100-102; Francois Allery, male, father, 26; Frederick, male, son, 4; Margaret, female, daughter, 2. (1889-TMC)

#93-96; Francois Allery, male, father, 22; Elize, female, mother, 18; Mareretta, female, daughter, 3; Frederick, male, son, 6. (1890-TMC)

Allery, Joseph

Joseph Allery, father, 22; Marurete, wife, 19; Joseph, son, 2. (November 1886-TMC)

Family 4, #21-26; Margarett Allery, female, wife, 25, mixed bloods on reservation; Joseph, male, husband, 30; Joseph, male, son, 7; Isidore, male, son, 5; Louis, male, son, 2; Margarett, female, daughter, 2 months. (1892-TMC)Allary, Louis

#25-31; Male, father, 33; Marie, female, wife, 27; Marie, female, daughter, 12; Harriet, female, daughter, 9; Simon, male, son, 8; Joseph, male, son, 5; Eugene, male, son, 3. (1889-TMC-off)

Allery, Michel

#114-117; Michel Allery, father, male, 71; Marie, wife, female, 67; Ellen, daughter, female, 31; Joseph, grandson, male, 7. (1885-TMC)

#750-756; Michael Henry, father, male, 72; Marie, wife, female, 68; Ellen, daughter, female, 32; Joseph, adopted son, male, 8; Rosine, granddaughter, female, 5; Virginie, granddaughter, female, 4; Marie, granddaughter, female, 2. (1886-TMC)

Michael Allery, father, 68; Mary, wife, 60; Rosie, daughter, 7; Virginie, daughter, 3; Marie, daughter, 3; Ellen, (mother of children), daughter, 30; Henry, adopted son, 7. (28 May 1887-TMC)

#32-35; Michael Allary, male, father, 70; Maria, female, wife, 60; Pierre, male, son, 29; Rosin, female, granddaughter, 13. (1889-TMC-off)

Family 3; #12-15; Michael Allery, male, father, 77; mixed bloods in vicinity of reservation; Marie, female, wife, 75; Henry, male, grandson, 10; Rosin, female, granddaughter, 8. (1892-TMC)

Allery, Napoleon

Family 12; #60; Napoleon Allery, male, single, 27, mixed bloods in vicinity of reservation. (1892-TMC)

Allery, Pierre

#118-119; Pierre Allery, father, male, 29; Marie Rose, wife, female, 23. (1885-TMC)

#757-758; Pierre Henry, father, male, 30; Marie Rose, wife, female, 24. (1886-TMC)

#42-46; Pierre Allary, male, father, 58; Angelic, female, wife, 55; Pierre, male, son, 12; Mary Jane, female, daughter, 14; Mary Rose, female, daughter, 10. (1889-TMC)

Allery, Pierre

#675-679; Pierre Allery, father, male, 45; Angelic, wife, female, 40; Mary, daughter, female, 10; Pierre, son, male, 9; Marie Rose, daughter, female, 8. (1886-TMC)

#78-82; Pierre Allery, father, 57; Angelic, wife, 52; Mary Jane, daughter, 13; Mary Rose, daughter, 9; Pierre, son, 11. (1888-TMC)

#39-43; Pierre Allery, male, father, 55; Angelique, female, mother, 56; Paul, male, son, 13; Mary Jane, female, daughter, 15; Mary Rose, female, daughter, 14. (1890-TMC)

Amyotte, Anastasie

#590-592; Anastasie Amyotte, mother, female, 30; Theodore, son, male, 6; Louis, son, male, 2. (1885-TMC)

Family 5; #22-26; Astasia Amyott, female, widow, 39, mixed bloods in vicinity of reservation; Theodore, male, son, 11; Louis, male, son, 8. (1892-TMC)

Amyotte, Francois Jr.

Francois Amyotte, father, 44; Celina, wife, 34; Napoleon, son, 14; Joseph, son, 11; Marierose, daughter, 8; Celina, daughter, 5; Justine, daughter, 3; Francois, son, 1; Albert son, 4 months, (June 1886). (1884-TMC)

#465-472; Francois Amyotte Jr., father, male, 45; Celina, wife, female, 35; Napoleon, son, male, 15; Joseph, son, male, 12; Marie Rose, daughter, female, 9; Celina, daughter, female, 6; Justine, daughter, female, 4; Francois, son, male, 2. (1885-TMC)

#689-697; Francois Amyotte Jr., father, male, 46; Selina, wife, female, 36; Napoleon, son, male, 16; Joseph, son, male, 13; Marie Rose, daughter, female, 10; Selina, daughter, female, 7; Justine, daughter, female, 5; Francois, son, male, 3; Albert, son, male, 4 months. (1886-TMC)

#9-15; Francois Amyott, male, father, 46; Celina, female, wife, 35; Marie Elise, female, daughter, 14; Celina, female, daughter, 12; Christine, female, daughter, 11; Francois, male, son, 8; ...., male, son, 1-1/2. (1889-TMC-off)

Family 11; #51-59; Francois Amyott, male, father, 51, mixed bloods in vicinity of reservation; Celina, female, wife, 41; Joseph, male, son, 20; Celina Mary, female, daughter, 14; Justine, female, daughter, 11; Francois, male, son, 9; John, male, son, 6; Daniel, male, son, 3; Josephine, female, daughter, 4 months. (1892-TMC)

Amyotte, Francois Sr.

Francois Amyotte (Sr.), father, 66; Louise, wife, 62. (1884-TMC)

#477-478; Francois Amyotte Sr., father, male, 67; Louise Amyotte, wife, female, 63. (1886-TMC)

#786-787; Francois Amyotte Sr., father, male, 68; Louise, wife, female, 64. (1886-TMC)

Amyotte, Gabriel

Gabriel Amyotte, father, 26; Betsy, wife, 26; Marierose, daughter, 4; Joseph, son, 1; one house, 5 tons hay, 2 horses, 2 carts. (1884-TMC)

#473-476; Gabriel Amyotte, father, male, 27; Betsy, wife, female, 27; Marie Rose, daughter, female, 5; Joseph, son, male, 2. (1885-TMC)

#685-688; Gabriel Amyotte, father, male, 28; Betsy, wife, female, 28; Marie Rose, daughter, female, 6; Joseph, son, male, 3. (1886-TMC)

#1-5; Gabriel Amyott, male, father, 30; Betsy, female, wife, 31; Mary Rose, female, daughter, 7; Joseph, male, son, 5; Rosalie, female, daughter, 3. (1889-TMC-off)

Family 4; #16-21; Gabriel Amyott, male, father, 35, mixed bloods in vicinity of reservation; Betsy, female, wife, 32; Mary Rose, female, daughter, 9; Rosalie, female, daughter, 5; Gabriel, male, son, 7; Claudia, female, daughter, 3. (1892-TMC)

Amyotte, Louis

Louis Amyotte, father, 42; Isabel, wife, 42; Julienne, daughter, 19; Marierose, daughter, 17; Louis, son, 14; St.Pierre, son, 11; Adele, daughter, 9; Virginie, daughter, 7; Veronique, daughter, 4; Elise, 2; one DB shot gun. (1884-TMC)

#455-464; Louis Amyotte, father, male, 43; Isabel, wife, female, 43; Julienne, daughter, female, 20; Marie Rose, daughter, female, 18; Louis, son, male, 16; St.Pierre, son, male, 12; Adele, daughter, female, 10; Elise, daughter, female, 8; Veronique, daughter, female, 5; Virginie, daughter, female, 3. (1885-TMC)

#698-707; Louis Amyotte, father, male, 44; Isabelle, wife, female, 44; Julianne, daughter, female, 21; Marie Rose, daughter, female, 19; Louis, son, male, 16; St.Pierre, son, male, 13; Adelle, daughter, female, 11; Virginia, daughter, female, 9; Veronique, daughter, female, 6; Eliza, daughter, female, 4. (1886-TMC)

#16-24; Louis Amyott, male, father, 45; Isabel, female, wife, 45; Louis, male, son, 18; Peter, male, son, 15; Adelin, female, daughter, 13; Adel, female, daughter, 11; Veronica, female, daughter, 8; Virginie, female, daughter, 6; Laura, female, daughter, 3. (1889-TMC-off)

Family 1, #1-7; Louis Amyott, male, father, 50, mixed bloods in vicinity of reservation; Isabell, female, wife, 50; Peter, male, son, 20; Adelain, female, daughter, 16; Adel, female, daughter, 14; Veronica, female, daughter, 12; Virginie, female, daughter, 10. (1892-TMC)

Amyott, Louis

Family 13; #61-62; Louis Amoyott, jr., male, father, 22, mixed bloods in vicinity of reservation; Marie, female, wife, 19. (1892-TMC)

Azure, Adelaide

Deleaide Azure (x), 1 woman, 2 girls, 3 total, $5.00 a share, $15.00 total. (1869 TM annuity)

Delaide Azure (x), 1 man, 1 total, $10.50 a share, $10.50 paid. (1872 TM annuity)

Azure, Agathe

Agat Azure (x), 1 woman, 1 total, $3.00 a share, $3.00 paid. (1868 TM annuity)

Azure, Alexandre

#665-668; Alexandre Azure, father, male, 38; Lalouise, wife, female, 36; Genevieve, adopted daughter, female, 13; Angelic, daughter, female, 2 months. (1886-TMC)

Azure, Alexandre

#876-878; Alexandre Azure, father, male, 29; Catche, daughter, female, 3; Eliza, daughter, female, 2 months. (1886-TMC)

#83-84; Alexander Azure, father, 33; Eliz, daughter, 2. (1888-TMC)

#40-41; Alexander Azure, male, father, 34; Virginie, female, wife, 25. (1889-TMC)

#37-38; Alexandre Azure, male, father, 35; Virginia, female, mother, 26. (1890-TMC)

Family 6; #31-32; Alexander Azure, male, father, 37, mixed bloods on reservation; Virgine, female, wife, 26. (1892-TMC)

Azure, Andre

#91-92; Andre Azure, father, 22; Clemma, wife, 18. (1888-TMC)

#116-117; Andre Azure, male, father, 23; Clemenia, female, wife, 18. (1889-TMC)

#109-110; Andre Azure, male, father, 23; Clemencia, female, mother, 18. (1890-TMC)

Family 19, #74-75; Andre Azure, No.1, male, father, 26, mixed blood on reservation; Clemence, female, wife, 20. (1892-TMC)

Azure, Andre No. 2

#122-123; Andre Azure No. 2, male, father, 19; Emily, female, mother, 18. (1890-TMC)

Family 13; #58-60; Andre Auzre, 2d, male, father, 22, mixed bloods on reservation; Emily, female; William, male, son, 1-1/2. (1892-TMC)

Azure, Antoine

Family 8, #38-42; Antoine Azure, male, son, 38, mixed bloods in vicinity of reservation; Margaret, female, mother, 60; Moses, male, nephew, 5; Joseph, male, nephew, 3. (1892-TMC)

Azure, Antoine (La Belle)

Antoine Auzure (x), 1 man, 1 total, $3.00 a share, $3.00 paid. (1868 TM annuity)

Antoine Auzure (x), 1 man, 1 total, $5.00 a share, $5.00 paid. (1870 TM annuity)

Antoine La Belle (x), 1 man, 1 woman, 1 child, 3 total, $8.50 a share, $25.50 paid. (1871 TM annuity)

Azure, Antoine (No.1)

Antoine Azure, father, 33; Marie, wife, 27; Veronique, daughter, 7; Christine, daughter, 5; Andre, son, 2; one D. B. shotgun. (1884-TMC)

#152-156; Antoine Azure, father, male, 34; Marie, wife, female, 28; Veronique, daughter, female, 6; Christine, daughter, female, 4; Andre, son, male, 2. (1885-TMC)

#245-249; Antoine Azure, father, male, 35; Marie, wife, female, 29; Veronique, daughter, female, 7; Christine, daughter, female, 5; Andre, son, male, 2. (1886-TMC)

#43-47; Antoine Azure (No.1), father, 35; Marie, wife, 30; Veronique, daughter, 8; Christine, daughter, 5; Andrew, son, 3. (1887-TMC)

#40-44; Antoine Azure No. 1, father, 37; Marie, wife, 32; Veronique, daughter, 8; Christine, daughter, 6; Andrew, son, 4. (1888-TMC)

#1-5; Antoine Azure, male, father, 36; Andre, male, son, 5; Theodore, male, son, 6 months; Veronic, female, daughter, 9 years; Christine, female, daughter, 7. (1889-TMC)

#1-4; Antoine Azure, male, husband, 37; Andre, male, son, 6; Veronica, female, daughter, 10; Christine, female, daughter, 9. (1890-TMC)

Family 2; #8-11; Antonio Azure 1st, male, father, 40, mixed bloods on reservation; Veronic, female, daughter, 12; Christine, female, daughter, 10; Andre, male, son, 8. (1892-TMC)

Azure, Antoine (No.2) (Tu Shish)

Tu Shish Azzure (x), 1 man, 1 woman, 2 children, 4 total, $8.50 a share, $34.00 paid. (1871 TM annuity)

#51-58; Antoine Azure (No. 2), father, 65; Victoria, wife, 63; Justine, daughter, 18; Andre, son, 16; Gabriel, son, 13; Alexandre, son, 10; Christine, daughter, 7; Cecilia, daughter, 22. (1887-TMC)

#47-51; Antoine Azure No. 2, father, 70; Victoria, wife, 65; Andre, son, 17; Gabriel, son, 15; Alexandre, son, 10. (1888-TMC)

#74-77; Antoine Azure No.2, male, father, 70; Andre, male, son, 18; Gabriel, male, son, 16; Alexander, male, son, 13. (1889-TMC)

#72-74; Antoine Azure No. 2, male, father, 66; Gabriel, male, son, 17; Alex, male, son, 13. (1890-TMC)

Family 12; #52-55; Antoini Azure, No. 2, male, father, 68, mixed bloods on reservation; Gabriel, male, son, 16; Alexander, male, son, 17; Virginie, female, grand daughter, 16. (1892-TMC)

Azure, Benjamin

#128; Benjamin Azure, male, 22. (1890-TMC)

Family 24, #91-92; Benjamin Azure, male, father, 23, mixed bloods on reservation; Mary, female, wife, 18. (1892-TMC)

Azure, Charles

#692-693; Charles Azure, father, male, 25; Rosalie, wife, female, 41. (1885-TMC)

#536-537; Charles Azure No. 2; Father, male, 27; Rosalie, wife, female, 43. (1886-TMC)

Azure, Charles Jr.

Chas. Azure (x), 1 man, 1 woman, 3 children, 5 total, $3.00 a share, $15.00 paid. (1868 TM annuity)

#69-74; Charles Azure Jr., father, 45; Jossett, wife, 48; Francois, son, 24; St.Pierre, son, 18; Virginia, daughter, 16; Ramel, son, 8. (1887-TMC)

#62-66; Chas. Azure Jr., father, 49; Jossett, wife, 53; St.Pierre, son, 17; Virginie, daughter, 15; William, son, 17. (1888-TMC)

#103-108; Charles Azure Jr, male, father, 53; Josette, female, wife, 57; Pierre, male, son, 18; William, male, son, 9; Margarett, female, niece, 12; Isabel, female, niece, 7. (1889-TMC)

#97-101; Charles Azure Jr., male, father, 45; Josette, female, mother, 40; Pierre, male, son, 20; Remeal, male, son, 10; Virginie, female, daughter, 18. (1890-TMC)

Family 17, #67-70; Charles Azure, jr., male, father, 55, mixed bloods on reservation; Jossett, female, wife, 53; Virginie, female, daughter, 20; Remeal, male, son, 12. (1892-TMC)

Azure, Charles No. 1

Charles Azure (x), 1 man, 1 woman, 9 children, 11 total, $3.00 a share, $33.00 paid. (1868 TM annuity)

Charlinse Azzure (x), 1 man, 1 total, $8.50 a share, $8.50 paid. (1871 TM annuity)

Charles Azure (x), 1 man, 1 total, $10.50 a share, $10.50 paid. (1872 TM annuity)

Charles Azure, father, 67; Nancy, wife, 52; Jerome, son, 22; St.Pierre, son, 17, (died June 1886); one house, one stable, 2 acres broke, 10 tons hay. (1884-TMC)

#728-731; Charles Azure, father, male, 56; Marguerite [?], wife, female, 50; Jerome, son, male, 23; Francois, son, male, 9. (1885-TMC)

#579-581; Charles Azure (No. 1), father, male, 69; Nancy, wife, female, 54; Jerome, son, male, 24. (1886-TMC)

#48-50; Charles Azure, father, 71; Nancy, wife, 65; Baptist, son, 26. (1887-TMC)

#45-46; Chas. Azure Sr., father, 72; Nancy, wife, 66. (1888-TMC)

#55-56; Chas, Azure, male, father, 73; Nancy, female, wife, 62. (1889-TMC)

#52-53; Charles Azure, male, father, 74; Mary, female, mother, 63. (1890-TMC)

Family 16, #65-66; Charles Azure, sr., male, father, 76, mixed bloods on reservation; Nancy, female, wife, 64. (1892-TMC)

Azure, Clement

#883-886; Clemon Azure, father, male, 27; Marguerite, wife, female, 22; Isidore, son, male, 3; Joseph, son, male, 9 months. (1886-TMC)

#35-38; Clement Azure, father, 29; Margaret, wife, 28; Isidore, son, 4; Mary Celina, daughter, 2 months. (1887-TMC)

#31-34; Clement Azure, father, 32; Margaret, wife, 30; Isidore, son, 6; Mary Claudia, daughter, 1 month. (1888-TMC)

#11-14; Clemence Azure, male, father, 33; Margaret, female, wife, 30; Isidore, male, son, 7; Marie, female, daughter, 1. (1889-TMC)

#12-15; Clemence Azure, male, father, 35; Margaret, female, mother, 34; Isidore, male, son, 7; Marie, female, daughter, 2. (1890-TMC)

Azure, Francois (No. 1)

#59-64; Francois Azure (No. 1), father, 33; Marie, wife, 29; Eliza [Elie], daughter, [son], 8; St.Pierre, son, 6; Thomas, son, 3; John Louis, son, 1-4 months. (1887-TMC)

#57-61; Francois Azure No. 1, father, 33; Marie, wife, 30; Eliza [Elie], girl [?], 9; St.Pierre, son, 6; Thomas, son, 4; John Louis, son, 2. (1888-TMC)

#68-73; Francois Azure, No. 1, male, father, 31; Marie, female, wife, 30; Elie, male, son, 10; Pierre, male, son, 7; Thomas, male, son, 4; Jean Louis, male, son, 2. (1889-TMC)

#66-71; Francois Azure, male, father, 35; Marie, female, mother, 32; Elie, male, son, 11; Pierre, male, son, 2; John, male, son, 4; Mary, female, daughter, 1. (1890-TMC)

Family 11, #45-51; Francois Azure, No. 1; male, father, 37, mixed bloods on reservation; Marie, female, wife, 34; Elie, male, son, 13; Pierre, male, son, 11; John Louis, male, son, 6; Louise Ann, female, daughter, 3; Josephine, female, daughter, 8 months. (1892-TMC)

Azure, Francois (No. 2)

Francois Azur (No. 2), father, 31; Julia, wife, 31; Josephine, daughter, 7; Pierre son, 4; Terrese, daughter, 3; Marie, daughter, 1. (15 May 1887-TMC)

#85-90; Francois Azure No. 2, father, 35; Julia, wife, 30; Josephine, daughter, 9; St.Pierre, son, 7; Marie Teresa, daughter, 5; Marie Julia, daughter, 3. (1888-TMC)

#109-115; Francois Azure, No. 2, male, father, 34; Julia, female, wife, 34; Josephine, female, daughter, 10; Pierre, male, son, 8; Maria Theresa, female, daughter, 5; Marie Julia, female, daughter, 3; Joseph, male, son, 4 months. (1889-TMC)

#102-108; Francois Azure No. 2, male, father, 34; Julia, female, mother, 34; Josephine, female, daughter, 11; Pierre, male, son, 8; Theresa, female, daughter, 6; Julia, female, daughter, 4; Joseph, male, son, 1. (1890-TMC)

Family 26; #98-104; Francois Azure, No. 2, male, father, 36, mixed bloods on reservation; Julia, female, wife, 36; #100, Josephine, female, daughter, 11; Pierre, male, son, 10; Marie Theresa, [female], [daughter], 8; Marie Julia, female, daughter, 6; Joseph, male, son, 3. (1892-TMC)

Azure, Frezene

Family 9, #39-39-1/2; Frezene Azure, female, widow, 34, mixed bloods on reservation; Norbert, male, son, 13. (1892-TMC)

Azure, Gabriel

Gabriel Azure (x), 1 man, 1 total, $3.00 a share, $3.00 paid. (1868 TM annuity)

Gabriel Azure, father, 42; Virginia, wife, 25; Jean Baptiste, son, 16, one house, one stable, 10 tons hay, ½ acre potatoes, one cart, 5 horses, 2 colts, one [..] cattle, 3 cows, 5 head young stock, D. B. shotgun. (1884-TMC)

#75-77; Gabriel Azure, father, male, 43; Virginie, wife, female, 26; Jean Baptiste, son, male, 17. (1885-TMC)

#90-92; Gabriel Azure, father, male, 44; Virginia, wife, female, 27; Jean Baptiste, son, male, 18. (1886-TMC)

#21-23; Gabriel Azure, father, 44; Virginie, wife, 30; John Baptist, son, 17. (1887-TMC)

#19-20 (no # for son); Gabriel Azure, father, 44; Virginie, wife, 31; John Baptist, son, 18. (1888-TMC)

#120-122; Gabriel Azure, male, father, 44; Virgnie, female, wife, 35; John Baptist, male, son, 17. (1889-TMC)

#117-119; Gabriel Azure, male, father, 45; Virginia, female, mother, 36; John B., male, son, 20. (1890-TMC)

Family 18; #71-73; Gabriel Azure, male; father, 48, mixed blood on reservation; Virginie, female, wife, 37; John Baptist, male, son, 22. (1892-TMC)

Azure, Isidore

#879-882; Isidore Azure, Father, male, 24; Carolina, wife, female, 22; Octavie, daughter, female, 2, Simion Patier [Paquin], brother-in-law, male, 8. (1886-TMC)

#39-42; Isidore Azure, father, 26; Caroline, wife, 24; Octavia, daughter, 3; Josephine, daughter, 1. (1887-TMC)

#35-39; Isidore Azure, father, 26; Caroline, wife, 25; Octavia, daughter, 6; Josephine, daughter, 3; Joseph, son, 4 months. (1888-TMC)

#6-10; Isidore Azure, male, father, 27; Caroline, female, wife, 26; Octavia, female, daughter, 7; Josephine, female, daughter, 4; Joseph, male, son, 1-1/2. (1889-TMC)

#5-11; Isidore Azure, male, father, 27; Caroline, female, mother, 28; Octavia, female, daughter, 7; Josephine, female, daughter, 5; Joseph, male, son, 2; Joseph Delorme, male, son, 6 months; Patrice Sampson [Samson Paquin], male, son, 13. (1890-TMC)

Family 8; #36-38; Isidore Azure, male, father, 32, mixed bloods on reservation; Octavie, female, daughter, 9; Josephine, female, daughter, __. (1892-TMC) Part of Family No. 8: #1105-1107, Joseph Baptist Azure, male, son, 3; Joseph Delorme, male, son, 3; Sampson Patie, male, brother-in-law, 15. (1892-TMC)

Azure, James

#76-77; James Azure, father, 23; Elize, wife, 20. (1888-TMC)

#6-8; James Azure, male, father, 26; Elise, female, wife, 20; Joseph, male, son, 1. (1889-TMC-off)

Family 10; #46-50; James Azure, male, father, 29, mixed bloods in vicinity of reservation; Elisa, female, wife, 25; Joseph, male, son, 3; Clemence, female, daughter, 2; William, male, son, 6 months. (1892-TMC)

Azure, Jean Baptiste

Jean Baptiste Azure, father, 27; Virginie, wife, 19, (died); Claude, son, 9; St.Pierre, son, 2, (died); Hyacinth, son, 2, (died); Jerome, son, 2, (died); one house, 1/4 acre potatoes, ½ acre vegetables, 2 tons hay, one mare, one colt, one cow. (1884-TMC)

#66-71; Jean Baptiste Azure, father, male, 27; Virginie, wife, female, 21; Claude, son, male, 4; Pierre, son, male, 2; Hyacinth, son, male, 2 months; Jerome, son, male, 2 months. (1885-TMC)

#250-251; Jean Baptist Azure, father, male, 28; Claude, son, male, 6. (1886-TMC)

#19-20; John Baptist Azure, father, 29; Claud, son, 7. (1887-TMC)

#118-119; J. B. Azure, male, father, 30; Claud, male, son, 8. (1889-TMC)

#114-116; J. Baptist, male, father, 31; Julia, female, mother, 16; Claude, male, son, 9. (1890-TMC)

Family 20; #76-78; J. B. Azure, male, father, 38, mixed bloods on reservation; Elise, female, wife, 17; Claud, male, son, 11. (1892-TMC)

Azure, Jean Baptist (No. 2)

#904-905; Jean Baptist Azure (No. 2), father, male, 25; Robert, son, male, 2. (1886-TMC)

#70-75; Baptist Azure, father, 39; Frezme, wife, 29 [?]; Norbert, son, 8; Ursule, daughter, 7; Moses, son, 5; William, son, 4. (1888-TMC)

#57-63; Baptist Azure, male, father, 28; Frezine, female, wife 30; Alexander, male, son, 3 months; Norbert, male, step son, 10; Ursule, female, step daughter, 9; Moise, male, step son, 7; William, male, step son, 4. (1889-TMC)

#54-60; Baptist Azure, male, father, 28; Frezene, female, mother, 31; Alexander, male, son, 1-1/2; Norbert, male, son, 11; Ursule, female, daughter, 10; Moses, male, son, 7; William Male, son, 6. (1890-TMC)

Azure, Jerome

#75-76; Jerome Azure, father, 23; Margarette, wife, 23. (1887-TMC)

#67-69; Jerome Azure, father, 24; Margaret, wife, 24; John Baptist, son, 2 months. (1888-TMC)

#64-67; Jerome Azure, male, female, 25; Margaret, female, wife, 25; Jean Baptist, male, son, 2; Herman, male, nephew, 3. (1889-TMC)

#61-65; Jerome Azure, male, father, 26; Margaret, female, mother, 26; J. Baptist, male, son, 3; Norman L, male, son, 4; January, male, son, 6 months. (1890-TMC)

Family 15, #62-64-1/2; Jerome Azure, male, father, 28, mixed bloods on reservation; Margarett, female, wife, 28; J. Baptist, male, son, 5; Simeon Herman, male, adopted nephew, 6. (1892-TMC)

Azure, Jonas

#597-598; Jonas Azure, father, male, 24; Adelle, wife, female, 20. (1886-TMC)

#38-40; Jonas Azure, male, father, 30; Eliza, female, wife, 21; Clemence, female, daughter, 1 year. (1889-TMC-off)

Family 9; #42-45; Jonas Azure, male, father, 83 (sic), mixed bloods in vicinity of reservation; Adalaid, female, wife, 23; Marie, female, daughter, 4; Joseph, male, son, 2. (1892-TMC)

Azure, Joseph

Joseph Auzure (x), 1 man, 2 women, 1 child, 4 total, $5.00 a share, $20.00 paid. (1870 TM annuity)

Azure, Joseph (No. 1)

Joseph Azure (No. 1), father, 76; Josephte, wife, 70; Antoine, son, 26; Charles, son, 24; Jonas, son, 22; Octavie, daughter, 20; Virginie Cross, adopted daughter, 16. (1884-TMC)

#694-699; Joseph Azure, father, male, 77; Josephte, wife, female, 71; Antoine, son, male, 27; Jonas, son, male, 23; Octavie, daughter, female, 21; Virginie Cross, adopted daughter, female, 17. (1885-TMC)

#524-527; Joseph Azure (No. 1), father, male, 78; Josepht, wife, female, 73; Antoine, son, male, 28; Virginia Cross, adopted daughter, female, 18. (1886-TMC)

#36-37; Mrs. Joseph Azure, female, mother, 70; Antoine, male, son, 40. (1889-TMC-off)

Azure, Joseph (No. 2)

Joseph Azure (x), 1 man, 1 woman, 7 children, 9 total, $3.00 a share, $27.00 paid. (1868 TM annuity)

Josa Auzure (x), 4 men, 4 women, 1 child, 7 total, $5.00 a share, $35.00 paid. (1870 TM annuity)

#887-892; Joseph Azure (No. 2), father, male, 50; Angelic, wife, female, 48; Benjamin, son, male, 18; Marie, daughter, female, 17; Ambroise, son, male, 8; Gabriel, son, male, 7. (1886-TMC)

#27-34; Joseph Azure, father, 63; Angelic, wife, 49; Benjamin, son, 19; Theodesia, daughter, 15; Ambroise, son, 11; Gabriel, son, 8; Thathilt, niece, 6; Elizabeth, niece, 1. (1887-TMC)

#24-30; Joseph Azure, father, 58; Angelic, wife, 51; Benjamin, son, 18; Theodisie, daughter, 17; Ambroise, son, 12; Gabriel, son, 8; Elizabeth, 7, niece. (1888-TMC)

#15-20; Joseph Azure, male, father, 62; Angelique, female, wife, 56; Benjamin, male, son, 20; Ambroise, male, son, 14; Gabriel, male, son, 11; Elize, female, granddaughter, 3. (1889-TMC)

#16-20; Joseph Azure, male, father, 63; Angelique, female, mother, 57; Ambroise, male, son, 15; Gabriel, male, son, 12; Elize, female, daughter, 4. (1890-TMC)

Family 5, #27-30; Joseph Azure, male, father, 64, mixed bloods on reservation; Angelique, female, wife, 50; Ambroise,male, son, 18; Elize, female, daughter, 13. (1892-TMC)

Azure, Joseph (No. 3)

#893-895; Joseph Azure (No. 3), father, male, 27; Marie, wife, female, 24; Mary Jane, daughter, female, 7. (1886-TMC)

Azure, Joseph

#77-78; Joseph Azure, father, 23; Elize, wife, 20. (1887-TMC)

Azure, Mrs. Joseph

Mrs. Joseph Azzure (x), 1 woman, 1 child, 2 total, $8.50 a share, $17.00 paid. (1871 TM annuity)

Azure, Louis Bruno

#65-68; Louis Bruno Azure, father, 24; Madaleine, wife, 27; Justine, daughter, 5; Moses, son, 3. (1887-TMC)

#52-56; Madalein Azure, mother, 25; (Husband in prison); Justine, daughter, 5; Moses, son, 3; Marie St.Ann, daughter, 1; Marie, daughter, 9 months. (1888-TMC)

#78-81; Madalaine Azure, female, mother, 29; Justine, female, daughter, 7; Moses, male, son, 5; Marie St.Ann, female, daughter, 1. (1889-TMC)

#75-77; Madeleine Azure, female, mother, 31; Justine, female, daughter, 8; Moses, male, son, 6. (1890-TMC)

Family 22, #82-86; Bruno Azure, male, father, 29, mixed bloods on reservation; Madalain, female, wife, 33; Justin, female, daughter, 10; Moses, male, son, 6; Baptist, male, son, 2. (1892-TMC)

Azure, Marguerite

Marguerite Azure, mother, 25; Joseph, son, 1; Susan, daughter, 8 months. (1884-TMC)

#11-13, Marguerite Azure, mother, female, 26; Joseph, son, male, 2; Susanne, daughter, female, 1 month. (1885-TMC)

#93-95; Marguerite Azure, mother, female, 27; Joseph, son, male, 3; Susan, daughter, female, 1. (1886-TMC)

Family 7, #33-35, Margaret Azure, female, widow, 29, mixed bloods on reservation; Isidor, male, son, 9; Clodel, female, daughter, 5. (1892-TMC)

Azure, Marie

Madam Auzure (x), 1 woman, 11 children, 12 total, $3.00 a share, $36.00 paid. (1868 TM annuity)

#59-61; Widow Azure, mother, female, 66; Julienne, daughter, female, 24; Andre, son, male, 19. (1885-TMC)

#23-25; Widow Azure, mother, female, 67; Julianne, daughter, female, 25; Andre, son, male, 20. (1886-TMC)

#24-26; Widow Azure, mother, 68; Andre, son, 21; Julienne, daughter, 26. (1887-TMC)

#31-23; Charlotte Azure [Marthe ?], widow, 69; Claude [grandson], 8; Julienne, daughter, 28. (1888-TMC)

#82-84; Mary Azure, female, widow, 60; Juliane, female, daughter, 25; Frederick, male, grandson, 5. (1889-TMC)

#111-113; Marie Azure, female, mother, 69; Julia, female, daughter, 22; Frederick Grant, male, grandson, 6. (1890-TMC)

Family 21, #79-81; Mary Azure, female, widow, 71, mixed bloods on reservation; Julien, female, daughter, 29; Frederick, male, grandson, 8. (1892-TMC)

Azure, Moses

#124-127; Moses Azure, male, father, 30; Margaret, female, mother, 25; Antoine, male, son, 6; Joseph, male, son, 1. (1890-TMC)

Family 23; #87-90; Moses Azure, male, father, 33, mixed bloods on reservation; Margarett, female, wife, 25; Joseph, male, son, 7; Antoine, male, son, 3. (1892-TMC)

Azure, Pauline

Pauline Auzure (x), 1 woman, 2 children, 3 total, $3.00 a share, $9.00 paid. (1868 TM annuity)

Azure, Pierre

Pierre Azure, father, 39; Clemence, wife, 30; Domitile, daughter, 11; Pierre, son, 9; Jean Baptiste, son, 7; Fredrick, son, 5; Israel, son, 1; Patrice, son, 5; Marie, daughter, 3 months (June 1886) one house, 2 stables, 10 tons hay, one mare, one cart, 2 cows, 2 calves, one acre broke, ½ acre potatoes, D. B. shot gun. (1884-TMC)

#430-437; Pierre Azure, father, male, 40; Clemence, wife, female, 31; Pierre, son, male, 12; Domitile, daughter, female, 10; Jean Baptiste, son, male, 8; Patric, son, male, 6; Frederick, son, male, 4; Isreal, son, male, 2. (1885-TMC)

#236-244; Pierre Azure, father, male, 41; Clemence, wife, female, 32; Domitile, daughter, female, 13; Pierre, son, male, 11; Jean Baptist, son, male, 9; Fredrick, son, male, 5; Patrice, son, male, 7; Israel, son, male, 3; Marie, daughter, female, 3 months. (1886-TMC)

#1-9; Pierre Azure, father, 42; Clemna, wife, 35; Pierre, son, 15; Demojail, daughter, 13; John Baptist, son, 10; Patrice, son, 8; Frederick, son, 6; Israel, son, 4, Marie, daughter, 6 months. (1887-TMC)

#1-10; Pierre Azure, father, 41; Clemence, wife, 34; Pierre, son, 15; Demojail, daughter, 13; John Baptist, son, 11; Patrice, son, 9; Frederick, son, 7; Israel, son, 5; Marie, daughter, 2; Clemence, daughter, 5 months. (1888-TMC)

#30-39; Pierre Azure, male, father, 45; Clemena, female, wife, 35; Pierre, male, son, 15; Jean Baptist, male, son, 12; Patrice, male, son, 10; Frederick, male, son, 8; Isreal, male, son, 6; Dometil, female, daughter, 13; Marie, female, daughter, 3; Clemena, female, daughter, 1-1/2. (1889-TMC)

#28-36; Pierre Azure, male, father, 46; Pierre Jr., male, son, 16; J. B., male, son, 14; Frisk, male, son, 8; Israel, male, son, 9; Dometide, female, daughter, 15; Marie, female, daughter, 4; Clemence, female, daughter, 3. (1890-TMC)

Family 3, #12-20; Peter Azure, male, father, 45, mixed bloods on reservation; Pierre, male, son, 11; Dometil, female, daughter, 16; John B., male, son, 14; Beatrice, female, daughter, 12; Frederick male, son, 10; Israel, male, son, 8; Mary, female, daughter, 6; Clemence, female, daughter, 8. (1892-TMC)

Azure, Pierre

Family 14, #59-61; Pierre Azure, 2d, male, father, 24, mixed bloods on reservation; Mary, female, wife, 22; Emerze, female, daughter, 6 months. (1892-TMC)

Azure, Ursule

Ursule Azure, female, daughter, 11, mixed bloods on reservation; #41-44; Moses, male, son, 10; William, male, son, 8; Alexander, male, son, 3; Francois Ladux No. 1; male, father, 37. (See Francois Ladux) (1892-TMC)

Azure, Widow

Veuve Azure, mother, 67; Andre, son, 20; Julienne, daughter, 25; one house, one stable, 20 tons hay, 3 mares, one horse, 2 colts, 7 cows, 6 head young stock. (1884-TMC)

Turtle Mountain Chippewa Pembina Band 1865-1892

Baker, George

#123-125; Geo. Baker, male, father, 45; Susan, female, wife, 27; Napoleon, male, son, 2. (1889-TMC)

#129-132; Geo. Baker (white man), male, father, 40; Susan (Chippewa), female, mother, 28; Napoleon, male, son, 2; Josephine, female, daughter, 8 months. (1890-TMC)

Family 27; #105-109; Jossett Baker, female, wife, 31, mixed bloods on reservation; George, male, husband, 46; Napoleon, male, son, 3; Josephine, female, daughter, 2; Louise Ann, female, daughter, 9 months. (1892-TMC)

Batosh, Antoine

Antoine Batosh (x), 1 man, 1 woman, 2 total, $8.50 a share, $17.00 paid. (1871 TM annuity)

Batoche, Marguerite

Margarite Battosh (x), 2 men, 2 women, 2 children, 6 total, $3.00 a share, $18.00 paid. (1868 TM annuity)

Margaret Batosh (x), 1 woman, 2 boys, 2 girls, 5 total, $5.00 a share, $25.00 paid. (1869 TM annuity)

Mararette Babaush (x), 1 woman, 4 children, 5 total, $5.00 a share, $25.00 paid. (1870 TM annuity)

Baton, Margarette

Margarette Baton (x), 1 woman, 1 child, 2 total, $8.50 a share, $17.00 paid. (1871 TM annuity)

Beauchamp, David

David Beauchamp (x), 1 man, 1 woman, 2 total, $5.00 a share, $10.00 total. (1869 TM annuity)

Beauchemin, Gabriel

Gabriel Boshmain, father, 45; Margurette, wife, 38; Dolphis, son, 15; Marie, daughter, 12; Julie, daughter, 8; Gabriel, son, 7; Saintan, daughter, 5; Margarete, daughter, 3. (June 1886-TMC)

#136-144; Gabriel, Boshman, father, 46; Margueritte, wife, 39; Dolphis, son, 14; Marie, daughter, 13; Julie, daughter, 9; Gabriel, son, 8; St.Ann, daughter, 6; Margueritte, daughter, 4; Thomas, son, 1. (1887-TMC)

#139-147; Gabriel Boshman, father, 49; Marguerite, wife, 36; Dolphis, son, 16; Marie, daughter, 14; Juli, daughter, 13; Gabriel, son, 11; St.Ann, daughter, 9; Margueritte, daughter, 7; Thomas, son, 2. (1888-TMC)

#143-149; Gabriel Beauchmain, male, father, 50; Margerte, female, wife, 38; Marie, female, daughter, 15; Gabriel, male, son, 11; Marguerette, female, daughter, 7; Thomas, male, son, 2; Adolphus, male, son, 18. (1889-TMC)

#149-154; Gabriel Beauchmin, male, father, 50; Margaret, female, mother, 38; Gabriel, male, son, 12; Margaret, female, daughter, 9; Thomas, male, son, 2; Adolphus, male, son, 19. (1890-TMC)

Family 37; #151-156; Gabriel Beauchman, male, father, 53, mixed bloods on reservation; Margaret, female, wife, 42; Gabriel, male, son, 15; Thomas, male, son, 6; Joseph, male, son, 4; Louis, male, son, 8 months. (1892-TMC)

Beaver, Baptist

#669-674; Baptist Beaver, father, male, 48; Mary, wife, female, 48; Baptist, son, male, 18; Gregory, son, male, 15; Marie Rose, daughter, female, 8; Napoleon, son, male, 6. (1886-TMC)

Belgarde, Alexis

Alex Bellegarde (x), 1 man, 2 women, 3 boys, 3 girls, 9 total, $5.00 a share, $45.00 paid. (1869 TM annuity)

Alexis Bellegarde (x), 2 men, 2 women, 2 children, 6 total, $5.00 a share, $30.00 paid. (1870 TM annuity)

Alexis Belgarde (x), 1 man, 1 woman, 1 child, 3 total, $8.50 a share, $25.50 paid. (1871 TM annuity)

Alexis Belgard, father, 61; Suzanne, wife, 53; Gilbert, son, 17; Antoine, son, 21; Mary Jane, daughter, 15; one house, one stable, 10 tons hay, one acre barley, one acre vegetables, one mare, one colt, one cow, one cart, 2 calves, one cook stove. (1884-TMC)

#240-244; Alexis Belgard, father, male, 62; Susanne, wife, female, 54; Antoine, son, male, 22; Gilbert, son, male, 18; Mary Jane, daughter, female, 16. (1885-TMC)

#125-128; Susan Belgarde, widow, 56; Antoine, son, 24; Norbert [Gilbert], son, 20; Mary Jane, daughter, 18. (1887-TMC)

#126-127; Susan Belgarde, mother, 57; Gilbert, son, 21. (1888-TMC)

#126; Susan Belgarde, female, widow, 56. (1889-TMC)

#133-134; Susan Belgarde, female, mother, 60; Gilbert, male, son, 23. (1890-TMC)

Family 30; #123, Susan Belgarde, female, widow, __, mixed bloods on reservation. (1892-TMC)

Belgarde, Alexis

Alexis Belgard, (dead), father, 34; Marierose, wife, 30; Adele, daughter, 7; Josephine, daughter, 6; Jean Baptiste, son, 2; (June 1886, married to ....); one house, 2 tons hay, 2 mares, one.., one cow, two calves. (1884-TMC)

Belgarde, Alphonsine Widow

See Norbert Belgarde

Belgarde, Antoine

#142-145; Antoine Belgard, son, male, 23; Susanna, mother, female, 55; Gilbert, brother, male, 19; Mary Jane, sister, female, 17. (1886-TMC)

#128-129; Antoine Belgarde, father, 25; Julia, wife, 22. (1888-TMC)

#211-213; Antoine Belgarde, male, father, 25; Julia, female, wife, 22; Antoine, male, son, 7 months. (1889-TMC)

#217-219; Antoine Belgarde, male, father, 26; Julia, female, mother, 23; Antoine, male, son, 1. (1890-TMC)

Family 21; #90-94, Antoine Belgarde, male, father, 30, mixed bloods in vicinity of reservation; Julie, female, wife, 26; Antoine, male, son, 3; Julian, male, son, 1-1/2; Name unknown, female, daughter, 10 days. (1892-TMC)

Belgarde, Augustin

Augustin Belgard, father, 47; Madeleine, wife, 33; Augustin, son, 18; Larose, daughter, 16; John, son, 14; Ambroise, son, 12; Joseph, son, 10; Josephine, daughter, 8; Elizabeth, daughter, 6; Michel, son, 4; Philomene, daughter, 2; Mary, daughter, 1; Zobeide, daughter, 1 months (June 1886); on horse, one carbine. (1884-TMC)

#547-558; Augustin Belgard, father, male, 48; Madeleine, wife, female, 35; Augustin, son, male, 19; Larose, daughter, female, 17; John, son, male, 15; Ambroise, son, male, 13;

Joseph, son Male, 11; Elisabeth, daughter, female, 9; Josephine, daughter, female, 7; Michel, son, male, 5; Philomene, daughter, female, 3; Mary, daughter, female, 1. (1885-TMC)

#791-803; Augustin Belgard, father, male, 49; Madeline, wife, female, 35; Augustin, son, male, 20; Louise, daughter, female, 18; John Son, male, 16; Ambroise, son, male, 14; Joseph, son, male, 12; Josephine, daughter, female, 10; Elizabeth, daughter, female, 8; Michael, son, male, 6; Philomene, daughter, female, 4; Mary, daughter, female, 3; Zobeide, daughter, female, 1 month. (1886-TMC)

#58-68; Augustin Belgarde, male, father, 54; Madalain, female, wife, 37; John, male, son, 21; Ambroise, male, son, 18; Joseph, male, son, 14; Josephine, female, daughter, 12; Elizabeth, female, daughter, 10; Michael, male, don, 8; Philomene, female, daughter, 7; Mary, female, daughter, 5; Zobieth, female, daughter, 3. (1889-TMC-off)

Belgarde, Baptiste

Baptiste Belgard, father, 44; Marie, wife, 42; James, son, 16; Elionore, daughter, 14; Louis, son, 10; Matilda, daughter, 7; William, son, 4; Marie, daughter, 1; one single B gun. (1884-TMC)

#525-532; Baptiste Belgard, father, male, 45; Marie, wife, female, 43; James, son, male, 17; Elionore, daughter, female, 15; Louis, son, male, 11; Matilda, daughter, female, 8; William son, male, 5; Marie, daughter, female, 2. (1885-TMC)

#778-785; Baptist Belgarde, father, male, 46; Marie, wife, female, 44; James, son, male, 18; Elinor, daughter, female, 16; Louis, son, male, 12; Matilda, daughter, female, 9; William, son, male, 6; Marie, daughter, female, 3. (1886-TMC)

#128-135; Baptist Belgarde, male, father, 47; Marie, female, wife, 47; Jaque, male, son, 20; William, male, son, 19; Louis, male, son, 12; Mathilda, female, daughter, 14; Marie, female, daughter, 6; La Rose,l Female, daughter, 4. (1889-TMC)

#135-139; Baptiste Belgarde, male, father, 49; Marie, female, mother, 47; Jacques, male, son, 21; William, male, son, 9; Matilda, female, daughter, _; Marie, female, daughter, 7; LaRose, female, daughter, 4. (1890-TMC)

Family 29; #116-122; Baptiste Belgarde, male, father, 51, mixed bloods on reservation; Mary, female, wife, 51; Mathiel, female, daughter, 17; Louis, male, son, 15; William, male, son, 12; Mary, female, daughter, 10; La Rose, female, daughter, 8. (1892-TMC)

Belgarde, Bazile

Bazil Belgard, father, 23; Marie, wife, 21; one cart, one horse. (1884-TMC)

#245-246; Bazile Belgard, father, male, 24; Marguerite, wife, female, 22. (1885-TMC)

#171-172; Bazil Belgard, father, male, 25; Marie, wife, female, 23. (1886-TMC)

#129-130; Bazil Belgarde, father, 26; Marie, wife, 24. (1887-TMC)

#137-138; Bazile Belgarde, father, 27; Virginie, wife, 25. (1888-TMC)

#150-151; Bazil Belgarde, male, father, 28; Virginie, female, wife, 23. (1889-TMC)

#155-156; Bazil Belgarde, male, father, 29; Virginie, female, mother, 24. (1890-TMC)

Family 34; #140-141; Bazil Belgarde, male, father, 31, mixed bloods on reservation; Virginie, female, wife, 27. (1892-TMC)

Belgarde, Charles

Charles Belgard (x), 1 man, 1 woman, 1 child, 3 total, $5.00 a share, $15.00 paid. (1865 TM annuity)

Charles Bellegard (x), 1 man, 1 woman, 2 children, 4 total, $3.00 a share, $12.00 paid. (1868 TM annuity)

Belgarde, Charles

#103-104; Chas. Belgarde, male, father, 24; Virginie, female, wife, 20. (1889-TMC-off)

Family 18; #78-79, Charles Belgarde, male, father, 27, mixed bloods in vicinity of reservation; Viriginie, female, wife, 24. (1892-TMC)

Belgarde, Euphrosine

Frizien Belgarde (x), 1 man, 1 woman, 6 children, 9 total, $4.00 a share, $32.00 paid. (1868 TM annuity)

Belgarde, Francois

#522-524; Francois Belgard, father, male, 24; Marie Rose, wife, female, 18; William, son, male, 5 months. (1885-TMC)

#765-767; Francois Belgard, father, male, 25; Marie Rose, wife, female, 19; William, son, male, 1. (1886-TMC)

Belgarde, Frank

#900-903; Frank Belgard, father, male, 29; Genevieve, wife, female, 30; Mary, daughter, female, 4; Louis, son, male, 2. (1886-TMC)

Belgarde, Gilbert

#127; Gilbert Belgarde, male, 21. (1889-TMC)

Family 32; #132-134, Gilbert Belgarde, male, father, 25, mixed bloods on reservation; Sabra, female, wife, 20; Emma, female, daughter, 9 months. (1892-TMC)

Belgarde, Jacques

Family 46; #201-203, Jacques Belgarde, male, father, 23; Jossett, female, wife, 22; Jacques, male, son, 1-1/2. (1892-TMC)

Belgarde, Joseph

#220-221; Joseph Belgarde, male, father, 26; Sahra, female, mother, 19. (1890-TMC)

Family 40; #170-173; Joseph Belgarde, male, father, 28, mixed bloods on reservation; Sabra, female, wife, 20; Frank, male, son, 1-1/2; Mary, female, daughter, 3 months. (1892-TMC)

Belgarde, Josette

Josette Belgarde (x), 1 woman, 2 children, 3 total, $4.00 a share, $12.00 paid. (1868 TM annuity)

Josette Bellgard (x), 1 woman, 2 children, 3 total, $5.00 a share, $15.00 paid. (1870 TM annuity)

Belgarde, Louis

#896-899; Louis Belgard, father, male, 26; Eliza, wife, female, 23; Pierre, son, male, 2; Mary, daughter, female, 8 months. (1886-TMC)

#151-154; Louis Belgarde, father, 27; Eliza, wife, 24; Pierre, son, 3; Mary, daughter, 1-8 months. (1887-TMC)

#151-155; Louis Bellgarde Jr. father, 26; Eliza, wife, 26; St.Pierre, son, 4; Mary Delphine, daughter, 2; Juliene, daughter, 5 months. (1888-TMC)

#208-210; Louis Belgarde, male, father, 27; Eliza, female, wife, 27; St.Pierre, male, son, 4. (1889-TMC)

#213-216; Louis Belgarde, male, father, 28; Eliza, female, mother, 28; St.Pierre, male, son, 5; Baptiste, male, son, 4 months. (1890-TMC)

Family 41; #174-178, Louis Belgarde, male, father, 30, mixed bloods on reservation; Elisa, female, wife, 30; St.Pierre, male, son, 6; Baptist, male, son, 3; Bruno, male, son, 8 months. (1892-TMC)

Belgarde, Louis Jr.

#41-42; Louis Belgarde Jr., male, father, 33; Rachel, female, daughter, 5. (1889-TMC-off)

Belgarde, Louis Sr.

Louis Belgard, father, _, Betsy, wife, 46; Frank, son, 21; Augustin, son, 18; Rosin, daughter, 16; Ovelia, son, 11; Alex, son, 9; Roger, _; Elizabeth, daughter 6. (Jun 1886-TMC)

#43-52; Louis Belgarde Sr., male, father, 50; Eliza, female, wife, 50; Francois, male, son, 24; Augustin, male, son, 22; Alphonsine, female, daughter, 17; Lavila, F [?], dau [?], 14-1/2; Alexis, male, son, 11-1/2; Roger, male, son, 9; Elizabeth, female, daughter, 7; Peter, male, son, 30. (1889-TMC-off)

Family 16; #69-72, Louis Belgarde, sr., male, father, 50, mixed bloods in vicinity of reservation; Eliza, female, wife, 52; Elizabeth Mary, female, daughter, 13; Acela, male, son, 18. (1892-TMC)

Belgarde, Madelaine

Family 31; #124-131, Madalaine Belgarde, female, widow, 42, mixed bloods on reservation; John, male, son, 23; Joseph, male, son, 18; Isabella, female, daughter, 15; Michael, male, son, 12; Philomene, female, daughter, 9; Marie, female, daughter, 8; Zobiach, female, daughter, 1-1/2. (1892-TMC)

Belgarde, Marguerite

Margaritte Bellgard (x), 1 man, 1 woman, 4 children, 6 total, $3.00 a share, $18.00 paid. (1868 TM annuity)

Margurete Belgard, 115 years, (...1887?-TMC)

Belgarde, Mary Rose

#247-250; Marie Rose Belgard, mother, female, 31; Adele Belgard, daughter, female, 9; Josephine, daughter, female, 7; Jean Baptiste, son, male, 3. (1886-TMC)

Belgarde, Norbert

#225-227; Alphonsine Belgarde, Widow [?], female, mother, 25; Anna, female, daughter, 2; Marcel, male, son, 5 months. (1890-TMC)

Family 35; #142-146; Norbert Belgarde, male, father, 26, mixed bloods on reservation; Alphonsine, female, wife, 24; Annie, female, daughter, 5; Marcial, male, son, 3; Louis, male, son, 1 month. (1892-TMC)

Belgarde, Theodore Jr.

#228-230; Theo Belgarde Jr., male, father, 40; Louise, female, mother, 30; Louis, male, son, 6. (1890-TMC)

Family 38; #157-161, Theodore Belgarde, jr; male, father, 35, mixed bloods on reservation; Louise, female, wife, 31; Edward, male, son, 2; Mary Jane, female, daughter, 2; Gabriel, male, son, 10 months. (1892-TMC)

Belgarde, Theodore Sr.

Theodore Belgard, father, 60; Madeline, wife, 58; Joseph, son, 22; one house, one stable, 20 tons hay, one horse, one pr. cattle. (1884-TMC)

#220-222; Theodore Belgard, father, male, 61; Madeleine, wife, female, 59; Joseph, son, male, 23. (1885-TMC)

#109-111; Theodore Belgard, father, male, 62; Madeline, wife, female, 61; Joseph, son, male, 24. (1886-TMC)

#145-147; Theodore Belgarde, father, 63; Madaliene, wife, 61; Joseph, son, 25. (1887-TMC)

#148-150; Theo Belgarde, father, 63; Madeleine, wife, 61; Joseph, son, 23. (1888-TMC)

#196-200; Theo Belgarde Sr., male, father, 64; Madalain, female, wife, 62; Marie, female, granddaughter, 7; Louis, male, grandson, 5; Joseph, male, son, 24. (1889-TMC)

#209-212; Theo Belgarde Sr., male, father, 65; Madelaine, female, mother, 68; Marie, female, granddaughter, 8; Louis, male, grandson, 5. (1890-TMC)

Family 36; #147-150, Theo. Belgarde, sr.; male, father, 68, mixed bloods on reservation; Madalain, female, wife, 65; Marie, female, grandaughter, 11; Louis, male, grandson, 9. (1892-TMC)

Bellehumeur, Antoine

Antoine Bellehemeur, Chief Nephew (x), 1 man, 1 woman, 1 child, 3 total, $5.00 a share, $15.00 paid. (1865 TM annuity)

Antoine Bellhemeur (x), 1 man, 1 woman, 3 children, 5 total, $3.00 a share, $15.00 paid. (1868 TM annuity)

Antoine Bellehumur (x), 1 man, 1 woman, 1 boy, 2 girls, 5 total, $5.00 a share, $25.00 total. (1869 TM annuity)

Antoine Belhumurse (x), 1 man, 1 women, 2 total, $5.00 a share, $10.00 paid. (1870 TM annuity)

Antoine Belimeure (x), 1 man, 1 total, $10.50 a share, $10.50 paid. (1872 TM annuity)

Bellehumeur, Francois

Francois Belemeure (x), 1 woman, 1 total, $8.50 a share, $8.50 paid. (1871 TM annuity)

Bellehumeur, Joseph

Joseph Bellhemeur (x), 1 man, 1 woman, 6 children, 8 total, $3.00 a share, $24.00 paid. (1868 TM annuity)

Bellehumeur, Margaret

Margaret Bellheimeur (x), 1 woman, 3 boys, 1 daughter, 5 total, $5.00 a share, $25.00 total. (1869 TM annuity)

Bellehumeur, Michael Monette or

Michael Bellhemeur (x), 1 man, 1 woman, 8 children, 10 total, $3.00 a share, $30.00 paid. (1868 TM annuity)

Michael Bellehumeur (x), 1 man, 2 women, 4 boys, 2 girls, 9 total, $5.00 a share, $45.00 total. (1869 TM annuity)

Michael Belcuire (x), 1 man, 1 woman, 2 children, 4 total, $5.00 a share, $20.00 paid. (1870 TM annuity)

Michael Monette (x), 1 man, 1 child, 2 total, $8.50 a share, $17.00 paid. (1871 TM annuity)

Michael Belimeure (x), 1 man, 1 woman, 2 total, $10.50 a share, $21.00 paid. (1872 TM annuity)

Bellmere, Gregory

#131-135; Gregory Bellmere, father; 40; Philomene, wife, 38; Sahra, daughter, 13; Dion, son, 11; Louisa, daughter, 6. (1887-TMC)

Bercier, Alexander

Alexander Bercier, father, 50, (died 1885); Thibault, son, 17; Mary, daughter, 15; Jean, son, 12; Elizie, daughter, 8; Joseph, son, 4; Mary Bercier, mother, 76; 1 house, 1 stable, 5 ½ acres broke, 5 tons hay, 3 ½ acres wheat, 1 acre oats, 1 acre potatoes, 1 mare, 1 colt, heifer, 1 cook stove. (1884-TMC)

Bercier, Cuthbert

Cuthberth Bercier, father, 32; Justine, wife, 19; Jonas, son, 8; Theodore, son, 3; Pierre, son, 1; Matilda, niece, (June 1885), 5; Madeline, niece, (June 1885), 1; one house, two stables, one cook stove, 4 ½ acres broke, 2 ½ acres wheat, 1 ½ acres [..], ½ acre vegetables, one mare, one horse, two cows, two calves. (1884-TMC)

#14-20; Curthberth Bercier, father, male, 33; Justine, wife, 20; Jonas, son, male, 9; Theodore, son, male, 4; Pierre, son, male, _; Matilda, niece, female, 14; Madeleine, niece, female, 10. (1885-TMC)

#16-22; Cutbert Bercier, father, male, 34; Justine, wife, female, 21; Jonas, son, male, 10; Theodore, son, male, 5; Pierre son, male, 3; Matilda, niece, female, 14; Madeline, niece, female, 10. (1886-TMC)

#115-121; Culbert Bercier, father, 35; Justine, wife, 22; Jonas, son, 11; Theodore, son, 6; Pierre, son, 4; Matilda, niece, 16; Madeline, niece, 7. (1887-TMC)

#130-136; Culbert Bercier, father, 36; Justine, wife, 23; Jonas, son, 12; Pierre, son, 4; Matilda, niece, 18; Madalain, niece, 14; Philomene, daughter, 2. (1888-TMC)

#201-207; Corbert Bercier, male, father, 36; Justine, female, wife, 26; Jonas, male, son, 13; Pierre, male, son, 6; Philomene, female, daughter, 6; Virgini, female, daughter, 2 months; Madalain, female, niece, 15. (1889-TMC)

#203-207; Corbett Bercier, male, father, 38; Jusine, female, mother, 26; Jonas, male, son, 13; Pierre, male, son, 6; Philomene, female, daughter, 5; Virginie, female, daughter, 2. (1890-TMC)

Bercier, Euphrosine

#9-15; Fresine Bercier, mother, female, 28; Norbert, son, male, 6; Moise, son, male, 4; Usule, daughter, female, 3; William, son, male, 1; Usule Lafreniere, mother, female, 57, Joseph, brother, male, 17. (1886-TMC)

#110-114; Frezine Bercier, widow, 29; Norbert, son, 7; Ursule, daughter, 6; Moses, son, 4; William, son, 2. (1887-TMC)

Bercier, Jean Baptiste

Jean Baptiste Bercier, father, 54; Marguerite, wife, 47; Hyacint, son, 18; Mary, daughter, 15; Louis, son, 12; Madelaine, daughter, 7; Emily, daughter, 3; one horse, two stables, 8 acres broke, one cook stove, two carts, one plough, one horse, one mare, one colt, two cows, one gun, one [?]. (1884-TMC)

#51-57; Jean Baptiste Bercier, father, male, 55; Marguerite, wife, female, 49; Hyacinth, son, male, 17; Marie, daughter, female, 16; Louis, son, male, 13; Madeleine, daughter, female, 8; Emily, daughter, female, 4. (1885-TMC)

#1-7; Jean Baptiste Bercier, father, male, 56; Marguerite, wife, female, 49; Hyacinth, son, male, 20; Mary, daughter, female, 17; Louis, son, male, 14; Madeline, daughter, female, 9; Emily, daughter, female, 5. (1886-TMC)

#79-85; John Baptist Bercier, father, 55; Margueritt, wife, 49; Mary, daughter, 16; Hyacinth, son, 19; Louis, son, 13; Madaleine, daughter, 8; Emily, daughter, 4. (1887-TMC)

#93-99; J. B. Bercier, father, 56; Margueret, wife, 53; Mary, daughter, 18; Hyacinth, son, 21; Louis, son, 16; Madaleine, daughter, 11; Emily, daughter, 6. (1888-TMC)

#179-185; J. B. Bercier, male, father, 60; Margaret, female, wife, 50; Hyacinth, male, son, 20; Louis, male, son, 18; Marie, female, daughter, 19; Madalain, female, daughter, 11; Amilia, female, daughter, 7. (1889-TMC)

#187-192; J. B. Bercier, male, father, 61; Margaret, female, mother, 54; Hyacinth, male, son, 23; Louis, male, son, 19; Madalaine, female, daughter, 13; Amelia, female, daughter, 9. (1890-TMC)

Bercier, Joseph

Joseph Bercier, father, 39; Felavie, wife, 47; Melanie, daughter, 20; Joseph, son, 18; Baptiste, son, 14; Marie, daughter, 13; Margrete, daughter, 10; Josue, son, 8; Rosedelima, daughter, 5; Tobias, son, 2; 3 ½ acres broke, one house, one stable, 3 tons hay, one cart, one cow, one stove, two acres wheat, one acre potatoes, ½ acre vegetables, D. B. shot gun broken. (1884-TMC)

#28-37; Joseph Bercier, father, male, 50; Felavie, wife, female, 48; Melanie, daughter, female, 21; Joseph, son, male, 19; Baptiste, son, male, 15; Marie, daughter, female, 13; Marguerite, daughter, female, 11; Josue, son, male, 9; Rose, daughter, female, 6; Tobie, son, male, 3. (1885-TMC)

#26-35; Joseph Bercier, father, male, 51; Flavie, wife, female, 49; Melanie, daughter, female, 22; Joseph, son, male, 20; Baptiste, son, male, 17; Marie, daughter, female, 15; Josue, son, male, 14; Rose Delima, daughter, female, 7; Tobias, son, male, 4. (1886-TMC)

#100-109; Joseph Bercier, father, 52; Felavie, wife, 50; Melanie, daughter, 23; Joseph, son, 21; Baptiste, son, 17; Marie, daughter, 16; Marguerett, daughter, 13; Jesue, son, 18; Tobias, son, 5; Rosaline, daughter, 8. (1887-TMC)

#115-124; Joseph Bercier, father, 53; Felavie, wife, 51; Melanie, daughter, 24; Joseph, son, 17; Baptiste, son, 19; Marie, daughter, 16; Margueret, daughter, 18; Josue, son, 10; Rosaline, daughter, 8; Tobias, son, 5. (1888-TMC)

#186-195; Joseph Bercier, male, father, 54; Marie, female, wife, 50; Joseph, male, son, 21; Baptist, male, son, 17; Melani, female, daughter, 22; Marie, female, daughter, 14; Margarette, female, daughter, 11; Joshua, male, son, 10; Rosaline, female, daughter, 8; Adolph, male, son, 6. (1889-TMC)

#193-202; Joseph Bercier, male, father, 52; Marie, female, mother, 51; Joseph, male, son, 24; Baptiste, male, son, 20; Melanie, female, daughter, 26; Marie, female, daughter, 15; Margeritte, female, daughter, 14; Joseph Louis, male, son, 13; Delina, female, daughter, 12; Adolphus, male, son, 10. (1890-TMC)

Bercier, Mary

#95-99; Mary Bercier, widow, 78; Mary, [grand] daughter, 18; John, [grand] son, 16; Elise, [grand] daughter, 13; Joseph, [grand] son, 7. (1887-TMC)

#111-114; Mary Bercier, mother, 58; Mary, daughter, 19; Elise, daughter, 14; Joseph, boy, 8. (1888-TMC)

#176-178; Mary Bercier, female, widow, 70; Mary, female, granddaughter, 17; Elise, female, granddaughter, 13. (1889-TMC)

#183-185; Mary Bercier, female, mother, 80; Mary, female, granddaughter, 18; Elise, female, granddaughter, 16. (1890-TMC)

Bercier, Moise

#58; Moise Bercier, __, male, 37. (1885-TMC)

#8; Moise Bercier, widower, male, 36. (1886-TMC)

#122; Moses Bercier, man, 40. (1887-TMC)

#110; Moses Bercier, man, 41. (1888-TMC)

#170; Moses Bercier, male, 37. (1889-TMC)

#176; Moses Bercier, male, father, 38. (1890-TMC)

Bercier, Napoleon

Napoleon Bercier, father, 24; Emily, wife, 24; Moise, son, 2; Rose Emily (twins), 2, (died June 1885), Jean, son, 6 months, (June 1886); one house, 1 stable, 3 acres broke, 2 acres wheat, ½ oats, ½ acre potatoes, 1 cow, 1 calf. (1884-TMC)

#48-50; Napoleon Bercier, father, male, 25; Emily, wife, female, 25; Moise, son, male, 3. (1885-TMC)

#50-53; Napoleon Bercier, father, male, 26; Emily, wife, female, 26; Moise, son, male, 4; Jean, son, male, 6 months. (1886-TMC)

#86-89; Napoleon Bercier, father, 27; Emily, wife, 27; Moses, son, 5; John Simon, son, 1-6 months. (1887-TMC)

#100-104; Napoleon Bercier, father, 28; Emily, wife, 28; Moses, son, 6; John Simon, son, 3; Joseph, son, 10 months. (1888-TMC)

#165-169; Napoleon Bercier, male, father, 30; Emilie, female, wife, 30; Moses, male, son, 7; Jean, male, son, 3; Joseph, son, 2. (1889-TMC)

#170-175; Napoleon Bercier, male, father, 31; Emily, female, mother, 31; Moses, male, son, 8; Jean, male, son, 4; Joseph, male, son, 3; Israel, male, son, 4 months. (1890-TMC)

Bercier, Paul

Paul Bercier, father, 30; Frezine, wife, 26; Norbert, son, 4; Moise, son, 3; Ursule, daughter, 1; Ursule Lafrenier, mother-in-law, 49; Joseph, brother-in-law, 15; (June 1885) William, son, 2 months; one house, two stables, three acres broke, five tons hay, one cook stove, two mares, two colts, three cows, four calves, one light wagon. (1884-TMC)

#21-27; Paul Bercier, father, male, 31; Frizine, wife, female, 27; Norbert, son, male, 5; Ursula, daughter, female, 4; Moise, son, male, 2; Urusula Lafreniere, mother, female, 56; Joseph Lafreniere, nephew, male, 16. (1885-TMC)

Bercier, Thibault

#42-47; Thibault Bercier, brother, male, 18; Marie, sister, female, 16; Jean, brother, male, 13; Elise, sister, female, 9; Joseph, brother, male, 5; Mary, grandmother, female, 77. (1885-TMC)

#40-45; Thibault Bercier, brother, male, 19; Mary, sister, female, 17; Jean, brother, male, 14; Eliza, sister, female, 8; Joseph, brother, male, 6; Mary Bercier, grandmother, female, 78. (1886-TMC)

Bercier, William

William Bercier, father, 27; Madeleine, wife, 23; Zachary, son, 3; Antoine, son, 1; one house, one stable, 10 acres broke, 6 acres wheat, 2 ½ acres oats, one acre potatoes, ½ acre vegetables, 10 tons hay, 1 cow, 1 calf, 1 yoak cattle, 2 carts, 1 cook stove. (1884-TMC)

#38-41; William Bercier, father, male, 28; Madeleine, wife, female, 24; Zachary, son, male, 4; Antoine, son, male, 2. (1885-TMC)

#36-39; William Bercier, father, male, 29; Madeleine, wife, female, 25; Zachary, son, male, 5; Antoine, son, male, 3. (1886-TMC)

#90-94; William Bercier, father, 30; Madalaine, wife, 26; Zacharay, son, 6; Antoine, son, 4; Edward, son, 7 months. (1887-TMC)

#105-109; William Bercier, father, 31; Madalain, wife, 25; Zachary, son, 8; Antoine, son, 6; Edward, son, 2. (1888-TMC)

#171-175; William Bercier, male, father, 26; Madalaine, female, wife, 20; Zachary, male, son, 8; Antoine, male, son, 6; Edward, male, son, 3. (1889-TMC)

#177-182; William Bercier, male, father, 35; Madalain, female, mother, 27; Zachary, male, son, 9; Antoine, male, son, 6; Edward, male, son, 4; Alex, male, son, 9 months. (1890-TMC)

Berger, Judrick [nee Judith Wilkie]

Judrick Berger (x), 1 woman, 3 girls, 4 total, $5.00 a share, $20.00 total. (1869 TM annuity)

Berger, Pierre

Pierre Bergler (x), 1 man, 1 woman, 11 children, 13 total, $3.00 a share, $39.00 paid. (1868 TM annuity)

Berthelet, Antoine

Family 22; #95-99, Helen Bairhelette, female, wife, 38, mixed bloods on reservation; Antoine, male, husband, 38; Virginia, female, daughter, 8; Marie, female, daughter, 6; Flora, female, daughter, 3. (1892-TMC)

Birston/Baston/Beston

Beston, Charles

#53-54; Chas. Beston, male, [father], 26; Justine, female, wife, 23. (1889-TMC-off)

Family 15, #66-68, Justine Baston, female, wife, 24, mixed bloods in vicinity of reservtion; Charles, male, husband, and 27, Joseph, male, son, 3. (1892-TMC)

Baston, Widow

#306-308; Widow Baston [Birston], mother, female, 56; Charles, son, male, 20; Alexandre, son, male, 16. (1885-TMC)

#788-790; Widow Bastow, mother, female, 57; Alexandre, son, male, 17; Eliza, grand daughter, female, 2. (1886-TMC)

#55-57; Madalain Beston, female, widow, 50; Elise, female, granddaughter, 6; Alex, male, son, 30. (1889-TMC-off)

Blackbird, Margaret

Family 39; #162-169, Margaret Blackbird, female, widow, 40, mixed bloods on reservation; John Baptist, male, son, 20; Joseph, male, son, 18; Victorie, female, daughter, 14; Mary Jane, female, daughter, 10; Adele, female, daughter, 7; William, male, son, 10; John Louis, male, son, 16. (1892-TMC)

Blue, Peter and Albert

#514-515; Peter Blue, brother, male, 12; Albert, brother, male, 10. (1886-TMC)

#123-124; Peter Blue, orphan, 12; Albert, orphan, 11. (1887-TMC)

Blue, Peter

#125; Peter Blue, father [?], 12. (1888-TMC)

Blue, Margurete

Margurete Blue, (died June 1886), mother, 41; Peter, son, 11; Albert, son, 9. (January 1886)

Boisvert, John Baptiste

John Babtiste Boisvert (x), 1 man, 1 woman, 3 boys, 1 daughter, 6 total, $5.00 a share, $30.00 total. (1869 TM annuity)

Boisvert, Susan

Susan Boisvert (x), 3 men, 3 women, 2 children, 8 total, $5.00 a share, $40.00 paid. (1870 TM annuity)

Susane Boivert (x), 1 woman, 1 total, $8.50 a share, $8.50 paid. (1871 TM annuity)

Bonga, Pierre

Pierre Bonga (x), 2 men, 2 women, 2 children, 6 total, $5.00 a share, $30.00 paid. (1870 TM annuity)

Bonneau, Joseph

#95-96; Joseph Bonneau, male, father, 68; Madalain, female, daughter, 21. (1889-TMC-off)

Bonneau, Magloire

#97-102; LaGloue Bonneau, male, father, 36; Victoria, female, wife, 30; Marie Rose, female, daughter, 12; Alex, male, son, 8; Marie Jane, female, daughter, 5; Ezear, male, son, 7 months. (1889-TMC-off)

Family 19; #80-86, Victoria, female, wife, 37, mixed bloods in vicinity of reservation; L. Glone, male, husband, 37; Marie Rose, female, daughter, 15; Alexis, male, son, 12; Mary Jane, female, daughter, 7; Reylard, male, son, 3; Virginie, female, daughter, 1. (1892-TMC)

Bottineau, Angelique

Angelique Bottineau (x), 1 woman, 1 child, 2 total, $4.00 a share, $8.00 paid. (1868 TM annuity)

Bottineau, Charles

Charles Bottineau (x), 1 man, 1 woman, 1 child, 3 total, $4.00 a share, $12.00 paid. (1868 TM annuity)

Charles Bottineau (x), 1 man, 1 woman, 2 total, $5.00 a share, $10.00 paid. (1869 TM annuity)

Charles Bottineau (x), 1 man, 1 woman, 2 total, $5.00 a share, $10.00 paid. (1870 TM annuity)

C. Bottineau (x), 1 man, 1 woman, 2 total, $8.50 a share, $17.00 paid. (1871 TM annuity)

Bottineau, John Baptiste

John B. Bottineau (x), 1 man, 1 woman, 3 girls, 5 total, $5.00 a share, $25.00 paid. (1869 TM annuity)

Baptiste Bottineau (x), 1 man, 1 woman, 2 children, 4 total, $5.00 a share, $20.00 paid. (1870 TM annuity)

Batees Bottineau (x), 1 man, 1 woman, 2 children, 4 total, $8.50 a share, $34.00 paid. (1871 TM annuity)

Bottineau, Joseph

Joseph Bottineau (x), 1 man, 1 woman, 1 child, 3 total, $3.00 a share, $9.00 paid. (1868 TM annuity)

Joseph Bottineau (x), 1 man, 1 woman, 1 boy, 3 total, $5.00 a share, $15.00 total. (1869 TM annuity)

Bottineau, Joseph

Family 14; #63-65, Joseph Bottineau, male, father, 28, mixed bloods in vicinity of reservation; Marie Rose, female, wife, 26; Antoine, male, son, 11 months. (1892-TMC)

Bottineau, Pierrish

Pierrish Bottineau (x), 3 men, 3 women, 10 children, 16 total, $5.00 a share, $80.00 paid. (1870 TM annuity)

Boucher, Francois

Francis Boucher (x), 1 man, 1 woman, 4 children, 6 total, $4.00 a share, $24.00 paid. (1868 TM annuity)

Francois Bouchey (x), 2 men, 1 woman, 2 boys, 1 daughter, 6 total, $5.00 a share, $30.00 paid. (1869 TM annuity)

Francis Boshea (x), 2 men, 1 woman, 2 children, 5 total, $5.00 a share, $25.00 paid. (1870 TM annuity)

Francois Boucher (x), 1 man, 1 woman, 2 children, 4 total, $8.50 a share, $34.00 paid. (1871 TM annuity)

Francis Bouche (x), 1 man, 2 women, 2 children, 5 total, $5.00 a share, $25.00 paid. (1874 TM annuity)

Boucher, John

John Boucher (x), 1 man, 1 woman, 2 total, $4.00 a share, $8.00 paid. (1868 TM annuity)

John Bouchey (x), 1 man, 1 woman, 2 girls, 4 total, $5.00 a share, $20.00 paid. (1869 TM annuity)

Jean Bouche (x), 1 man, 2 women, 1 child, 4 total, $5.00 a share, $20.00 paid. (1874 TM annuity)

Bouvier, Antoine

#164-169; Antoine Bouvier Jr., father, 34; Elize, wife, 26; Joseph, son, 10; Elzeard, son, 6; Marie Genevieve, daughter, 4; Jean Antoine, son, 2. (1888-TMC)

#159-164; Antoine Bouvier, male, father, 32; Elise, female, wife, 27; Elizear, male, son, 7; Marie, female, daughter, 5; Antoine, male, son, 3; Henry, male, son, 2. (1889-TMC)

#164-169; Antoine Bouvier, male, father, 37; Elize, female, mother, 27; Elzear, male, son, 7; Genevieve, female, daughter, 5; Antoine, male, son, 4; Henry, male, son, 2. (1890-TMC)

Bouvier, Casimire

#69-78; Casiamire Bouvier, male, father, 40; Deliah, female, wife, 32; Sahra, female, daughter, 15; Eliza, female, daughter, 13; John B., male, son, 10; Melina, female, daughter, 8; Adolphus, male, son, 7; Clementine, female, daughter, 5; Francois, male, son, 4; Deliah, female, daughter, 7 months. (1889-TMC-off)

Bouvier, Paul

Paul Beauvier (x), 1 man, 1 woman, 4 children, 6 total, $3.00 a share, $18.00 paid. (1868 TM annuity)

Paul Bouvier (x), 1 man, 1 total, $10.50 a share, $10.50 paid. (1872 TM annuity)

Boyer, Abraham

Abraham Boyer, father, 43; Julie, wife, 40; Francoise, daughter, 16, (married 1886); Alfred, son, 14; Marie, daughter, 10; Johny, son, 7; Joseph, son, 1; 8 horses, 1 colt, 4 tons hay. (1884-TMC)

#324-329; Abraham Boyer, father, male, 49; Julie, wife, female, 41; Francoise, daughter, female, 17; Alfred, son, male, 15; Marie, daughter, female, 11; John, male, 8. (1885-TMC)

#257-262; Abraham Boier, father, male, 45; Julia, wife, female, 42; Alfred, son, male, 16; Marie, daughter, female, 12; John, son, male, 9; Joseph, son, male, 3. (1886-TMC)

#136-142; Abraham Boyer, male, father, 44; Julie, female, wife, 40; Alfred, male, son, 19; Marie, female, daughter, 16; John, male, son, 13; Joseph, male, son, 6; Alex. (1889-TMC)

#142-148; Abraham Boyer, male, father, 48; Julia, female, mother, 35; Alfred, male, son, 20; John, male, son, 13; Alex, male, son, 2; Frederick, male, son, 1 month. (1890-TMC)

Family 33; #135-139; Abraham Boyer, male, father, 44, mixed bloods on reservation; Juli, female, wife, 43; Alfred, male, son, 22; Joseph, male, son, 9; Alexander, male, son, 4. (1892-TMC)

Brenner, Christine

Family 248; #1104, Christine Brenner, female, single, 19, mixed bloods on reservation. (1892-TMC)

Brien, Alexandre

Ellen Brien, mother, 20; Theodore, son, 3; Ulric, son, 2; Alexandre Brien, father, 35, (June 1885). (1884-TMC)

#718-723; Alexandre Brien, father, male, 35; Ellen, wife, female, 26; Mary, daughter, female, 12; Joseph, son, male, 14; Theodore, son, male, 4; Ulric, son, male, 3. (1885-TMC)

#593-596; Alexandre Brien, father, male, 36; Ellen, wife, female, 22; Theodore, son, male, 5; Ulric, son, male, 4. (1886-TMC)

Brien, Antoine

Antoine Brien, father, 60; Josephtatee, wife, 50; Gregoire, son, 22; Agnor, son, 16; Adele, daughter 18, (married June 1886 to English H.B.); Baptiste, son, 11; Alexander, son, 9; one house, 2 stables, 20 acres oats, 15 acres wheat, one horse, one mare, one lumber wagon, one pr. cattle, 2 cows, 3 head young stock, one cook stove, one heating stove. (1884-TMC)

#708-713; Antoine Brien, father, male, 61; Josephte, wife, female, 50; Gregoire, son, male, 23; Adele, daughter, female, 19; Agenor, son, male, 17; Alexandre son, male, 10. (1885-TMC)

#582-587; Antoine Brien, father, male, 62; Josepht, wife, female, 52; Gregry, son, male, 24; Agnor, son, male, 18; Baptist, son, male, 13; Alexandre, son, male, 11. (1886-TMC)

#79-84; Antoine Brien, male, father, 64; Jossett, female, wife, 63; Jeannor, male, son, 20; Baptist Cline, male, grandson, 17; Alex, male, grandson, 9; Joseph, male, grandson, 9. (1889-TMC-off)

Family 45; #196-200, Antoine Brien, male, father, 67, mixed bloods on reservation; Josett, female, wife, 66; John (Kline), male, grandson, 20; Alexander, male, grandson, 10; Joseph, male, grandson, 14. (1892-TMC)

Brien, Jenoir

Family 44; #193-195, Jenoir Brien, __, mixed bloods on reservation; Marie, __; Rosalie, ___. (1892-TMC)

Brien, Theodore

Theodore Brien, father, 28; Mary Rose, wife, 22; Liza, daughter, 3; Louis Alfred, son, 1; Rozine, daughter 4 months (June 1885); one house, 2 stables, 3 horses, one ox, 3 cows, 2 calves, 20 tons hay, 8 acres wheat, 8 acres oats, one acre potatoes. (1884-TMC)

#703-707; Theodore Brien, father, male, 29; Mary Rose, wife, female, 23; Liza, daughter, female, 4; Louis, son, male, 2; Rozine, daughter, female, 4 months. (1885-TMC)

#588-592; Theodore Brien, father, male, 30; Marie Rose, wife, female, 24; Liza, daughter, female, 5; Louis Alfred, son, male, 3; Rozine, daughter, female, 1. (1886-TMC)

#89-94; Theo Brien, male, father, 30; Marie Rose, female, wife, 26; Eliza, female, daughter, 7; Alfred, male, son, 4; Robert, male, son, 2; Virginie, female, daughter, 2 months. (1889-TMC-off)

Family 43; #186-192, Theodore Brien, male, father, 35, mixed bloods on reservation; Marie Rose, female, wife, 30; Eliza, female, daughter, 10; Alfred, male, son, 8; Robert, male, son, 5; Virginie, female, daughter, 3; Philip, male, son, 1. (1892-TMC)

Briere, Angelic

#161-163; Angelic Briere, female, mother, 65; Cleophace, male, son, 34; Wm. Laplante, male, grandson, 12. (1890-TMC)

Brier, Baptiste

#85-88; Baptist Brier, male, father, 45; Baptist, male, son, 20; Gregory, male, son, 17; Mary Rose, female, daughter, 11. (1889-TMC-off)

Brieyer, Jerome

#152-158; Jerome Brieyer, male, father, 36; Eliza, female, wife, 29; Jean Napoleon, male, son, 10; Celina, female, daughter, 7; Angelic, female, mother, 64; Kitaface, male, brother, 33; William Male, nephew, 11. (1889-TMC)

#157-160; Jerome Briere, male, father, 36; Eliza, female, mother, 30; Napoleon, male, son, 10; Celina, female, daughter, 7. (1890-TMC)

Brown, Eliza

#148-150; Eliza Brown, widow, 31; George Edwin, son, 11; Susan, daughter, 9. (1887-TMC)

#222-224; Eliza Widow Brown, female, mother, 24, female, mother; George, male, son, 11; Angus, male, son, 3. (1890-TMC)

Bruce, Joseph

#156-163; Joseph Bruce, father, 44; Isabel, wife, 35; Pierre, son, 18; Alexander, son, 11; Rosalie, daughter, 10; Alphonsine, daughter, 7; Baptist, son, 3; John, son, 1. (1888-TMC)

Bruce, Rosalie

Family 28; #110-115, Rosalie Bruce, female, wife, 29, mixed bloods on reservation; Joseph, male, husband, 41; Joseph, male, son, 10; Mary, female, daughter, 7; Frederick, male, son, 3; Robert, male, son, 1. (1892-TMC)

Brunelle, John

Family 42; John Brunelle, #179-185, male, father, 46, mixed bloods on reservation; Julien, female, wife, 34; John, male, son, 12; Peter, male, son, 10; William, male, son, 8; Louis, male, son, 6; Ernest, male, son, 8 months. (1892-TMC)

Brunnell, Joseph

Family 20; #87-89, Jossett Brunnell, female, wife, 74, mixed bloods in vicinity of reservation; Joseph, male, husband, 74; Margaret Belgarde, female, grandmother, 110. (1892-TMC)

Cadotte/Cadot

Cadotte, Marian

Marian Cadotte (x), 1 woman, 4 children, 5 total, $3.00 a share, $15.00 paid. (1868 TM annuity)

Cadotte, Pierre

Pierre Cadotte, father, _; Catherine, wife, _; Alex Sinkler, nephew, 11; William Sinkler, nephew, 1; Moise Cadotte, nephew, 10; Alfred Bird, nephew, 3. (June 1886)

#106-111; Pierre Cadot, male, father, 46; Catherine, female, wife, 40; Alexander, male, son, 16; Moses, male, son, 13; William James, male, son, 7; Alfred James, male, son, 7. (1889-TMC-off)

Family 23; #100-103, Pierre Cadott, male, father, 49, mixed bloods in vicinity of reservation; Catharine, female, wife, 43; Moses, male, grandson, 16; William James, male, grandson, 10. (1892-TMC)

Canada, Alexis

#593; Alexis Canada, _, male, 22. (1885-TMC)

#710-711; Alexis Canada, father, male, 23; Marie, wife, female, 19. (1886-TMC)

Canada, Antoine

Antoine Canada, husband, 27; Celina, wife, 17; one house, 8 tons hay, 2 mules, one mare, one colt, one mower, one rake, one wago, one plough. (1884-TMC)

#572, Antoine Canada, _, male, 28. (1885-TMC)

#708-709; Antoine Canada, father, male, 29; Selina, wife, female, 17. (1886-TMC)

Caplette, Alexander

Family 56; #245-248, Alexander Caplett, male, father, 31; Dometil, female, wife, 40; Mary Ellen, female, daughter, 6; Maian de Couteau, female, mother-in-law, 86. (1892-TMC)

Caplette, Antoine

Antoine Caplet (x), 1 man, 1 woman, 2 children, 4 total, $3.00 a share, $12.00 paid. (1868 TM annuity)

Antoine Caplette (x), 2 men, 2 women, 1 child, 5 total, $5.00 a share, $25.00 paid. (1870 TM annuity)

Antoine Caplette (x), 1 man, 1 woman, 2 total, $8.50 a share, $17.00 paid. (1871 TM annuity)

Caplette, Baptiste

Batiste Caplette (x), 1 man, 1 woman, 2 children, 4 total, $8.50 a share, $34.00 paid. (1871 TM annuity)

Caplette, Louis

Louis Caplet (x), 1 man, 1 woman, 5 children, 7 total, $5.00 a share, $35.00 paid. (1865 TM annuity)

Louis Caplet (x), 1 man, 1 woman, 2 children, 4 total, $3.00 a share, $12.00 paid. (1868 TM annuity)

Louis Caplette (x), 2 men, 2 women, 2 children, 6 total, $5.00 a share, $30.00 paid. (1870 TM annuity)

Louison Caplette (x), 1 man, 1 woman, 2 total, $8.50 a share, $17.00 paid. (1871 TM annuity)

Turtle Mountain Chippewa Pembina Band 1865-1892

Louis Caplet (x), 1 man, 1 total, $10.50 a share, $10.50 paid. (1872 TM annuity)

Caplette, Modest

#155-156; Modest Caplett, father, 20; Rose, wife, 22. (1887-TMC)

#170-172; Modest Caplet, father, 21; Rose, wife, 23; Justine, daughter, 9 months. (1888-TMC)

#241-244; Modest Caplett, male, father, 21; Rosalie, female, wife, 24; Justine, female, daughter, 2; Pierre, male, son, 5 months. (1889-TMC)

#258-262; Modeste Caplette, male, father, 22; Rosalie, female, mother, 25; Justine, female, daughter, 3; Robert, male, son, 2; Marie L., female, daughter, 2 months. (1890-TMC)

Family 54; #236-241; Modest Caplette, male, father, 24, mixed bloods on reservation; Rose, female, wife, 26; Marie Justine, female, daughter, 5; Pierre, male, son, 3; Mary Louise, female, daughter, 2; Mary Elise, female, daughter, 10 months. (1892-TMC)

Caribou, Antoine

Antoine Carbo (x), 1 man 1 woman, 9 children, 11 total, $3.00 a share, $33.00 paid. (1868 TM annuity)

Antoine Carribo (x), 1 man, 3 women, 2 boys, 2 girls, 8 total, $5.00 a share, $40.00 total. (1869 TM annuity)

Antoine Carribeau (x), 3 men, 1 woman, 4 children, 8 total, $5.00 a share, $40.00 paid. (1870 TM annuity)

Antoine Carriboo (x), 1 man, 3 women, 2 children, 6 total, $5.00 a share, $30.00 paid. (1874 TM annuity)

Caribou, Francois

Francois Caribe (x), 1 man, 1 woman, 1 child, 3 total, $5.00 a share, $15.00 paid. (1865 TM annuity)

Francois Carribo (x), 1 man, 1 woman, 2 children, 4 total, $4.00 a share, $16.00 paid. (1868 TM annuity)

Francis Carribo (x), 1 man, 1 woman, 1 boy, 1 daughter, 4 total, $5.00 a share, $20.00 total. (1869 TM annuity)

Francis Carribeau (x), 1 man, 1 woman, 3 children, 5 total, $5.00 a share, $25.00 paid. (1870 TM annuity)

Francis Carriboo (x), 1 man, 1 woman, 1 child, 3 total, $5.00 a share, $15.00 paid. (1874 TM annuity)

Champagne, Charles

#196-199; Chas. Champagne, father, 27; Marie, wife, 27; Adele Rose, daughter, 2; Philomene, daughter, 9 months. (1888-TMC)

#214-217; Chas. Champagne, male, father, 49; Marie, female, wife, 29; Adele, female, daughter, 4; Philomene, female, daughter, 2. (1889-TMC)

#231-235; Chas. Champagne, male, father, 32; Marie, female, mother, 30; Adell, female, daughter, 7; Philomene, female, daughter, 9; Elizabeth, female, daughter, 9. (1890-TMC)

Champagne, Jean Baptiste Jr.

Baptiste Champagne, father, 25; Adele, wife, 25; Fredrick Charles, son, 9 months, Joseph Alfred, son, 9 months, Charlotte Parisien, mother, 79, (June 1885), one single B shot gun; (June 1886), one house, ½ acre potatoes, 8 tons hay, one winchester. (1884-TMC)

#342-346; Baptiste Champagne Jr., father, male, 26; Adele, wife, female, 24; Frederick, C., son, male, 2; Joseph A., son, male, 2; Charlotte Parisien, grandmother, female, 80. (1885-TMC)

#231-235; Baptist Champagne Jr., father, male, 27; Adella, wife, female, 25; Fredrick Charles, twin son, male, 3; Joseph Alfred, twin son, 3; Charlotte Parisien, grandmother, female, 81. (1886-TMC)

(1887-TMC)

#181-185; Baptist Champagne Jr., father, 30; Adele, wife, 26; Frederick, son, 5; Joseph, son, 5; Marie Isabel, daughter, 2. (1888-TMC)

#229-233; J. B. Champagne, Jr., male, father, 33; Adelle, female, wife, 32; Charles, male, son, 6; Frederick, male, son, 6; Isabel, female, daughter, 3. (1889-TMC)

#245-249; J. B. Champagne Jr., male, father, 34; Adele, female, mother, 32; Charles, male, son, 6; Fredk, male, son, 6; Isabell, female, daughter, 3. (1890-TMC)

Family 50; #213-218; J. B. Champagne, jr., male, father, 34, mixed bloods on reservation; Adele, female, wife, 31; Charles, male, son, 8; Frederick, male, son, 8; Isabel, female, daughter, 5; Louise Ann, female, daughter, 1. (1892-TMC)

Champagne, Jean Baptiste Sr.

Baptiste Champagne, father, 52; Madeleine, wife, 49; Louis, son, 13; Sara, daughter, 10; Jean Marie, son, 8; Louise, daughter, 7; Terese, daughter, 4; one house, one stable, one acre wheat, one acre potatoes, 4 mares, 2 horses, 3 head young stock, one DB shot gun. (1884-TMC)

#287-293; Baptiste Champagne Sr., father, male, 53; Madeleine, wife, female, 50; Louis, son, male, 14; Sara, daughter, female, 11; Jean, son, male, 9; Larose, daughter, female, 7; Terese, daughter, female, 5. (1885-TMC)

#345-351; Baptiste Champagne Sr., father, male, 54; Madeline, wife, female, 57; Louis, son, male, 15; Sarah, daughter, female, 12; Jeanmaria, son, male, 10; Louise, daughter, female, 9; Teresa, daughter, female, 6. (1886-TMC)

#157-164; Baptist Champagne, father, 53; Madaline, wife, 52; Louis, son, 16; Sahra, daughter, 13; Jean, son, 11; Louis, daughter, 10; Terrace, daughter, 7; Jerome, son, 3. (1887-TMC)

#173-179; Baptist Champagne Sr., father, 60; Madalaine, wife, 58; Louis, son, 18; Sahra, daughter, 15; Jean, son, 13; Louise, daughter, 13; Teresa, daughter, 9. (1888-TMC)

#219-225; J. B. Champagne, Sr., male, father, 57; Madalain, female, wife, 57; Louis, male, son, 17; Jean Marie, son, 14; Sahrah, female, daughter, 16; LaRose, female, daughter, 13; Theresa, female, daughter, 6. (1889-TMC)

#238-244; J. B. Champagne Sr., male, father, 58; Madalaine, female, mother, 58; Louis, male, son, 18; Jean M., male, son, 14; Sahrah, female, daughter, 15; LaRose, female, daughter, 12; Therese, female, daughter, 10. (1890-TMC)

Family 48; #205-211; J. B. Champagne sr., male, father, 60, mixed bloods on reservation; Madalain, female, wife, 54; Louis, male, son, 21; John M., male, son, 17; Sabra, male [?], son, 18; La Rose, female, daughter, 16; Theresa, female, daughter, 12. (1892-TMC)

Champagne, Jerome

#180; Jerome Champagne, man, 24. (1888-TMC)

#218; Jerome Champagne, male, 26. (1889-TMC)

#236-237; Jerome Champagne, male, father, 25; Propriatem [?], female, mother, 24. (1890-TMC)

Family 49; #212, Jerome Champagne, male, widower, 28, mixed bloods on reservation. (1892-TMC)

Champagne, Manuel

Manuel Champagne (x), 1 man, 1 woman, 1 boy, 3 total, $5.00 a share, $15.00 total. (1869 TM annuity)

Charbonneau, Antoine

Family 24; #104-107; Antoine Charbonneau, male, father, 38, mixed bloods on reservation; Frances, female, wife, 34; Victoria, female, daughter, 14; Jerome, male, son, 10. (1892-TMC)

Charbonneau, Pierre

#947-953; Pierre Charbonneau, father, male, 42; Rose, wife, female, 39; Mary, daughter, female, 12; Marguerite, daughter, female, 8; John, son, male, 6; Elisbert, daughter, female, 4; Justine, daughter, female, 2. (1886-TMC)

#249-252; Peter Charbonneau, male, father, 45; Mary, female, daughter, 16; Margaret, female, daughter, 11; Elizabeth, female, daughter, 8. (1889-TMC)

#267-270; Peter Charbonneau, male, father, 45; Mary, female, mother, 28; Mary, female, daughter, 16; Margaret, female, daughter, 11; Elizabeth, female, daughter, 8. (1890-TMC)

Family 55; #242-244; Peter Charbonneau, male, father, 49, mixed bloods on reservation; Angelique, female, wife, 38; Elizabeth, female, daughter, 10. (1892-TMC)

Charette, Alex

Alex Charette (x), 1 man, 1 woman, 3 children, 5 total, $3.00 a share, $15.00 paid. (1868 TM annuity)

Alex Charrette (x), 1 man, 1 total, $8.50 a share, $8.50 paid. (1871 TM annuity)

Alexander Chaurette (x), 1 man, 1 total, $10.50 a share, $10.50 paid. (1872 TM annuity)

Charette, Baptist

Baptiste Charrette (x), 1 man, 1 woman, 2 children, 4 total, $5.00 a share, $20.00 paid. (1870 TM annuity)

Baptiste Charette (x), 1 man, 1 woman, 1 child, 3 total, $8.50 a share, $25.50 paid. (1871 TM annuity)

Baptiste Chaurette (x), 1 man, 1 total, $10.50 a share, $10.50 paid. (1872 TM annuity)

Baptist Charette, father, 82; Josepht, wife, 60; Pierre, son, 18; Bertin, brother-in-law, 22. (June 1886-TMC)

#171-174; Baptist Charrett, father, 80; Josett, wife, 70; Delphin, granddaughter, 4; St.Pierre, son, 17. (1887-TMC)

#193-195; Baptist Charrett, father, 85; Jossett, wife, 55; St.Pierre, grandson, 19. (1888-TMC)

#245-248; Baptist Charett, male, father, 85; Jossett, female, wife, 66; Pierre, male, son, 20; Simmon, male, grandson, 17. (1889-TMC)

#263-266; Baptiste Charrette, male, father, 85; Josette, female, mother, 67; Pierre, male, son, 21; Francois, male, son, 28. (1890-TMC)

Family 53, #230-235; Baptiste Charrette, male, father, 88, mixed bloods on reservation; Jossette, female, wife, 70; Pierre, male, son, 23; Delphine, female, grand daughter, 14; Francois, male, son, 32; Moses, male, son, 30. (1892-TMC)

Charette, Josette

Josette Charette (x), 1 woman, 2 boys, 2 girls, 5 total, $5.00 a share, $25.00 total. (1869 TM annuity)

Chartrand, Ambroise

#175-180; Antoine [Ambroise] Chartrand, father, 31; Frances, wife, 27; Zachary, son, 9; Helen, daughter, 7; St.Pierre, son, 4; Josephine, daughter, 2. (1887-TMC)

#186-192; Ambroise Chartrand, father, 33; Francoise, wife, 30; Zachary, son, 10; Helen, daughter, 8; St.Pierre, son, 6; Josephine, daughter, 3; Joseph, son, 7 months. (1888-TMC)

#234-240; Ambroise Chartrand, male, father, 38; Francoise, female, wife, 33; Zachary, male, son, 10; St.Pierre, male, son, 5; Marie, female, daughter, 8; Josephine, female, daughter, 4; Joseph, male, son, 1. (1889-TMC)

#450-457; Ambroise Chartrand, male, father, 40; Frances, female, mother, 35; Zachary, male, son, 10; St.Pierre, male, son, 7; Joseph, male, son, 5; Marie, female, daughter, 8; Josephine, female, daughter, 6; Gabriel, male, son, 6 months. (1890-TMC)

Family 51; #219-224; Frances, female, wife, 26, mixed bloods on reservation; Ambroise, male, husband, 39; Zachary, male, son, 12; Marie Ellen, female, daughter, 10; Joseph, male, son, 4; Gabriel, female [?], daughter, 2. (1892-TMC)

Cloutier, Thomas

Family 47; #204, Thomas Cluthier, male, single, 55, mixed bloods on reservation. (1892-TMC)

Collin, Antoine

Antoine Collin (x), 1 man, 1 woman, 3 children, 5 total, $5.00 a share, $25.00 paid. (1865 TM annuity)

Collin, Antoine

Antoine Colin (x), 1 man, 1 total, $5.00 a share, $5.00 total. (1869 TM annuity)

Collin, Baptiste

Butis Cullah (x), 1 man, 1 woman, 3 children, 5 total, $5.00 a share, $25.00 paid.(1865 TM annuity)

Coloque, Margarette

Margarette Coloque (x), 1 woman, 1 total, $8.50 a share, $8.50 paid. (1871 TM annuity)

Cook, Alexis

Alexis Cook (x), 1 man, 1 total, $8.50 a share, $8.50 paid. (1871 TM annuity)

Courchene, John

John Curcine, father, 24; Mary, wife, 25; Philip, son, 2; Antoine, son, 4. (July 1886)

Cox, Alexis

Alexis Cox (x), 1 man, 1 woman, 2 children, 4 total, $3.00 a share, $12.00 paid. (1868 TM annuity)

Cyre, Alexander

#114; Alexander Cyre, male, 21. (1889-TMC-off)

Family 25; #108-109, Ester Cyre, female, wife, 18, mixed bloods in vicinity of reservation; Alexander, male, husband, 23. (1892-TMC)

Cyre, (Mrs.) Joseph

#112-113; Mrs. Joseph Cyre, female, Mother, 40; Geo., male, adopted son, 12. (1889-TMC-off)

Dagneau, Daniel

Daniel Dagneau, father, 50; Josephte, wife, 38; Virginie, daughter, 9; Mary Rose, daughter, 5; Gregorie, son, 3; Jean Baptiste, son, 1; Margurete, daughter, 2; one house, one stable, one cook stove, one cow, 3 head, ½ acre potatoes. (1884-TMC)

#685-691; Daniel Dagneau, father, male, 51; Josephte, wife, female, 41; Virginie, daughter, female, 10; Marie Rose, daughter, female, 6; Marguerite, daughter, female, 4; Gregoire, son, male, 3; Jean Baptiste, son, male, 2. (1885-TMC)

#558-564; Daniel Dagneau, father, male, 52; Josepht, wife, female, 40; Virginia, daughter, female, 11; Marie Rose, daughter, female, 7; Gregory, son, male, 5; Marguerite, daughter, female, 4; Jean Baptist, son, male, 2. (1886-TMC)

#149-155; Daniel Dagnon, male, father, 37; Susan, female, wife, 30; Virginie, female, daughter, 15; Marie Rose, female, daughter, 11; Margaret, female, daughter, 8; Gregory, male, son, 6; John B., male, son, 5. (1889-TMC-off)

Dauphinais/Duphinais/Dufinais

Dauphinais, Charles

Charles Duphinais, father, 36; Angelic, wife, 32; David, son, 10; Larmon, son, 8; Delphin, daughter, 6; Margurete, daughter, 4. (November 1886-TMC)

#317-322, 333; Chas. Duphinais, father, 37; Angelic, wife, 33; David, son, 16; Norman, son, 10; Delphenne, daughter, 8; Margaret, daughter, 3; Maria, daughter, 2 months. (1887-TMC)

#323-329; Chas. Dauphinaw, father, 37; Angelic, wife, 35; David, son, ..; Norman, son, 12, Delphene, daughter, 9; Margaret, daughter, 7; Baptist, son, 1. (1888-TMC)

#384-389; (Charles) Joseph Duffinais, male, father, 41; Angelic, female, wife, 30; David, male, son, 15; Herman, male, son, 13; Delphine, female, daughter, 11; Margarett, female, daughter, 3. (1889-TMC)

#390-397; Chas. Duffinais, male, father, 42; Angelic, female, mother, 31; Herman, male, son, 13; Delphine, female, daughter, 12; Margaret, female, daughter, 7; Francois Male, son, 5 months. (1890-TMC)

Family 76; #347-354; Charles Duffinais, male, father, 43, mixed bloods on reservation; Angelic, female, wife, 36; David, male, son, 17; Norman, male, son, 15; Delphine, female, daughter, 13; Margaret, female, daughter, 11; Bruno, male, son, 3; Mary Jane, female, daughter, 5 months. (1892-TMC)

Duphinais, John

#511-513; John Duphinais, father, male, 22; Josephte, wife, female, 20; Joseph, son, male, 1. (1886-TMC)

Dauphinais, Joseph

#334-337; Joseph Duffanaes, father, 30, Juli, wife, 23; Baptist, son, 6; Elise, daughter, 9. (1887-TMC)

Dauphinais, Joseph

#405-407; Joseph Duffinais, male, father, 50; Caroline, female, mother, 19; Bazzaw, male, son, 8. (1890-TM

Family 77; #355-358; Joseph Duffinais, male, father, 54, mixed bloods on reservation; Caroline, female, wife, 18; Melanie Pettier, female, daughter-in-law, 9 [?]; Francois, male, son, 11. (1892-TMC)

Duffenaise, Margaret

#138-139; Margaret Duffenais, female, mother, 46; Francois, male, stepson, 44. (1889-TMC-off)

Davis, Alexandre

#924-928; Alexandre Davis, father, male, 33; Eliza [?], wife, female, 25; Alexandre, son, male, 8; Philomene, daughter, 7; Jean Baptist, son, 1. (1886-TMC)

#211-216; Alexander Davis, father, 37; Elize, wife, 26; Filiman, daughter, 8; Alexander, son, 6; Napoleon, son, 2; Rosalie, daughter, 3 months. (1887-TMC)

#224-229; Alexander Davis, father, 37; Elize, wife, 26; Filimen, daughter, 10; Alexandre, son, 8; Napoleon, son, 3; Rosalie, daughter, 1. (1888-TMC)

#342-347; Alexander Davis, male, father, 36; Elize, female, wife, 26; Alexander, male, son, 7; Napoleon, male, son, 5; Marie, female, daughter, 10; Rosalie, female, daughter, 2. (1889-TMC)

#361-365; Alexander Davis, male, father, 27; Glize [Eulalie], female, mother, 32; Marie, female, daughter, 10; Rosalie, female, daughter, 3. (1890-TMC)

Family 66; #290-295, Alexander Davis, male, father, 36, mixed bloods on reservation; Elalie, female, wife, 36; Mary Philomene, female, daughter, 13; Alexander, male, son, 10; Rosinie, female, daughter, 2; Louis, male, son, 4 months. (1892-TMC)

Davis, Augustus

Augustus Davis (x), 1 man, 1 total, $10.00 a share, $10.00 paid. (1873 TM annuity)

Augustus Davis (x), 1 man, 1 total, $5.00 a share, $5.00 paid. (1874 TM annuity)

Davis, Genevieve

#640-642; Genevieve Davis, mother, female, 52; Melvina, daughter, female, 14; Teresa, daughter, female, 9. (1886-TMC)

#267-270; Genevieve Davis, widow, 53; Meloma, daughter, 10; Terrasa, daughter, 11; Michia, daughter, 14. (1887-TMC)

#354-356; Genevieve Davis, female, mother, 50; Gene-ton, Little Brother, male, Grandson, 16; Virginie, female, granddaughter, 11. (1889-TMC)

Davis, Jean Baptist Jr.

#920-923; Baptist Davis, father, male, 36; Amrease, wife, female, 23; Adelle, daughter, female, 14; Jean Baptist, son, male, 2. (1886-TMC)

#260-265; Baptist Davis, father, 37; Emerize, wife, 24; Adele, daughter, 15; John Baptist, son, 3; Louise, daughter, 8 months; Francois Lavallee, adopted son, 15. (1887-TMC)

#275-279, Baptist Davis Jr., father, 40; Emerize, wife, 25; Adelle, daughter, 15; John B. son, 4; Louisa, daughter, 2. (1888-TMC)

#348-353; J. B. Davis, male, father, 41; Emereze, female, wife, 26; Baptist, male, son, 5; Adell, female, daughter, 16; Louisa, female, daughter, 3; Emereze, female, daughter, 2 months. (1889-TMC)

#366-372; J. B. Davis Jr., male, father, 42; Emereze, female, mother, 28; Baptiste, male, son, 6; Adell, female, daughter, 18; Louisa, female, daughter, 4; Emma M., female, daughter, 1; Francois Lavalie, male, brother-in-law, 18. (1890-TMC)

Family 92; #407-413, J. B. Davis, jr., male, father, 46; mixed bloods on reservation; Emerise, female, wife, 30; Mary Adele, female, daughter, 20; Louise Ann, female, daughter, 6; Mary, female, daughter, 3; Francois Lavallie, male, __, 21. (1892-TMC)

Davis, Jean Baptist Sr.

#334-338; J. B. Davis Sr., father, 70; Julie, wife, 69; Adele, daughter, 8; William, son, 6; Jerome, son, 3. (1888-TMC)

#296-297; J. B. Davis Sr., male, father, 72; Julia, female, wife, 70. (1889-TMC)

Family 70; #313-316, John Baptist Davis, sr., male, father, 73, mixed bloods on reservation; Julia, female, wife, 72; Adele, female, granddaughter, 12; Jerome Lafocernaise, male, grandson, 8. (1892-TMC)

Davis, Jerome

Jerome Davis (x), 1 man, 1 women, 1 child, 3 total, $10.00 a share, $30.00 paid. (1873 TM annuity)

Jerome Davis (x), 1 man, 2 women, 3 children, 6 total, $5.00 a share, $30.00 paid. (1874 TM annuity)

#680-684; Jerome Davis, father, male, 39; Charlotte, wife, female, 39; Liza, daughter, female, 19; Anastasie, daughter, female, 7; Marie, daughter, female, 1. (1886-TMC)

#415-420; Jerome Davis, male, father, 40; Charlotte, female, mother, 40; Anastasie, female, daughter, 10; Marie, female, daughter, 4; Eliza, female, daughter, 12; William, male, son, 1. (1890-TMC)

Family 68; #302-306; Jerome Davis, male, father, 44, mixed bloods on reservation; Charlotte, female, wife, 44; Anastasi, female, daughter, 12; Mary, female, daughter, 6; Napoleon, male, son, 12. (1892-TMC)

Davis, Joseph

Joseph Davis, father, 21; Josephine, wife, 18; Joseph, son, 9 months, (June 1886); one house, 4 tons hay, one horse, one cart, one single B. gun. (1884-TMC)

#588-589; Joseph Davis, father, male, 22; Josephine, wife, female, 19. (1885-TMC)

#271-273; Joseph Davis, father, male, 23; Josephine, wife, female, 20; Joseph Norbert, son, male, 9 months. (1886-TMC)

#118-122; Joseph Davis, male, father, 25; Josephine, female, wife, 23; Joseph, male, son, 4; Frank, male, son, 3; Jerome, male, son, 2. (1889-TMC-off)

Family 26; #110-116, Joseph Davis, male, father, 28, mixed bloods in vicinity of reservation; Josephine, female, wife, 25; Joseph, male, son, 7; Francois, male, son, 5; Jerome, male, son, 3; David, male, son, 2; Louis Ann, female, daughter, 4 months. (1892-TMC)

Davis, Leander

Family 89; #401-402, Leander Davis, male, father, 23; mixed bloods on reservation; Josephine, female, wife, 16. (1892-TMC)

Davis, Louis

#187-193; Louis Davis, father, 30; Terrace, wife, 32; Pierre, son, 9; Isidore, son, 8; Laoela, son, 5; Marie Rose, daughter, 4; Josephine, daughter, 3. (1887-TMC)

#203-209; Louis Davis, father, 30; Teresa, wife, 32; Pierre, son, 11; Isidore, son, 6; Lavela, son, 9; Marie Rose, daughter, 4; Josephine, daughter, [...] (1888-TMC)

#298-305; Louis Davis, male, father, 31; Theresa, female, wife, 30; Pierre, male, son, 10; Lasela, male, son, 8; Ezear, male, son, 6; Rosalie, female, daughter, 2; Marie Rose, female, daughter, 5; Josephine, female, daughter, 3. (1889-TMC)

Family 65; #287-289, Louis Davis, male, father, 22, mixed bloods on reservation; Mary Rose, female, wife, 20; Mary Rose, female, daughter, 1-1/2. (1892-TMC)

Davis, Michel

Michel Davis (x), 1 man, 1 total, $10.00 a share, $10.00 paid. (1873 TM annuity)

Michel Davis (x), 1 man, 1 total, $5.00 a share, $5.00 paid. (1874 TM annuity)

Michael Davis, father, 30; Felavie, wife, 22; Michel, son, 4; Marierose, daughter, age 10 months, (June 1886); one house, 2 horses, 6 tons hay. (1884-TMC)

#544-546; Michel Davis, father, male, 31; Felavie, wife, female, 23; Michel, son, male, 3. (1885-TMC)

#267-270; Michael Davis, father, male, 32; Flora, wife, female, 24; Michael, son, male, 4; Marie Rose, daughter, female, 10 months. (1886-TMC)

#194-198; Michael Davis, father, 33; Clara, wife, 25; Michael, son, 4; Marie Rose, daughter, 3; Patrice, son, 1. (1887-TMC)

#230-234; Michael Davis, father, 33; Clara, wife, 25; Michael, son, 5; Marie Rose, daughter, 4; Patrice, son, 2. (1888-TMC)

#337-341; Michael Davis, male, father, 37; Clara, female, wife, 27; Michael, male, son, 7; Patrice, male, son, 3; Marie Rose, female, daughter, 5. (1889-TMC)

#356-360; Michael Davis, male, father, 36; Clara, female, mother, 28; Michael, male, son, 7; Patrice, male, son, 4; Marie Rose, female, daughter, 6. (1890-TMC)

Family 69; #307-312; Michael Davis, male, father, 39, mixed bloods on reservation; Flavit, female, wife, 29; Michael, male, son, 10; Mary, female, daughter, 7; Patrice, male, son, 5; Philomene, female, daughter, 5 months. (1892-TMC)

Davis, St.Mathe

#408-409; St.Mathe Davis, male, father, 19; Marie Rose, female, mother, 17. (1890-TMC)

Davis, William Jr.

Wm. Davis Jr. (x), 1 man, 1 woman, 3 children, 5 total, $10.00 a share, $50.00 paid. (1873 TM annuity)

William Davis Jr. (x), 1 man, 1 woman, 4 children, 6 total, $5.00 a share, $30.00 paid. (1874 TM annuity)

William Davis, father, 59; Sara, wife, 50; Leandre, son, 15; Sara, daughter, 13; Agath, daughter, 11; Louis, son, 2; Marierose, daughter, 8 months (June 1885); one single B. shot gun. (1884-TMC)

#232-239, (236 missing); William Davis Jr., father, male, 40; Sara, wife, female, 31; Leandre, son, male, 16; Sara, daughter, female, 14; Agathe, daughter, female, 12; Louis, son, male, 3; Marie Rose, daughter, female, 8 months. (1885-TMC)

#219-225; William Davis Jr. father, male, 41; Sarah, wife, female, 32; Leandre, son, male, 17; Sarah, daughter, female, 15; Agatha, daughter, female, 13; Louis, son, male, 4; Marie Rose, daughter, female, 2. (1886-TMC)

#253-259; Wm. Davis Jr., father, 42; Sahrah, wife, 33; Landry, son, 18; Sahra, daughter, 17; Agatha, daughter, 14; Marie Rose, daughter, 3; Maxim, son, 1 month. (1887-TMC)

#261-267; Wm. Davis Jr., father, 43; Sarah, wife, 33; Leander, son, 19; Sahra, daughter, 18; Agatha, daughter, 16; Marie Rose, daughter, 3; Maxime, son, 1. (1888-TMC)

#262-269; Wm. Davis, male, father, 44; Sahrah, female, wife, 34; Leander, male, son, 20; Maxim, male, son, 2; Sahrah, female, daughter, 18; Agatha, female, daughter, 16; Marie Rose, female, daughter, 4; No Name, female, daughter, 1 month. (1889-TMC)

#285-291; Wm. Davis Jr., male, father, 45; Sarah, female, mother, 38; Leander, male, son, 21; Maxime, male, son, 3; Sahra, female, daughter, 19; Agatha, female, daughter, 17; Marie Rose, female, daughter, 5. (1890-TMC)

Family 72; #321-325; William Davis, jr., male, father, 47, mixed bloods on reservation; Sabra, female, wife, 38; Sabra, female, daughter, 22; Maxim, male, son, 5; William Jerome, male, grandson, 8 months. (1892-TMC)

Davis, William Sr.

Wm. Davis (x), 1 man, 2 women, 6 children, 9 total, $10.00 a share, $90.00 paid. (1873 TM annuity)

William Davis Sr. (x), 1 man, 2 women, 6 children, 9 total, $5.00 a share, $45.00 paid. (1874 TM annuity)

William Davis (Sr.), father, 61; Marie, wife, 49; Louis, son, 14; Francois, son, 12; Anastasie, daughter, 9; Milka, daughter, 3. (1884-TMC)

#583-587; William Davis Sr., father, male, 62; Marie, wife, female, 50; Louis, son, male, 15; Francois, son, male, 13; Anastasie, daughter, female, 10; Milka, daughter, female, 4. (1885-TMC)

#226-230; William Davis Sr., father, male, 63; Marie, wife, female, 51; Louis, son, male, 16; Francois, son, male, 14; Anastasie, daughter, female, 11. (1886-TMC)

#218-223; Wm. Davis Sr., father, 65; Marie, wife, 53; Louis, son, 18; Francois, son, 17; Anastasie, daughter, 12; Edward, adopted son, 6. (1888-TMC)

#332-336; Wm. Davis, Sr., male, father, 66; Louis, male, son, 18; Frank, male, son, 17; Anastasie, female, daughter, 13; Leander, male, son, 6. (1889-TMC)

#349-355; Wm. Davis Sr., male, father, 67; Madalaine, female, mother, 60; Frank, male, son, 18; Anastasie, female, daughter, 14; Leander, male, grandson, 7; Alex Gonville, male, N., 25; Elise Gonville, female, granddaughter, 5. (1890-TMC)

Family 67; #206-208, 299-301; William Davis sr., male, father, 69, mixed bloods on reservation; Madalain, female, wife, 61; Francois, male, son, 20; Anastasi, female, daughter, 17; Leander, male, son, 9; Elise, female, daughter, 9. (1892-TMC)

Dease, John

John Das (x), 1 man, 1 woman, 1 child, 3 total, $5.00 a share, $15.00 paid. (1865 TM annuity)

John Dees (x), 1 man, 1 woman, 1 boy, 1 daughter, 4 total, $5.00 a share, $20.00 total. (1869 TM annuity)

Dease, Madame

Madame Desse (x), 1 man, 1 woman, 2 total, $3.00 a share, $6.00 paid. (1868 TM annuity)

Dease, Michael

Michael Dease, father, 37; Lucy, wife, 37; John, son, 16; Marie Rose, daughter, 14; Adele, daughter, 12; Louis, son, 10; Ellen, daughter, 7; Clarisse, daughter, 5; Virginie, daughter, 3; Joseph, son, 4 months; left the country June 1886. (1884-TMC)

#573-582; Michel Dease, father, male, 39; Lucy, wife, female, 38; John, son, male, 17; Marie Rose, daughter, female, 15; Adele, daughter, female, 13; Louis, son, male, 11; Ellen, daughter, female, 8; Claris, daughter, female, 6; Virginie, daughter, female, 4; Jsoeph, son, male, 1. (1885-TMC)

Decoteaux, Augustin

Augustin Dakota (x), 1 man, 2 women, 3 total, $10.00 a share, $30.00 paid. (1873 TM annuity)

Decoteaux, Baptiste

#157-163; Baptiste Decouteaux, father, male, 41; Marguerite, wife, female, 43; Patrice, son, male, 15; Francois, son, male, 13; Alexandre, son, male, 11; Andre, son, male, 8; Marie Ann, daughter, female, 2. (1885-TMC)

#163-170; Baptist Decoteaux, father, male, 42; Marguerite, wife, female, 44; Patrice, son, male, 16; Francois, son, male, 14; Alexandre, son, male, 12; Andre, son, male, 9; Mary Ann, daughter, female, 3; Lenore, daughter, female, 2. (1886-TMC)

DeCouteau, Daniel

Family 59, #258-260, Daniel De Couteau, male, father, 20 [sic], mixed bloods on reservation; Julie, female, wife, 34; Francois, male, son, 19. (1892-TMC)

Decouteau, Elzear

#255-256; Ezear DeCouteau, father, 23; Adele, wife, 17. (1888-TMC)

#329-331; Ezear DeCouteau, male, father, 23; Adel, female, wife, 22; Joseph, male, son, 2 months. (1889-TMC)

#348; Ezear Widower Decouteau, male, 26. (1890-TMC)

Family 30; #124-125, Ezear Decouteau, male, father, 27, mixed bloods in vicinity of reservation; Mary Rose, female, wife, 19. (1892-TMC)

DeCouteau, Frank

Family 62; #272-275, Frank De Couteau, male, father, 24, mixed bloods on reservation; Agnes, female, wife, 20; Celina, female, daughter, 1; Mary, female, daughter, 3 months. (1892-TMC)

Decouteau, James

Family 79, #398-400, James Decouteau, male, father, 21, mixed bloods on reservation; Madalain, female, wife, 21; Madalain, female, daughter, 1 month. (1892-TMC)

DeCouteau, Jean Baptiste

Baptist Decoteau, father, 40; Margurete, wife, 42; Patrice, son, 14; Francois, son, 12; Alexandre, son, 10; Andre, son, 7; Marie Anne, daughter, 1, (June 1886) Lyenore, daughter, 8 months; one single B gun. (1884-TMC)

#421-428; Patrice Decouteau [J. B.], male, father, 40; Margaret, female, mother, 35; Patrice, male, son, 20; Francois, male, son, 18; Alex, male, son, 17; Justine [?], female, daughter, 15; Marie, female, daughter, 7; Eleonore, female, daughter, 6. (1890-TMC)

Family 57; #249-255; John B. De Couteau, male, father, 49, mixed bloods on reservation; Margaret, female, wife, 49; Patrick male, son, 23; Alexander, male, son, 19; Andre, male, son, 16; Mary, female, daughter, 8; Eleanore, female, daughter, 7. (1892-TMC)

Decouteau, Joseph

Joseph Decoteau (x), 1 man, 1 woman, 4 children, 6 total, $3.00 a share, $18.00 paid. (1868 TM annuity)

#292-293; Joseph De Couteau, father, 89; Mary, wife, 80. (1888-TMC)

#400-401; Joseph De Couteau, male, father, 90; Mary, female, wife, 81. (1889-TMC)

#404-405; Joseph Decouteau, male, father, 91; Mary, female, mother, 81. (1890-TMC)

Family 58, #256; Joseph De Couteau, male, father, 100, mixed bloods on reservation; #257, Mary, female, wife, 80. (1892-TMC)

Decoteau, Laurie

Laurie Decoteau (x), 1 woman, 1 child, 2 total, $3.00 a share, $6.00 paid. (1868 TM annuity)

Decoteaux, Louis Jr.

Louis Decoteau (x), 1 man, 1 woman, 3 children, 5 total, $4.00 a share, $20.00 paid. (1868 TM annuity)

#496-501; Louis Decoteaux Jr., father, male, 41; Genevieve, wife, female, 25; St.Pierre, son, male, 12; Napoleon, son, male, 8; Marie, daughter, female, 4; William, son, male, 2. (1886-TMC)

#210-216; Louis DeCouteau Jr., father, 43; Genevive, wife, 27; St.Pierre, son, 14; Napoleon, son, 10; Marie, daughter, 6; William, son, 4; Julia, daughter, 2. (1888-TMC)

#306-313; Louis Decouteau Jr., male, father, 50; Genevive, female, wife, 35; Pierre, male, son, 13; Napoleon, male, son, 10; William, male, son, 4; Marie, female, daughter, 7; Julien, M [?], son [?], 3; Matilda, female, daughter, 2 months. (1889-TMC)

Family 64; #280-286; Louis Decouteau jr., male, father, 53, mixed blood; on reservation; Genevieve, female, wife, 45; St.Pierre, male, son, 16; Napoleon, male, son, 12; William, male, son, 7; Mary Caroline, female, daughter, 9; Julian, male, son, 6. (1892-TMC)

Decoteaux, Louis Sr.

Louis Decouteaux (Sr.), father, 68; Isabel, wife, 62; Norbert, son, 34; Elzeard, son, 20; Joseph, son, 17; Louis, son, 15; (June 1886) one single B shot gun. (1884-TMC)

#102-107; Louis Decoteaux, father, male, 69; Isabel, wife, female, 63; Norbert, son, male, 35; Elzeard, son, male, 27; Joseph, son, male, 18; Louis, son, male, 16. (1885-TMC)

#433-438; Louis Decoteaux Sr., father, male, 70; Isabelle, wife, female, 64; Norbert, son, male, 36; Elsard, son, male, 22; Joseph, son, male, 19; Louis, son, male, 17. (1886-TMC)

#181-186; Louis De Couteau, Sr., father, 71; Isabel, wife, 65; Norbert, son, 37; Elzeard, son, 23; Joseph, son, 20; Louis, son, 18. (1887-TMC)

#200-202; Louis Decouteau Sr., father, 71; Isabel, wife, 68; Joseph, son, 22. (1888-TMC)

#324-326; Louis DeCouteau, Sr., male, father, 73; Isabel, female, wife, 68; Joseph, male, son, 21. (1889-TMC)

#345-348; Louis Decouteau Sr., male, father, 70; Isabell, female, mother, 68; Joseph, male, son, 22; Ernest M., male, grandson, 2 months. (1890-TMC)

Family 63; #276-279, Louis De Couteau, sr., male, father, 75, mixed bloods on reservation; Isabel, female, wife, 69; Joseph, male, son, 26; Mary Angel, female, daughter [?], 3. (1892-TMC)

Decouteau, Louis 2d

#330-331; Louis De Couteau 2d, father, 19; Marie Rose, wife, 16. (1888-TMC)

#314-315; Louis DeCouteau 2nd, male, father, 20; Marie, female, daughter, 2 months. (1889-TMC)

Family 91; #405-406, Louis De Couteau, male, father 24, mixed bloods on reservation; A., female, wife, 20. (1892-TMC)

Decoteau, Marian [nee Lafournaise ?]

Marian Decoteau (x), 1 woman, 1 boy, 2 girls, 4 total, $5.00 a share, $20.00 paid. (1869 TM annuity)

Decoteaux, Moise

Moise Decouteau, father, 36; Marie, wife, 37; Genevieve, daughter, 1. (1884-TMC)

#164-166; Moise Decouteaux, father, male, 37; Marie, wife, female, 38; Genevieve, daughter, female, 2. (1885-TMC)

#173-175; Moise Decoteaux, father, male, 38; Marie, wife, female, 39; Genevieve, daughter, female, 3. (1886-TMC)

#283-286, 289; Moise De Couteau, father, 39; Marie, wife, 40; Genevia, daughter, 4; Marie, daughter, 4; Joseph, son, 2. (1887-TMC)

#294-298; Moses De Couteau, father, 39; Marie, wife, 39; Genevieve, daughter, 5; Jean, son, 3; Patrice, son, 1. (1888-TMC)

#256-262; Moses De Couteau, male, father, 40; Mary, female, wife, 35; Joseph, male, son, 4; Patrice, male, son, 2; Genevieve, female, daughter, 7; Peter Blue, male, nephew, 13. (1889-TMC)

#279-284; Moses Decouteau, male, father, 40; Wife, female, mother, 35; Joseph, male, son, 6; Genevieve, female, daughter, 7; Peter Blue, male, nephew, 16; Marie, female, daughter, 5 months. (1890-TMC)

Family 61; #267-271; Moses De Couteau, male, father, 42, mixed bloods on reservation; Mary, female, wife, 39; Joseph, male, son, 8; Genevieve, female, daughter, 8;Marie, female, daughter, 2-1/2. (1892-TMC)

Decouteau, Norbert

#227-228; Norbert DeCouteau, male, father, 37; La Rose, female, wife, 33. (1889-TMC)

#345-347; Norbert Decouteau, male, father, 38; LaRose, female, mother, 38; Madalaine, female, daughter, 10 months. (1890-TMC)

Family 84; #380-383, Norbert DeCouteau, male, father, 47, mixed bloods on reservation; La Rose, female, wife, 25; Madalaine, female, daughter, 3; Norbert, male, son, 1. (1892-TMC)

Decoteau, Pierre

Pierre De Coto (x), 1 man, 2 women, 2 children, 5 total, $5.00 a share, $25.00 paid. (1874 TM annuity)

Delorme, Bazil

Bazil Delorme (x), 1 man, 2 women, 1 child, 4 total, $5.00 a share, $20.00 paid. (1870 TM annuity)

Bazil Delorme (x), 1 man, 1 woman, 2 total, $10.50 a share, $21.00 paid. (1872 TM annuity)

Delorme, Bernard

#257-260; Berhardt Delorme, father, 30; Jossett, wife, 30; Pauline, daughter, 1; Agathe, daughter, 3. (1888-TMC)

Family 75; #345-346, Bernharet Delorme, male, father, 36, mixed blood on reservation; Sophie, female, daughter, 1. (1892-TMC)

Delorme, Betsy

Betsy Delorme (x), 1 woman, 1 child, 2 total, $5.00 a share, $10.00 paid. (1870 TM annuity)

Delorme, Cayince [Joseph]

Cayince Delorme (x), 1 man, 1 woman, 2 total, $8.50 a share, $17.00 paid. (1871 TM annuity)

Cayence (x), 1 man, 1 total, $10.50 a share, $10.50 paid. (1872 TM annuity)

Delorme, Francis

#247, Francis Delorme, widow, 91. (1888-TMC)

Delorme, Francois

Family 28; #118-119, Francis Delorme, male, father, 53, mixed bloods in vicinity of reservation; Keafeal, female, daughter, 21. (1892-TMC)

Delorme, Isabelle

Isabelle Delorme (x), 1 man, 2 women, 1 child, 4 total, $5.00 a share, $20.00 paid. (1870 TM annuity)

Delorme, Joseph

Joseph Delorme (Jr.) (x), 1 man, 1 woman, 2 children, 4 total, $3.00 a share, $12.00 paid. (1868 TM annuity)

Joseph Delorme (x), 1 man, 1 woman, 1 boy, 1 daughter, 4 total, $5.00 a share, $20.00 total. (1869 TM annuity)

Joseph Delorme (x), 6 men, 2 women, 1 child, 9 total, $5.00 a share, $45.00 paid. (1870 TM annuity)

Joseph Delorme (x), 1 man, 1 woman, 2 total, $8.50 a share, $17.00 paid. (1871 TM annuity)

Joseph Delorme (x), 1 man, 1 total, $10.50 a share, $10.50 paid. (1872 TM annuity)

Joseph Delorme, father, 44; Angelic, wife, 40; Larose, daughter, 17; Joseph, son, 15; Francois, son, 13; Adele, daughter, 11; Charlotte, daughter, 9; Frederick, son, 7; Virginie, daughter, 5; Liza, daughter, 3; Jane, daughter, 3; Marie, daughter, 1; 2 houses, 2 stables, 45 tons hay, 2 acres wheat, ½ acre potatoes, 2 mares, 4 cows, 1 pr. Cattle, 25 head young stock, 1 wagon, one stove-cook, 1 heating, DB S single B. shot gun. (1884-TMC)

#176-187; Joseph Delorme, father, male, 45; Angelic, wife, female, 41; Larose, daughter, female, 18; Joseph, son, male, 16; Francois, son, male, 14; Adele, daughter, female, 12; Scolastique, daughter, female, 10; Frederick, son, male, 8; Virginie, daughter, female, 6; Liza, daughter, female, 4; Marie Virginie [Angelique], daughter, female, 4; Marie, daughter, female, 1. (1885-TMC)

#151-162; Joseph Delorme, father, male, 46; Angelic, wife, female, 42; La Rose, daughter, female, 19; Joseph, son, male, 17; Francois, son, male, 15; Adella, daughter, female, 13; Charlotte, daughter, female, 11; Frederick, son, male, 9; Virginia, daughter, female, 7; Eliza, daughter, female, 5; Jane, daughter, female, 5; Marie, daughter, female, 3. (1886-TMC)

#271-282; Joseph Delorme, father, 50; Angelic, wife, 43; Larose, daughter, 20; Joseph, son, 18; Francis, son, 16; Adele, daughter, 14; Pierre, son, 12; Charlotte, daughter, 10; Virginie, daughter, 8; Liza, daughter, 6; Jane, daughter, 6; Marie, daughter, 4. (1887-TMC)

#280-291, Joseph Delorme, father, 50; Angelic, wife, 43; Larose, daughter, 22; Joseph, son, 20; Francois, son, 18; Adele, daughter, 16; Pierre Frederick, son, 14; Scolastique, daughter, 12; Virginie, daughter, 10; Liza, daughter, 6; Jane, daughter, 6; Marie, daughter, 4. (1888-TMC)

#270-281; Joseph Delorme, male, father, 51; Angelic, female, wife, 44; Joseph, male, son, 21; Francis, male, son, 19; Frederick, male, son, 19; LaRose, female, daughter, 23; Adel, female, daughter, 17; Scholastique, female, daughter, 13; Virginie, female, daughter, 11; Liza, female, daughter, 7; Angelic, female, daughter, 7; Marie, female, daughter, 5. (1889-TMC)

#292-302; Joseph Delorme, male, father, 52; Angelic, female, mother, 45; Joseph, male, son, 22; Francois, male, son, 20; Frederick, male, son, 12; Adele, female, daughter, 15; Scolastique, female, daughter, 13; Virginie, female, daughter, 11; Eliza, female, daughter, 10; Angelic, female, daughter, 10; Marie, female, daughter, 9. (1890-TMC)

Family 73; #326-335; Joseph Delorme 1st, male, father, 51, mixed bloods on reservation; Angelique, female, wife, 46; Frederick, male, son, 14; Scholastic, female, daughter, 13; Virginie, female, daughter, 12; Elizabeth, female, daughter, 11; Angelique, female, daughter, 11; Mary, female, daughter, 8; Elise, female, daughter, 4; Christine, female, daughter, 2. (1892-TMC)

Delorme, Joseph (Sr.)

Joseph Delorme (Sr.) (x), 1 man, 1 woman, 7 children, 9 total, $3.00 a share, $27.00 paid. (1868 TM annuity)

Delorme, Joseph 2nd

#217; Joseph Delorme 2d, man, 19. (1888-TMC)

Family 27; #117, Joseph Delorme jr., male, single, 23, mixed bloods in vicinity of reservation. (1892-TMC)

Delorme, Nancy

Nancy Delorme (x), 1 woman, 2 children, 3 total, $5.00 a share, $15.00 paid. (1870 TM annuity)

Delorme, Patrice

Patrice Delorme, father, 27; Madline, wife, _; Joseph, brother, 29. (June 1886-TMC)

#410-414; Patrice Delorme, male, father, 36; Madalaine, female, mother, 28; Julie, female, daughter, 4; Cecilia, female, daughter, 2; John, male, son, 5 months. (1890-TMC)

Family 60; #261-266; Patrice Delorme, male, father, 25, mixed bloods on reservation; Madalain, female, wife, 27; Julie, female, daughter, 5; Cecil, female, daughter, 3; Patrice, male, son, 2; Betsey, female, daughter, 8 months. (1892-TMC)

Delorme, Urbain

Urbain Delorme, father, 50; Elize, wife, 38; Elize, daughter, 17; Collin, son, 15; Alphosine, daughter, 14; Louis, son, 12; Adeline, daughter, 10; Zilan, daughter, 9; Velina, daughter, 7; Mary Ann, daughter, 5; Urbain, son, 4; William, son, 2; Francois, son, 1; Joseph, son, 10 months (1886); one acre broke, one horse, 4 tons hay; one single B gun. (1884-TMC)

#294-305; Urbain Delorme, father, male, 51; Elize, wife, female, 39; Elize, daughter, female, 18; Collin, son, male, 16; Alphonsine, daughter, female, 13; Louis, son, male, 11; Adeline, daughter, female, 10; Vilina, daughter, female, 8; Mary Ann, daughter, female, 6; Urbain, son, male, 5; William, son, male, 3; Francois, son, male, 2. (1885-TMC)

#278-291; Urbain Delorme, father, male, 52; Eliza, wife, female, 41; Eliza, daughter, female, 19; Colin, son, male, 17; Alfonsine, daughter, female, 16; Louis, son, male, 14; Adeline, daughter, female, 12; Zilda, daughter, female, 11; Vilina, daughter, female, 9; Mary Anna, daughter, female, 7; Urbain, son, male, 6; William, son, male, 4; Francois, son, male, 3; Joseph, son, male, 10 months. (1886-TMC)

#222-234, Urban Delorme, father, 53; Elize, wife, 41; Collin, son, 18; Alphonsine, daughter, 17; Louis, son, 15; Adeline, daughter, 13; Zilda, daughter, 12; Velina, daughter, 10; Mary Ann, daughter, 8; Urban, son, 7; William, son, 5; Francois, son, 4; Joseph, son, 1-10 months. (1887-TMC)

#238-247; Urban Delorme, father, 55; Elize, wife, 42; Adeline, daughter, 14; Louis, son, 16; Zilda, daughter, 12; Velma, daughter, 10; Mary Ann, daughter, 8; Urbane, son, 6; William, son, 4; Francois, son, 2. (1888-TMC)

#284-295; Urbane Delorme, male, father, 56; Elize, female, wife, 43; Joseph, male, son, 19; Louis, male, son, 16; Urbane, male, son, 8; John, male, son, 7; William, male, son, 5; Frances, male, son, 4; Adelain, female, daughter, 14; Zilda, female, daughter, 12; Sielina, female, daughter, 10; Marie Anne, female, daughter, 3. (1889-TMC)

#303-309; Urbain Delorme, male, father, 57; Elize, female, mother, 44; Joseph, male, son, 21; Louis, male, son, 17; Urbane, male, son, 11; William, male, son, 10; Adelaine, female, daughter, 15. (1890-TMC)

Demontigny, Charles Jr.

#369, Charles Demontignie Jr., father, male, 42; Nancy, wife, female, 40; Maxime, son, male, 15; Marie, daughter, female, 13; Melanie, daughter, female, 10; Alfred, son, male, 6; Madeleine, daughter, female, 4; Pierre, son, male, 2. (1885-TMC)

#570-578; Charles Demontigne Jr., father, male, 43; Nancy, wife, female, 41; Maxime, son, male, 16; Marie, daughter, female, 14; Melanie, daughter, female, 11; Alfred, son, male, 7; Madeline, daughter, female, 5; Pierre, son, male, 3; Patrice, son, male, 3 months. (1886-TMC)

#296-304; Chas. Demontigne Jr., father, 45; Nancy, wife, 43; Maxim, son, 18; Filaman, daughter, 13; Milanie, daughter, 13; Alfred, son, 8; Madalin, daughter, 6; Pierre, son, 4; Patrice, son, 2. (1887-TMC)

#305-312; Chas. Demontigne Jr., father, 46; Nancy, wife, 44; Maxime, son, 19; Filamon, daughter, 16; Melanie, daughter, 14; Alfred, son, 9; Madalain, daughter, 7; Patrice, son, 5. (1888-TMC)

#376-381; Chas. Demontigne Jr., male, father, 46; Maxim, male, son, 18; Philomene, female, daughter, 15; Alfred, male, son, 11; Madalaine, female, daughter, 7; St.Pierre, male, son, 5. (1889-TMC)

Demontigny, Charles Sr.

#362-364; Charles Demontignie Sr., father, male, 67; Cadiz, wife, female, 71; Ernest [Thorn], grandson, male, 10. (1885-TMC)

#712-713; Charles Demontigne Sr., father, male, 68; Marie, wife, female, 72. (1886-TMC)

#332-333; Chas. Demontigne Sr., father, 70; Marie, wife, 75. (1888-TMC)

#382-383; Chas. Demontigne Sr., male, father, 75; Marie Rose, female, granddaughter, 13. (1889-TMC)

#389; Chas. Demontigne Widower, male, 76. (1890-TMC)

Demontigny, Hermance

Hermance Demontigny, father, 36; Cadiz, wife, 30; Ambroise, son, 3; Napoleon, son, 1; Sainton, daughter, 2 months (June 1886); one house, one stable, ½ acre vegetables, 4 tons hay, one mare, one cart. (1884-TMC)

#365-368; Hermance Demontignie, father, male, 37; Cadiz, wife, female, 31; Embroise, son, male, 4; Napoleon, son, male, 2. (1885-TMC)

#263-266; Hermance Demontigne, father, male, 38; Cadiz, wife, female, 32; Ambroise, son, male, 5; Napoleon, son, male, 2 months. (1886-TMC)

#235-241; H. Demontigne, father, 39; Cadiz, wife, 34; Ambroise, son, 6; Napoleon, son, 4; St.Ann, daughter, 1; Charles Demontgne, father, 70; Marie, mother, 75. (1887-TMC)

#235-237; Herman Demontigne, father, 40; Ambroise, son, 7; Napoleon, son, 5. (1888-TMC)

#372-375; Hermance Demontigny, male, father, 40; Ambroise, male, son, 9; Napoleon, male, son, 7; Philomene, daughter, 4. (1889-TMC)

Demontigny, Patrice

#663-666; Patrice Demontignie, father, male, 28; Rozine, wife, female, 27; Joseph, son, male, 3; Francois, son, male, 1. (1885-TMC)

#565-569; Patrice Demontigne, father, male, 29; Rozine, wife, female, 28; Joseph, son, male, 4; Francois, son, male, 2; Susanna, daughter, female, 9 months. (1886-TMC)

#156-160; Patrice Demontigne, male, father, 35; Rosin, female, wife, 30; Joseph, male, son, 7; Xavier, male, son, 6; Adel Rose, female, daughter, 4. (1889-TMC-off)

Desjarlais, Abraham

Abraham Desjarlais (x), 1 man, 1 woman, 7 children, 9 total, $3.00 a share, $27.00 paid. (1868 TM annuity)

Desjarlais, Andre

#644-649; Andre Desjarlais, father, male, 45; Adelaide, wife, female, 41; Pierre, son, male, 14; John, son, male, 8; Josephine, daughter, female, 6; Marie Rose, daughter, female, 1. (1885-TMC)

#538-543; Andre Desjarlais, father, male, 46; Adellie, wife, female, 42; John, son, male, 15; Pierre, son, male, 9; Josephine, daughter, female, 7; Marie Rose, daughter, female, 7. (1886-TMC)

#354-360; Andre Dejarlais, father, 58; Adelaide, wife, 44; John, son, 17; Pierre, son, 11; Josephine, daughter, 6; Marie Rose, daughter, 4; Ellen, daughter, 2. (1888-TMC)

#402-408; Andre Dejarlais, male, father, 48; Adelaide, female, wife, 44; John, male, son, 17; Pierre, male, son, 11; Josephine, female, daughter, 9; Marie Rose, female, daughter, 5; Ellen, female, daughter, 2. (1889-TMC)

Desjarlais, Andre

Andre Desjarlais (No. 2); father, 63; Josephte, wife, 63; Napoleon, son, 15. (June 1886-TMC)

#339-341; Andre Dejarlais, father, 60; Josett, wife, 52; Napoleon, son, 17. (1888-TMC)

#161-163; Andre Dejarlais (Co Co), male, father 70; Susan, female, wife, 60; Napoleon, male, son, 17. (1889-TMC-off)

Family 74; #336-344, Andre Dejarlais, male, father, 47, mixed bloods on reservation; Adele, female, wife, 42; John, male, son, 22; St. Pierre, male, son, 15; Josephine, female, daughter, 15; Marie Rose, female, daughter, 11; Ellen, female, daughter, 10; Caroline, female, daughter, 8; Patrice, male, son, 1½. (1892-TMC)

Desjarlais, Antoine

#315-316; Antoine Dejarlais, father, 24; Mary, wife, 30. (1887-TMC)

#321-322; Antoine Dejarlais, father, 26; Mary, wife, 28. (1888-TMC)

#390-392; Antoine Dejarlais, male, father, 26; Maria, wife, 30; Rose, female, daughter, 10 days. (1889-TMC)

#398-401; Antoine Dejarlais, male, father, 27; Marie, female, mother, 31; Mary Martin, female, sister-in-law, 15; George Martin, male, brother-in-law, 12. (1890-TMC)

Desjarlais, Antoine

#147-148; Antoine Dejarlais, male, father, 29; Ursul, female, wife, 28. (1889-TMC-off)

Family 82; #373-376, Antoine Dejarlais, male, father, 31, mixed blood on reservation; Ursul, female, wife, 34; Antoine John, male, son, 1-1/2; Frank, male, son, 11 months. (1892-TMC)

Desjarlais, Francois

#399; Francois Dejarlais, male, 25. (1889-TMC)

#402-403; Francois Dejarlais, male, father, 25; Marie, female, mother, 20. (1890-TMC)

Family 78; #359-360; Francois Dejarlais, Jr., male, father, 27, mixed bloods on reservation; Marie, female, wife, 24. (1892-TMC)

Desjarlais, Francois Jr.

Francois Desjarlais (Jr.), father, 52; Mary, wife, 45; Francois, son, 23; Louise, daughter, 18; Jemy, son, 13; Mary, daughter, 10; William, son, 6; Caroline, daughter, 4; Patrice, son, 2; one house, one stable, one horse, one mare, 2 carts, 2 cows, one calf, 2 stears, 8 tons hay, one acre potatoes, one plough, one tight wagon. (1884-TMC)

#676-684; Francois Desjarlais Jr., father, male, 53; Marie, wife, female, 46; Francois, son, male, 24; Louise, daughter, female, 19; James, son, male, 15; Marie, daughter, female, 11; William, son, male, 7; Caroline, daughter, female, 5; Patrice, son, male, 3. (1885-TMC)

#549-557; Francois Desjarlais Jr. Father, male, 54; Mary, wife, female, 47; Francois, son, male, 25; Louise, daughter, female, 20; Jennie, daughter, female, 15 [?]; Mary, daughter, female, 12; William, son, male, 8; Carolina, daughter, female, 6; Patrice, son, male, 4. (1886-TMC)

#128-134; Francois Dejarlais, male, father, 65; Marie, female, wife, 42, James, male, son, 18; Marie, female, daughter, 16; William, male, son, 11; Caroline, female, daughter, 8; Patrice, male, son, 6. (1889-TMC-off)

#429-434; Francois Dejarlais, male, father, 70; Marie, female, mother, 51; James, male, son, 19; William, male, son, 12; Caroline, female, daughter, 11; Patrice, male, son, 7. (1890-TMC)

Family 85; #384-388; Francois Dejarlais sr., male, father, 65, mixed bloods on reservation; Marie, female, wife, 50; James, male, son, 21; William, male, son, 15; Patrice, male, son, 9. (1892-TMC)

Desjarlais, Francois Sr.

Francis Dejarlais (x), 1 man, 4 women, 1 child, 6 total, $3.00 a share, $18.00 paid. (1868 TM annuity)

Francois Desjarlais (x), 2 men, 2 women, 3 children, 7 total, $5.00 a share, $35.00 paid. (1874 TM annuity)

Francois Desjarlais (Sr.), father, 84; Marie, wife, 80. (1884-TMC)

#667-668; Francois Desjarlais Sr., father, male, 85; Marie, wife, female, 81. (1885-TMC)

#494-495; Francois Desjarlais Sr., father, male, 86; Marie, wife, female, 82. (1886-TMC)

Desjarlais, Francois Xavier

#861-867; Francois Xavier Desjarlais, father, male, 30; Racheal, wife, female, 28; Louis, son, male, 12; Moise, son, male, 8; Marie, daughter, female, 5; Baptist, son, male, 2; Joseph, son, male, 6 months. (1886-TMC)

#316-323; F. X. Dejarlais, male, father, 37; Rachel, female, wife, 36; Louis, male, son, 14; Moses, male, son, 12; Leander, male, son, 8; Joseph, male, son, 6; Marie, female, daughter, 10; Catherine, female, daughter, 1. (1889-TMC)

#337-344; F. X. Dejarlais, male, father, 38; Rachel, female, mother, 37; Moses, male, son, 15; Leander, male, son, 9; Joseph, male, son, 7; Marie, female, daughter, 10; Catherine, female, daughter, 2. (1890-TMC)

Family 87; #391-397; F. X. Dejarlaris, male, father, 39, mixed blood on reservation; Rachel, female, wife, 39; Louis, male, son, 18; Moses, male, son, 15; Joseph, male, son, 8; Catharine, female, daughter, 6; Joseph, male, son, 6 months. (1892-TMC)

Desjarlais, Marguerite

#854-860; Marguerite Desjarlais, mother, female, 55; Alexandre, son, male, 24; Jean Marion, son, male, 21; Jean Baptist, son, male, 16; Veronique, granddaughter, female, 16; Collin, grandson, male, 14; Joseph, grandson, male, 12. (1886-TMC)

Family 81; #369-372, Margaret Dejarlais, female, widow, 63, mixed bloods on reservation; John Baptist, male, son, 22; #371, male, son, 20; Joseph, male, son, 18. (1892-TMC)

Desjarlais, Olivier

#357-362; Olivier Desjarlais, father, male, 35; Lachal, wife, female, 30; Francois, son, male, 13; Baptist, son, male, 10; Louis, son, male, 8; Eliza, daughter, female, 6. (1886-TMC)

Desjarlais, Pierre

Pierre Desjarlais (x), 1 man, 2 women, 3 children, 6 total, $5.00 a share, $30.00 paid. (1874 TM annuity)

Pierre Desjarlais, father, 50; Sara, wife, 42; Antoine, son, 21; Roger, son, 15; Cicele, daughter, 10; Celina, daughter, 5; Joseph, son, 3; Norbert, son, 1; one DB shot gun. (1884-TMC)

#251-258; Pierre Desjarlais, father, male, 51; Sara, wife, female, 43; Antoine, son, male, 22; Roger, son, male, 16; Cecile, daughter, 11; Celina, daughter, female, 6; Joseph, son, male, 4; Norbert, son, male, 2. (1885-TMC)

#528-535; Pierre Desjarlais, father, male, 52; Sarah, wife, female, 44; Antoine, son, male, 23; Roger, son, male, Cecile, daughter, female, 12; Celina, daughter, female, 7; Jsoeph, son, male, 5; Norbert, son, male, 3. (1886-TMC)

#246-252; Pierre Dejarlais, father, 51; Sahra, wife, 43; Roger, son, 16; Cecile, daughter, 6; Joseph, son, 4; Norbert, son, 2; Celina, daughter, 6. (1887-TMC)

#248-254; Pierre Dejarlais, father, 50; Sahra, wife, 46; Roger, son, 18; Cecile, daughter, 15; Celina, daughter, 10; Joseph, son, 7; Norbert, son, 4. (1888-TMC)

#393-398; Sahra Dejarlais, female, mother, 50; Roger, male, son, 20; Cecilia, female, daughter, 18; Celina, female, daughter, 12; Joseph, male, son, 10; Norbert, male, son, 4. (1889-TMC)

Desjarlais, Pierre 2nd

#135-137; Pierre Dejarlais 2d, male, father, 23; Harriett, female, wife, 19; Francois, male, son, 1. (1889-TMC-off)

Desjarlais, Rachel

#348-353, Rachel Dejarlais, mother, 33, deserted wife; Louis, son, 10; Moise, son, 8; Christine, daughter, 6; Joseph, son, 2; Christine, daughter, 2 months. (1888-TMC)

Desjarlais, Roger

Family 83; #377-379, Roger Dejarlais, male, brother, 25; Joseph, male, brother, 10; Norbert, male, brother, 8. (1892-TMC)

Desmarais, Alfred

#115-117; Alfred Demarais, male, father, 20; Nancy, female, wife, 21; Victoria Richards, female, niece, 13. (1889-TMC-off)

Desmarais, Francois Jr.

Francois Demarais (Jr.) (x), 1 man 1 woman, 3 children, 5 total, $3.00 a share, $15.00 paid. (1868 TM annuity)

Francis Desmarais (x), 2 men, 2 women, 2 children, 6 total, $5.00 a share, $30.00 paid. (1870 TM annuity)

Francois Desmarais (x), 1 man, 2 women, 3 children, 6 total, $5.00 a share, $30.00 paid. (1874 TM annuity)

#613-617; Francois Desmarais, father, male, 48; Marguerite, wife, female, 48; Esther, daughter, female, 12; Virginie, daughter, female, 9; Joseph, son, male, 7. (1885-TMC)

#544-548; Francois Desmarais, father, male, 49; Marguerite, wife, female, 49; Esther, daughter, female, 13; Virginia, daughter, female, 10; Joseph, son, male, 8. (1886-TMC)

#123-127; Francois Demarais, male, father, 50; Margaret, female, wife, 50; Esther, female, daughter, 16; Virginie, female, daughter, 14; Joseph, male, son, 11. (1889-TMC-off)

Family 29; #120-123, Francois Demarais, male, father, 53, mixed bloods in vicinity of reservation; Margarett, female, wife, 53; Virginie, female, daughter, 16; Joseph, male, son, 14. (1892-TMC)

Desmarais, Francois Sr.

Francois Demarais (Sen) (x), 1 man, 1 total, $3.00 a share, $3.00 paid. (1868 TM annuity)

Desmarais, John

#507-510; John Desmarais, father, male, 42; Clara [?}, daughter, female, 12; Norbert, son, male, 10; Isior, son, male, 4. (1886-TMC)

Desmarais, Joseph

#145-146; Joseph Demarais, male, father, 52; Deliad, female, wife, 53. (1889-TMC-off)

Desmarais, Margaret

Margeret Demarais (x), 1 man, 1 woman, 1 child, 3 total, $5.00 a share, $15.00 paid. (1865 TM annuity)

Margarette Desmarais (x), 1 woman, 1 child, 2 total, $5.00 a share, $10.00 paid. (1870 TM annuity)

Dionne, Moses

Family 90; #403-404, Mary Dionne, female, wife, 19, mixed bloods on reservation; Moses, male, husband 20. (1892-TMC)

Dionne, Pascal

#140-144; Pascal Dionne, male, father, 59; Philomena, female, wife, 50; Baptist, male, son, 22; Moses, male, son, 16; Louis, male, son, 5. (1889-TMC-off)

Ducept, Baptist

#342-346; Baptist Ducept, father, 30; Eliza, wife, 27; Caliste, son, 5; Pierre, son, 3; Marie Madalain, daughter, 7 months. (1888-TMC)

#367-371; Baptist Ducept, father, 30; Eliza, female, wife, 28; J. Baptist, male, son, 5; Pierre, son, 4; Madalaine, female, daughter, 1. (1889-TMC)

#383-388; Baptiste Ducept, male, father, 31; Eliza, female, mother, 29; J. B., male, son, 6; Pierre, male, son, 5; Madaleine, female, daughter, 3; Larose, female, daughter, 3 months. (1890-TMC)

Family 80; #365-368; Baptist Ducept, male, widower, 43, mixed bloods on reservation; Colin, male, son, 10; Pierre, male, son, 8; Mary, female, daughter, 6. (1892-TMC)

Ducept, Henry

#364-362; Henry Ducept, male, father, 24; Virginie, female, wife, 18; Henry, male, son, 4 months. (1889-TMC)

#380-382; Henry Ducept, male, father, 27; Virginie, female, mother, 19; Henry, male, son, 1. (1890-TMC)

Family 79; #361-364; Henry Ducept, male, father, 28, mixed bloods on reservation; Virginie, female, wife, 22; Henry, male, son, 4; Veronica, female, daughter, 2. (1892-TMC)

Ducept, Madelaine Widow

#255; Widow Ducept, female, Widow, 58. (1889-TMC)

#278; Madelaine Widow Ducept, female, 59. (1890-TMC)

Ducette, Michael

Michael Ducette (x), 1 man, 1 woman, 1 boy, 1 daughter, 4 total, $5.00 a share, $20.00 total. (1869 TM annuity)

Ducept, Pierre

#253-254; Pierre Ducept, male, father, 25; Celina, female, wife, 16. (1889-TMC)

#276-277; Pierre Ducept, male, father, 26; Celina, female, mother, 17. (1890-TMC)

Family 86; #389-390; Pierre Ducept, male, father, 32, mixed bloods on reservation; Celina, female, wife, 20. (1892-TMC)

Duchan, Baptist

Baptist Duchan, father, 35; Catharine, wife, 30; Baptist, son, 15; Milane, daughter, 14; Joseph, son, 13; Marie, daughter, 12; Madelin, daughter, 12; Caroline, daughter, 9. (January 1886-TMC)

#305-312; Baptiste Duchan, father, 36; Catherine, wife, 31; Baptist, son, 16; Malina, daughter, 14; Joseph, son, 12; Madaline, daughter, 8; Mary, daughter, 8; Caroline, daughter, 6. (1887-TMC)

Duchain, Isabelle

#313-314; Isabelle Duchan, widow, 62; Alexandre, son, 16. (1887-TMC)

#273-274; Isabell Duchain, widow, 70; Alexandre, son, 17. (1888-TMC)

Duchain, Laron

Laron Duchain, father, _; Marie Virginie, wife, 23; Marie, daughter, 2; Marie Rirginie, 2 months. (July 1886-TMC)

#242-245; Laron Duchain, father, 27; Mary, wife, 24; Marie Rose, daughter, 3; Marie Virginie, daughter, 1. (1887-TMC)

#268-272; Laron Duchain, father, 27; Virginie, wife, 22; Marie Rose, daughter, 3; Marie Virginie, daughter, 2; Alexander, son, 1. (1888-TMC)

#282-283; Laron Duchain, male, father, 27; Alex, male, son, 2. (1889-TMC)

Family 71; #317-320, Elise Duchan, female, wife, 20, mixed bloods on reservation; Larou, male, husband, 33; Virginie, female, daughter, 7; Alexander, male, son, 5. (1892-TMC)

Ducharme, Baptist

#477-480; Baptiste Ducharme, father, male, 33; Catherine, wife, female, 34; Baptist, son, male, 16; Melina, daughter, 14; William, son, male, 12; Marie, daughter, female, 10 (twin); Isabelle, daughter, female, 10 (twin), Marguerite, daughter, female, 8. (1886-TMC)

Ducharme, Chrisastom [Chrysostome]

#868-872; Chrisastom Ducharme, father, male, 33; Clemence, wife, female, 33; Rose, daughter, female, 8; Marie, daughter, female, 5; William, son, male, 2. (1886-TMC)

#290-295; Chym. Ducharb, father, 35; Clemence, wife, 25; Ruth, daughter, 9; Marie Rose, daughter, 6; William, son, 3; Maxim, son, 10 months. (1887-TMC)

#299-304; Chm. Ducharme, father, 36; Clemence, wife, 29; Rose de Lima, daughter, 10; Mary Rose, daughter, 7; William, son, 4; Maxime, son, 2. (1888-TMC)

#357-363; Chrisostom Ducharme, male, father, 37; Clemena, female, wife, 30; Rose Delima, female, daughter, 12; Marie Rose, female, daughter, 8; Maxime, male, son, 3; William, male, son, 5; Pierre, male, son, 7 months. (1889-TMC)

#373-379; Chytm Dcuharme, male, father, 38; Clemence, female, mother, 29; Rose D, female, daughter, 12; Mary R., female, daughter, 8; Maxime, male, son, 4; William, male, son, 6; Pierre, male, son, 2. (1890-TMC)

Duchaw, Baptist

#312-320; Baptist Duchaw, father, 43; Catherine, wife, 42; Baptist, son, 16; Melina, daughter, 14; Joseph, son, 12; Madalain, daughter, 7; Mary, daughter, 7; Caroline, daughter, 5. (1888-TMC)

Dumont, Isidore

#502-506; Isidore Dumont, father, male, 27; Marie, wife, female, 26; Veronique, daughter, female, 2; Fredrick, son, male, 1; Marie, daughter, female, 1 month. (1886-TMC)

Dusiame, Marie

Marie Dusiame, mother, 38; Marierose, daughter, _; Clamance, daughter, _; Rachael, daughter, 11; Joseph, son, 9; Baptist, son, 7. (1884-TMC)

Enno, Alexander [See also Alexis Canada]

#409-410; Alexander Enno, male, father, 25; Marie, female, wife, 22. (1889-TMC)
Family 93, #414-415, Mary Rose Enno, female, wife, 28, mixed bloods on reservation; Alexander, male, husband, 21. (1892-TMC)

Enno, Antoine

#361-365; Antoine Enno, father, 56; Caroline, wife, 55; Virginie, daughter, 24; Louis, son, 19; Jerome, son, 14. (1888-TMC)
#411-414; Antoine Enno, male, father, 56; Catherine, female, wife, 56; Louis, male, son, 20; Jerome, male, son, 15. (1889-TMC)
#435-437; Antoine Enno, male, father, 58; Catherine, female, mother, 58; Louis, male, son, 21. (1890-TMC)
Family 94; #416-418; Antoine Enno, male, father, 60, mixed bloods on reservation; Catharine, female, wife, 60; Louis, male, son, 22. (1892-TMC)

Enno, Antoine Jr. (See also Antoine Canada)

#164-166; Antoine Enno Jr., male, father, 27; Marie, female, wife, 18; Philomene, female, daughter, 6. (1889-TMC-off)
Family 31; #126-130, Antoine Enno, jr., male, father, 38, mixed bloods in vicinity of reservation; Mary Celina, female, wife, 23; Philomene, female, daughter, 3; Alexander, male, son, 2; Mary, female, [daughter], 10 days. (1892-TMC)

Enno, Baptiste

#438-439; Baptiste Enno, male, father, 25; Theresa, female, mother, 18. (1890-TMC)
Family 95; #419-421; Theresa Enno, female, wife, 20, mixed bloods on reservation; Baptist, male, husband, 26; Adele, female, daughter 2. (1892-TMC)

Espagnol, Catherine

Catherine Espagnol (x), 1 woman, 2 boys, 2 girls, 6 total, $5.00 a share, $30.00 total. (1869 TM annuity)

Fagnant, Jean Louis

#634-638; Jean Louis Fagnant, father, male, 57; Madeleine, wife, female, 41; Pierre, son, male, 20; Isabel, daughter, female, 15; John, son, male, 13. (1885-TMC)
#599-602; Jean Louis Fagnean, father, male, 58; Madeline, wife, female, 42; Pierre, son, male, 21; Isabelle, daughter, female, 16. (1886-TMC)
#174-176; J. L. Fagnant, male, father, 58; Madalain, female, wife, 45; St.Pierre, male, son, 20. (1889-TMC-off)

Fagnant, William

#873-875; William Fagneau, father, male, 33; Justine, wife, female, 18; Jerome Lafountain, brother-in-law, male, 7. (TMC-1886)

#340-342; William Falcon [Fagnant], father, 34; Susan [Justine], wife, 19; Jerome Lafontaine, brother-in-law, 8. (1887-TMC)

#369-372; Wm. Fagnant, father, 34; Julia, wife, 22; Victor, son, 2; Madalain Fagnant, mother, 85. (1888-TMC)

#426-429; William Fagnant, male, father, 34; Julia, female, wife, 23; Victor, male, son, 3; Antoine, male, son, 1. (1889-TMC)

#451-455; Wm. Fagnant, male, father, 35; Julia, female, mother, 24; Victor, male, son, 4; Antoine, male, son, 2; Emerice, female, daughter, 1 month. (1890-TMC)

Family 99; #436-441; William Fagnant, male, father, 40, mixed bloods on reservation; Julia, female, wife, 26; Victor, male, son, 7; Antoine, male, son, 4; Mary Elise, female, daughter, 2; Alexander, male, son, 2 months. (1892-TMC)

Falcon, Elie

Eleha Falcon, father, 38; Amely, daughter, 12; Frezine, daughter, 10; Virginia, daughter, 7; Eleha, son, 3. (1884-TMC)

#906-910; Eleha Falcon, father, male, 40; Amely, daughter, female, 14; Freisien, daughter, female, 12; Virginia, daughter, female, 9; Eleha, son, male, 5. (1886-TMC)

#353-357; Eleha Falcon, father, 40; Emily daughter, 15; Frizine, daughter, 13; Virginia, daughter, 9; Eli, son, 5. (1887-TMC)

#383-386; Eleha Falcon, father, 40; Emily, daughter, 15; Frezene, daughter, 13; Eli, son, 7. (1888-TMC)

#432-435; Elie Falcon, male, father, 43; Emilie, female, daughter, 17; Frezine, female, daughter, 15; Elie, male, son, 3 [sic]. (1889-TMC)

#456-458; Elie Falcon Widower, male, father, 44; Frezene, female, daughter, 15; Elie, male, son, 8. (1890-TMC)

Family 101; #444-446, Elie Falcon, male, father, 45, mixed bloods on reservation; Frezene, female, daughter, 16; Elie, male, son, 11. (1892-TMC)

Falcon, Job

#177-181; Job Falcon, male, father, 37; Marie, female, wife, 28; Antoine, male, son, 6; Rafel, male, son, 4; Alphonse, male, son, 1. (1889-TMC-off)

Fiddler, Francois

#358-360; Francois Fiddler, father, 22; Celina, wife, 22; Mary, daughter, 6 months. (1887-TMC)

Fiddler, (Mrs.) Frank

#182-184; Mrs. Frank Fiddler, female, mother, 25; Moses, male, son, 3; Joseph, male, son, 1-1/2. (1889-TMC)

Fidney, James

James Fidney (x), 1 man, 1 total, $3.00 a share, $3.00 paid. (1868 TM annuity)

Flavias, Pierre

#430-431; Pierre Flavias [?], male, father, 28; Amerise, female, daughter, 2. (1889-TMC)

Flamand, Pierre

Pierre Flamand (x), 1 man, 1 woman, 1 boy, 3 total, $5.00 a share, $15.00 paid. (1869 TM annuity)

Fleury, Andre

#171-173; Andre Fleury, male, father, 26; Catharine, female, wife, 26; Agatha, female, daughter, 5. (1889-TMC-off)

Fleury, Antoine

Antoine Fleury (x), 1 man, 1 woman, 2 boys, 4 total, $5.00 a share, $20.00 total. (1869 TM annuity)

Fleury, Betsy

Betsy Fleury (x), 1 man, 1 woman, 4 children, 6 total, $3.00 a share, $18.00 paid. (1868 TM annuity)

Fleury, Joseph

#167-170; Joseph Fleury, male, father, 64; Julie, female, wife, 54; William, male, son, 22; Bernard, male, son [?], 3. (1889-TMC-off)

Fleury, Patrice

Pautrice Fleury (x), 1 man, 1 woman, 1 child, 3 total, $3.00 a share, $9.00 paid. (1868 TM annuity)

Pautrice Fleury (x), 1 man, 1 woman, 4 boys, 1 daughter, 7 total, $5.00 a share, $35.00 total. (1869 TM annuity)

Foie, Pierre

Pierre Foie, father, 45; Betsy, wife, 42; Louis Vizina, adopted son, 17. (1884-TMC)

#215-217; Pierre Foie, father, male, 46; Betsy, wife, female, 43; Louis Vezina, adopted son, male, 18. (1885-TMC)

#96-98; Pierre Foie, father, male, 47; Betsy, wife, female, 44; Louis Vizina, son, male, 19. (1886-TMC)

#350-352; Pierre Foi, father, 48; Betsy, wife, 45; Louis, adopted son, 20. (1887-TMC)

#380-382; Pierre Foy, father, 50; Betsy, wife, 47; Louis, adopted son, 22. (1888-TMC)

#436-437; Pierre Foi, male, father, 51; Betsy, female, wife, 47. (1889-TMC)

#459-460; Pierre Foi, male, father, 52; Betsy, female, wife, 48. (1890-TMC)

Family 100; #442-443; Pierre Foi, male, father, 53; Betsy, female, wife, 51. (1892-TMC)

Foster, Mrs. Henry

Mrs. Henry Foster (x), 1 woman, 3 children, 4 total, $10.00 a share, $40.00 paid. (1873 TM annuity)

Fournier, Antoine

#393-395; Antoine Fournier, father, 33; Rosalie, wife, 25; Victoria, daughter, 8. (1888-TMC)

#444-446; Antoine Fournier, male, father, 38; Rosalie, female, wife, 22; Victoria, female, daughter, 8. (1889-TMC)

#466-467; Antoine Fournier, male, father, 34; Rosalie, female, mother, 25. (1890-TMC)

Fournier, Francois

#389-392; Francois Fournier, father, 58; Madalain, wife, 50; Jean, son, 9; Henriette, granddaughter, 6. (1888-TMC)

#438-443; Francois Fournier, male, father, 58; Madalaine, female, wife, 48; Norbert, male, son, 18; Florestine, female, daughter, 17; Jean, male, son, 11; Henriatta, female, granddaughter, 8. (1889-TMC)

#461-465; Francois Fournier, male, father, 60; Madelaine, female, mother, 52; Norbert, male, son, 20; Jean, male, son, 11; Henrietta, female, daughter, 9. (1890-TMC)

Fournier, Norbert

Family 102; #447, Nobert Fournier, male, father, 23, mixed bloods on reservation; #448, Mary, female, wife, 19. (1892-TMC)

Frederick, Dion

#361-362; Dion Frederick, father, 19; Susan, wife, 18. (1887-TMC)

#387-388; Dion Frederick, father, 20; Susan, wife, 19. (1888-TMC)

#417-418; Dion Frederick, male, father, 19; Susan, female, wife, 19. (1889-TMC)

Frederick, George

#396-397; Geo. Frederick, father, 23; Florestine, wife, 16. (1888-TMC)

Frederick, Joseph Jr.

Joseph Fredrick Jr., father, 38; Sara, wife, 35; Joseph, son, 7; Isabel, daughter, 5; Veronique, daughter, 3; (June 1886), Mary Jane, 2 months. (1884-TMC)

#137-142; Joseph Frederick Jr., father, male, 39; Sara, wife, female, 36; Joseph, son, male, 8; Isabel, daughter, female, 6; Veronique, daughter, female, 4; Mary Jane, daughter, female, 1. (1885-TMC)

#117-122; Joseph Frederick Jr., father, male, 40; Sarah, wife, female, 37; Joseph, son, male, 9; Isabella, daughter, female, 7; Veronique, daughter, female, 5; Mary Jane, daughter, female, 2 months. (1886-TMC)

#343-349; Joseph Frederick Jr., father, 41; Sahra, wife, 38; Joseph, son, 10; Isabel, daughter, 8; Veronique, daughter, 6; Mary Jane, 2; Josett, daughter, 2 months. (1887-TMC)

#373-379; Joseph Frederick Jr., father, 42; Sahra, wife, 39; Joseph son, 11; Isabel, daughter, 9; Veronique, daughter, 7; Mary Jane, daughter, 5; Jossett, daughter, 2. (1888-TMC)

#419-425; Joseph Frederick Jr., male, father, 40; Sahrah, female, wife, 42; Joseph, male, son, 11; Isabel, female, daughter, 9; Veronic, female, daughter, 7; Mary Jane, female, daughter, 5; Josette, female, daughter, 2. (1889-TMC)

#444-450; Joseph Frederick, male, father, 45; Sarah, female, mother, 43; Joseph, male, son, 12; isabelle, female, daughter, 11; Veronic, female, daughter, 7; Mary Jane, female, daughter, 6; Jossette, female, daughter, 4. (1890-TMC)

Family 96; #422-428; Joseph Frederick, male, father, 48, mixed bloods on reservation; Sabrah, female, wife, 46; Joseph, male, son, 15; Elizabeth, female, daughter, 12; Veronica, female, daughter, 10; Mary Jane, female, daughter, 8; Josett, female, daughter, 6. (1892-TMC)

Frederick, Joseph Sr.

Joseph Frederick (x), 1 man, 1 woman, 1 child, 3 total, $8.50 a share, $25.50 paid. (1871 TM annuity)

Joseph Fredrick, father, 67; Marie Anne, wife, 57; Josephte, daughter, 18, (married to white man June 1886); William son, 16 (married June 1886); Moise, grandson, 3 months, (born June 1885) (died); one house, one stable, 11 tons hay, one acre potatoes, one horse, 2 carts, one pr. cattle, yoak and chains, one plough B, one stove. (1884-TMC)

#259-262; Joseph Frederick Sr., father, male, 68; Marie, wife, female, 58; William, son, male, 18; Moise, grandson, male, 3 months. (1885-TMC)

#176-177; Joseph Fredrick Sr., father, male, 69; Mary Anne, wife, female, 59. (1886-TMC)

#338-339; Joseph Frederick, father, 70; Marian, wife, 60. (1887-TMC)

#366-368; Joseph Frederick Sr., father, 71; Marie Ann, wife, 61; Joseph DeCouteau, grandson, 15. (1888-TMC)

#415-416; Joseph Frederick Sr., male, father, 72; Marie Ann, female, wife, 63. (1889-TMC)

#440-443; Marie Anne Widow Frederick, female, mother, 70; Andre, male, grandson, 10; Xavier, male, N, 19; Suzanne, female, N, 20. (1890-TMC)

Family 97; #429-431, Mrs. Joseph Frederick, sr., female, widow, 84; Nancy Brown, female, __, 13; Edward Brown, male, __, 12. (1892-TMC)

Frederick, Louis

Louis Frederick (x), 1 man, 1 woman, 3 boys, 3 girls, 8 total, $5.00 a share, $40.00 total. (1869 TM annuity)

Frederick, William

#768-769; William Frederick, father, male, 18; Susanne, wife, female, 18. (1886-TMC)

Family 98; #432-435, ___ Frederick, male, father, 23, mixed blood on reservation; Susan, female, wife, 21; Christine, female, daughter, 3; Francois, male, son, 5 months. (1892-TMC)

Frockey, Baptiste

Baptiste Frockey (x), 1 man, 1 woman, 5 children, 7 total, $3.00 a share, $27.00 paid. (1868 TM annuity)

Gagar, Julia

Julia Gagar (x), 1 man, 1 woman, 2 total, $3.00 a share, $6.00 paid. (1868 TM annuity)

Gagnon, Joseph

#384-385; Joseph Gouneau, father, 77; Susan, wife, 75. (1887-TMC)

#398-399; Joseph Gouron, father, 77; Susan, wife, 73. (1888-TMC)

#484; Susan Widow Gagnon, 75. (1890-TMC)

Gardner, George

#528-534; Geo. Gardner, whiteman, male, father, 45; Anastasie, Chippewa, female, mother, 34; Charles, male, son, 15; Lucy, female, daughter, 9; William, male, son, 7; George, male, son, 3; Amilie, female, daughter, 4 months. (1890-TMC)

Family 117, #502-509; Anastasie Gardner, female, wife, 37, mixed bloods on reservation; George, male, husband, 47; Charles, male, son, 17; Emma, female, daughter, 15; Rachel, female, daughter, 13; Lucy, female, daughter, 11; William male, son, 9; George, male, son, 5; Emily, female, daughter, 3. (1892-TMC)

Gariepy, Francois

Francois Graudipie (x), 1 man, 1 woman, 2 boys, 1 daughter, 5 total, $5.00 a share, $25.00 total. (1869 TM annuity)

Gariepy, Joseph

Joseph Gardisan [Gariepy ?] (x), 1 man, 1 woman, 3 children, 5 total, $3.00 a share, $15.00 paid. (1868 TM annuity)

Joseph Gardisee [Gariepy ?] (x), 1 man, 1 woman, 3 children, 5 total, $3.00 a share, $15.00 paid. (1868 TM annuity)

Joseph Gardipie (x), 1 man, 1 woman, 2 boys, 1 daughter, 5 total, $5.00 a share, $25.00 total. (1869 TM annuity)

Joseph Gardepe (x), 1 man, 1 woman, 1 child, 3 total, $5.00 a share, $15.00 paid. (1870 TM annuity)

Gariepy, Norbert

Norbert Gardipie (x), 1 man, 1 woman, 1 daughter, 3 total, $5.00 a share, $15.00 total. (1869 TM annuity)

Gaugnon or Gangon, Susan

#463; Susan Gaugnon, female, widow, 72. (1889-TMC)

Family 116; #501, Susan Gangon, female, widow, 76, mixed bloods on reservation. (1892-TMC)

Gervais, Francois

Francis Garvis (x), 2 men, 2 women, 3 children, 7 total, $5.00 a share, $35.00 paid. (1870 TM annuity)

Gingras, Antoine

Antoine Gingras (x), 6 men, 1 woman, 4 girls, 11 total, $5.00 a share, $55.00 total. (1869 TM annuity)

Gingras, Marguerite [nee Trottier]

Madam Gingras (x), 1 woman, 1 total, $3.00 a share, $3.00 paid. (1868 TM annuity)

Margaret Gingras (x), 1 woman, 1 total, $5.00 a share, $5.00 total. (1869 TM annuity)

Gladu, Charles

Charles Gladue (x), 1 man, 1 woman, 5 children, 7 total, $3.00 a share, $21.00 paid. (1868 TM annuity)

Charles Gladeau (x), 1 man, 1 woman, 3 boys, 3 girls, 8 total, $5.00 a share, $40.00 total. (1869 TM annuity)

Charles Glaudue (x), 4 men, 4 women, 3 children, 11 total, $5.00 a share, $55.00 paid. (1870 TM annuity)

Charles Gladu, father, 54; Cadz, wife, 40; Charles, son, 16; Sara, daughter, 14; Marie Rosalie, daughter, 11; Marie Louise, daughter, 9; Claude, son, 5; Jean Moise, son, 3; Joseph, son, 1; James Azure, stepson, 22; Antoine Azure, son, 21; one house, one stable, 20 tons hay, 12 acres B, ½ acre potatoes, one wagon, one horse, one mare, one cow, 2 calves, one pr. cattle yoak and chain, one plough, one g. Stove, one stove H, one nickel gun. (1884-TMC)

#559-571; Charles Gladu, father, male, 55; Cadiz, wife, female, 41; James Azure, stepson, male, 23; Antoine Azure, stepson, male, 22; Charles Gladu, son, male, 17; Sara, daughter, female, 15; Marie, daughter, female, 12; Rosalie, daughter, female, 10; Louise, daughter, female, 8; Claude, son, male, 6; Jean, son, male, 4; Joseph, son, male, 2; William, son, male, 2 months. (1885-TMC)

#727; Charles [Gladu], Father, male, 56; Cadez, wife, female, 42; Charles, son, male, 18; Sarah, daughter, female, 16; Marie Rosalie, daughter, female, 13; Marie Louise, daughter, female, 11; Claude, son, male, 7; Jean Moise, son, male, 5; Joseph, son, male, 3; James Azure, stepson, male, 24; Antoine Azure, stepson, male, 23. (1886-TMC)

#200-209; Chas. Gladue, male, father, 59; Lesota, female, wife, 48; Charles, male, son, 20; Sahra, female, daughter, 18; Marie Louise, female, daughter, 12; Claud, male, son, 11; John, male, son, 7; Bruno, male, son, 6; William, male, son, 5; Louis, male, son, 2. (1889-TMC-off)

Family 34; #142-150, Charles Gladue, male, father, 70, mixed bloods in vicinity of reservation; Leviacded, female, wife, 46; Charles, male, son, 23; Marie Louise, female, daughter, 14; Claude, male, son, 12; John, male, son, 10; Bruno, male, son, 9; William, male, son, 7; Louis, male, son, 4. (1892-TMC)

Gladu, Frank

Family 36; #152-159, Julia Gladue, female, wife, 30, mixed bloods in vicinity of reservation; Frank (white), male, husband, 30; Rosalie, female, daughter, 10; __; Frank, male, son, 7; Adelia, female, daughter, 5; Mary, female, daughter, 3; Caroline, female, daughter, 2. (1892-TMC)

Gladu, Joseph

Joseph Gladu, father, 40; Madeleine, mother, 70; Anastazie Amyotte, widow, sister, 29; Theodore, son, 5; Louis, son, 1; one house, one stable, 8 tons hay, 5 acres wheat, ½ acre potatoes, one cook stove. (1884-TMC)

#125-126; Joseph Gladu, son, male, 43; Madeleine, mother, female, 71. (1885-TMC)

#714-718; Joseph Gladu, son, male, 42; Madeline, mother, female, 72; Anastasie Amyotte, sister [niece ?], female, 31; Theodore, nephew, male, 7; Louis, nephew, male, 3. (1886-TMC)

#185-189; Joseph Gladue, male, 40; Edasie Amyott, female, sister [niece], 33; Theodore, male, son, 9; Louis, male, son, 5; Madalaine, female, mother, 80. (1889-TMC-off)

Family 35; #151, Joseph Gladue, male, single, 44, mixed bloods in vicinity of reservation. (1892-TMC)

Gladue, Michael

Michael Glaudue (x), 1 man, 1 woman, 4 children, 6 total, $3.00 a share, $18.00 paid. (1868 TM annuity)

Michael Gladue (x), 1 man, 1 woman, 2 boys, 3 girls, 7 total, $5.00 a share, $35.00 total. (1869 TM annuity)

Michael Gladin (x), 3 men, 3 women, 2 children, 8 total, $5.00 a share, $40.00 paid. (1870 TM annuity)

Michael Gladue (x), 1 woman, 1 child, 2 total, $8.50 a share, $17.00 paid. (1871 TM annuity)

Michael Gladu (x), 1 man, 1 total, $10.50 a share, $10.50 paid. (1872 TM annuity)

Gladue, Michael

#191-193; Michael Gladue, male, father, 26; Marie, female, wife, 22; Joseph, male, son, 1. (1889-TMC-off)

Gladu, Mrs.

Mrs. Gladu (x), 1 woman, 1 child, 2 total, $8.50 a share, $17.00 paid. (1871 TM annuity)

Gladu, Pierre

Pierre Gladue (x), 1 man, 1 total, $10.50 a share, $10.50 paid. (1872 TM annuity)

Pierre Gladue, father, 47; Isabel, wife, 37; Marie Rose, daughter, 16; Justine, daughter, 14; Catharine, daughter, 12; Virginie, daughter, 3; Joseph, son, 1; Patrice, son, 6 months; one house, one single B shot gun. (1884-TMC)

#128-134; Pierre Gladu, father, male, 48; Isabel, wife, female, 39; Marie Rose, daughter, female, 17; Justine, daughter, female, 15; Catherine, daughter, female, 13; Virginie, daughter, female, 4; Joseph, son, male, 2. (1885-TMC)

#719-726; Pierre Gladu, father, male, 49; Isabelle, wife, female, 39; Marie Rose, daughter, female, 18; Justine, daughter, female, 16; Cathrine, daughter, female, 14; Virginia, daughter, female, 5; Joseph, son, male, 3; Patrice, son, male, 6 months. (1886-TMC)

#194-199; Peter Gladue, male, father, 52; Isabel, female, wife, 42; Virginie, female, daughter, 9; Joseph, male, son, 7; Patrice, male, son, 4; Napoleon, male, son 2. (1889-TMC-off)

Family 33; #136-141, Pierre Gladue, male, father, 60, mixed bloods in vicinity of reservation; Isabel, female, wife, 55; Virginie, female, daughter, 12; Joseph Peter, male, son, 9; Batrie, male, son, 7; Mary, female, daughter, 2. (1892-TMC)

Godon/Guddon/Godden

Guddon, Gilbert

#210-212; Gilbert Guddon, male, father, 40; Elize, female, wife, 24; Joseph, male, son, 3-1/2. (1889-TMC-off)

Godon, Joseph

Joseph Godon (x), 1 man, 1 woman, 2 total, $8.50 a share, $17.00 paid. (1871 TM annuity)

Godden, Louis

Family 106; #457-461, Louis Godden, male, father, 57, mixed blood on reservation; Mary, female, wife, 49; Philip, male, son, 21; Moses, male, son, 14; Veronie, female, daughter, 8. (1892-TMC)

#523-527; Louis Goddon, male, father, 50; Marie, female, mother, 45; Phillip, male, son, 19; Moses, male, son, 12; Veronique, female, daughter, 6. (1890-TMC)

Goneville, Antoine

#213-222; Antoine Goneville, male, father, 53; Elize, female, wife, 32; Elize, female, daughter, 12; Patrice, male, son, 11; Antoine, male, son, 5; John B., male, son, 3; Theresa, female, daughter, 4 months; Alexis Goneville, male, father, 80; Jossett, female, mother, 80. (1889-TMC-off)

Gossette, Rosalie

Family 37; #160-163, Rosalie Gossette, female, wife, 23, mixed bloods in vicinity of reservation; Alphonse, male, son, 5; Libby, female, daughter, 3; Samuel Paul, male, son, 8 months. (1892-TMC)

Goslin, Delos [?]

#223-224; Delos Goslin, male, father, 38; Mary, female, wife, 45; Joseph, male, son, 18; Jossett, female, daughter, 10; Roger, male, son, 10; Peter, male, son, 8. (1889-TMC-off)

Gourneau, Baptiste

#476; Baptiste Gourneau, male, 36. (1890-TMC)

Gourneau, Kashish pah [Gaspard Louis]

Kashish pah, halfbreed [Gaspard Louis Gourneau] (x), 1 man, 1 woman, 5 children, 7 total, $8.50 a share, $39.50 paid. (1871 TM annuity)

Gourneau, Joseph Sr.

Joseph Gourneau (x), 1 man, 1 woman, 8 children, 10 total, $3.00 a share, $30.00 paid. (1868 TM annuity)

Joseph Gornon (x), 1 man, 4 women, 5 boys, 3 girls, 13 total, $5.00 a share, $65.00 paid. (1869 TM annuity)

Joseph Gornon (x), 4 men, 6 women, 3 children, 13 total, $5.00 a share, $65.00 paid. (1870 TM annuity)

Joseph Gornoe (x), 2 men, 2 women, 9 children, 13 total, $8.50 a share, $110.50 paid. (1871 TM annuity)

Joseph Gurnoe (x), 1 man, 1 woman, 2 total, $10.50 a share, $21.00 paid. (1872 TM annuity)

Joseph Gorneau Sr., father, 65; Judith, wife, 60; Patrice, son, 28; Lendre, son, 28; Joseph, son, 26; Louis, son, 24; Alexandre, son, 22; Marie, daughter, 16; Cecile, daughter, 14; 2 Winchesters, one shot gun DB. (1884-TMC)

#143-151; Joseph Gourneau, father, male, 66; Judith, wife, female, 61; Patrice, son, male, 29; Leandre, son, male, 29; Joseph, son, male, 27; Louis, son, male, 25; Alexandre, son, male, 23; Marie, daughter, female, 17; Cecile, daughter, female, 15. (1885-TMC)

#178-186; Joseph Gourneau, father, male, 67; Judith, wife, female, 62; Patrice, son, male, 30; Lendre, son, male, 30; Joseph, son, male, 28; Louis, son, male, 26; Alexandre, son, male, 24; Marie, daughter, female, 18; Saline, daughter, female, 16. (1886-TMC)

#363-369; Joseph Gorneau Sr., father, 68; Judith, wife, 63; Leon, son, 29; Alexander, son, 22; Mary, daughter, 19; Cecilia, daughter, 17. (1887-TMC)

#400-405; Joseph Gourneau Sr., father, 69; Judith, wife, 64; Leon, son, 25; Alexander, son, 23; Mary, daughter, 20; Cecilia, daughter, 19. (1888-TMC)

#456-462; Joseph Gourneau Sr., male, father, 60; Judee, female, wife, 57; Leander, male, son, 30; Louis, male, son, 28; Alexander, male, son, 19; Marie, female, daughter, 18; Cecilia, female, daughter, 16. (1889-TMC)

#477-482; Joseph Gourneau Sr., male, father, 68; Judie, female, mother, 60; Leander, male, son, 36; Louis, male, son, 32; Alexander, male, son, 30; Cecile, female, daughter, 16. (1890-TMC)

Family 105; #453-456; Joseph Gourneau sr, male, father, 62, mixed bloods on reservation; Judie, female, wife, 56; Leonard, male, son, 35; Alexander, male, son, 24. (1892-TMC)

Gourneau, Joseph Jr. (No. 1) (2nd)

Joseph Gorneau Jr., father, 32; Jean, son, 4. (1884-TMC)

Joseph Gorneau Jr., father, son of Kaska, 34, Jean, son, 6. (1886-TMC)

#431-432; Joseph Gourneau Jr., father, 35; Angelic, wife, 26. (1888-TMC)

#452-454; Joseph Gourneau, male, father, 39; Angelic, female, wife, 26; Jean, male, son, 9. (1889-TMC)

#468-470; Joseph Gourneau No. 1, male, father, 40; Angelic, female, mother, 33; Jean Male, son, 9. (1890-TMC)

Family 109; #467-469, Joseph Gourneau, 2d, male, father, 43, mixed bloods on reservation; Angelique, female, wife, 35; John, male, son, 13. (1892-TMC)

Gourneau, Joseph Jr.

#487; Joseph Gourneau Jr., male, 26. (1889-TMC)

#483; Joseph Gourneau Jr., male, 34. (1890-TMC)

Family 104; #451-452; Joseph Gourneau jr., male, father, 26, mixed bloods on reservation; Elise, female, wife, 17. (1892-TMC)

Gourneau, Leon

#417-418; Leon Gourneau, father, 29; Monique, wife, 17. (1888-TMC)

Gourneau, Louis

Family 107; #462-464, Louis Gourneau, male, father, 30; Elise, female, wife, 18; Angelic, female, daughter, 10 months. (1892-TMC)

Gourneau, Marguerite

Margarette Gornoe (x), 1 man, 1 woman, 1 child, 3 total, $8.50 a share, $25.50 paid. (1871 TM annuity)

Gourneau, Patrice

#455; Patrice Gourneau, male, father, 30. (1889-TMC)

Family 108; #465, Patrice Gourneau, male, father, 35, mixed bloods on reservation; #466, La Rose, female, wife, 20. (1892-TMC)

Grandbois, Isidore

Isidore Grandbois, father, 37; Sara, wife, 28; Elzard, son, 10; Alexandre, son, 8; Sara, daughter, 7; David, son, 6; Isidore, son, 1; Lizie, daughter, 2 months, (June 1886). (1884-TMC)

#481-487; Isidore Grandbois, father, male, 38; Sara, wife, female, 29; Elziard, son, male, 11; Alexandre, son, male, 9; Sara, daughter, female, 7; David, son, male, 6; Isidore, son, male, 2. (1885-TMC)

#606-613; Isidore Grandbois, father, male, 39; Sarah, wife, female, 30; Elsard, son, male, 12; Alexandre, son, male, 10; Sarah, daughter, female, 9; David, son, male, 8; Isidore, son, male, 3; Liza, daughter, female, 2 months. (1886-TMC)

#386-393; Isidore Granbois, father, 40; Sahra, wife, 32; Elzard, son, 13; Alexandre, son, 12; Sahra, daughter, 10; David, son, 6; Isidore, son, 2; Eliza, daughter, 1. (1887-TMC)

#424-430; Isidore Granbois, father, 40; Sahra, wife, 32; Elzard, son, 15; Alexander, son, 13; David, son, 8; Eliza, daughter, 3; Joseph, son, 3 months. (1888-TMC)

#469-475; Isidor Granbois, male, father, 46; Sahra, female, wife, 34; Elizare, male, son, 16; Alex, male, son, 14; David, male, son, 3; Eliz, female, daughter, 3; Joseph, male, son, 1. (1889-TMC)

#500-507; Isidore Grandbois, male, father, 38; Sahra, female, wife, 36; Elizare, male, son, 16; Alexander, male, son, 14; David, male, son, 10; Elize, female, daughter, 4; Joseph, male, son, 2; Patrice, male, son, 2 months. (1890-TMC)

Family 111; #474-481; Isidore Granbois, male, father, 40, mixed bloods on reservation; Sabrah, female, wife, 39; Elizard, male, son, 19; Alexander, male, son, 16; David, male, son, 12; Eliza, female, daughter, 6; Patrice, male, son, 4; Genevieve, female, daughter, one month. (1892-TMC)

Grandbois, Patrice

#700-702; Patrice Grandbois, father, male, 23; Mary Jane, wife, female, 20; Alexandre, son, male, 3 months. (1885-TMC)

#603-605; Patrice Grandbois, father, male, 24; Mary Jane, wife, female, 21; Alexandre, son, male, 1. (1886-TMC)

#381-383; Patrice Granbois, father, 27; Mary Jane, wife, 22; Alexander, son, 2. (1887-TMC)

#419-423; Patrice Granbois, father, 24; Mary Jane, wife, 23; Alexander, son, 3; Michael, son, 1; John Morin, S L, 15. 1888-TMC)

#464-468; Patrice Granbois, male, father, 25; Marie Jane, female, wife, 25; Alexander, male, son, 4; Michael, male, son, 2; Zilda, female, daughter, 1 month. (1889-TMC)

#485-489; Patrice Grandbois, male, father, 26; Mary Jane, female, mother, 26; Alex, male, son, 5; Michael, male, son, 2, Zilda, female, daughter, 1. (1890-TMC)

Family 112; #482-487; Patrice Granbois, male, father, 29, mixed bloods on reservation; Mary Jane, female, wife, 27; Alexander, male, son, 7; Michael, male, son, 5; Zilda, female, daughter, 3; Emma, female, daughter, 1. (1892-TMC)

Grandbois, Paul

#521-522; Paul Granbois, male, father, 28; Margaret, female, mother, 20. (1890-TMC)

Family 103; #449-450; Paul Granbois, male, father, 30; Margaret, female, wife, 26. (1892-TMC)

Grant, Charles

Charles Grant (x), 1 man, 1 woman, 2 boys, 1 daughter, 5 total, $5.00 a share, $25.00 total. (1869 TM annuity)

Charles Grant (x), 2 men, 2 women, 3 children, 7 total, $5.00 a share, $35.00 paid. (1870 TM annuity)

C. Grant (x), 1 man, 1 woman, 2 total, $8.50 a share, $17.00 paid. (1871 TM annuity)

Chas. Grant (x), 1 man, 1 total, $10.50 a share, $10.50 paid. (1872 TM annuity)

Grant, Cuthbert

Cuthbert Grant (x), 1 man, 1 woman, 3 girls, 5 total, $5.00 a share, $25.00 total. (1869 TM annuity)

Cuthbert Grant (x), 2 men, 2 women, 1 child, 5 total, $5.00 a share, $25.00 paid. (1870 TM annuity)

Cuthbert Grant (x), 1 woman, 1 child, 2 total, $8.50 a share, $17.00 paid. (1871 TM annuity)

#433-436; Cuthbert Grant, father, 52; William, son, 18; James, son, 10; Charles, son, 8. (1888-TMC)

#447-450; Cuthbert Grant, male, father, 52; William, male, son, 16; James, male, son, 11; Charles, male, son, 9. (1889-TMC)

Family 110; #470-472, Cuthbert Grant, male, father, 57, mixed bloods on reservation; William, male, son, 20; James, male, son, 14; Charles, male, son, 12. (1892-TMC)

Grant, James

James Grant (x), 1 man, 1 woman, 1 boy, 3 girls, 6 total, $5.00 a share, $30.00 total. (1869 TM annuity)

Jim Grant (x), 1 man, 2 women, 2 children, 5 total, $5.00 a share, $25.00 paid. (1870 TM annuity)

Grant, Jean Baptiste

Jean Baptiste Grant, father, 22; Margarite, wife, 20; Joseph, 2; Frederick, 1; Sintow, daughter, 7 months; one house, 7 tons hay, ½ acre potatoes, ½ acre vegetables, one mare, one colt, one cow. (1884-TMC)

#62-65; Jean Baptiste Grant, father, male, 25; Marguerite, wife, female, 21; Joseph, son, male, 3; Frederick, son, male, 1. (1885-TMC)

#46-50; Jean Baptist Grant, father, male, 26; Marguerite wife, female, 22; Joseph, son, male, 4; Fredrick, son, male, 3; Sautow, daughter, female, 6 months. (1886-TMC)

#376-380; Jean Baptist Grant, father, 27; Margueritte, wife, 23; Joseph, son, 5; Frederick, son, 4; Smitow [?], daughter, 1-7 months. (1887-TMC)

#412-416; J. B. Grant, father, 38; Margarett, wife, 24; Joseph, son, _; Frederick, son, _, Julia, 8 months. (1888-TMC)

#482-486; J. B. Grant, male, father, 28; Margaret, female, wife, 25; Joseph, male, son, 7; Frederick, male, son, 5; Julie, female, daughter, 2. (1889-TMC)

#513-518; J. B. Grant, male, father, 29; Margarette, female, mother, 27; Joseph, male, son, 7; Julie, female, daughter, 3; Josephine, female, daughter, 9 months. (1890-TMC)

Family 115; #495-500; John Baptist Grant, male, father, 31, mixed bloods on reservation; Margaret, female, wife, 28; Joseph, male, son, 10; Julie, female, daughter, 5; Josephine, female, daughter, 3; Louis, male, son, 1. (1892-TMC)

Grant, Joseph

#519-520; Joseph Grant, male, father, 21; Marie R., female, mother, 20. (1890-TMC)

Family 114; #493-494; Joseph Grant, male, father, 23, mixed bloods on reservation; La Rose, female, wife, 21. (1892-TMC)

Grant, Julia

Julia Grant (x), 1 woman, 1 child, 2 total, $8.50 a share, $17.00 paid. (1871 TM annuity)

Grant, Pierre

Pierre Grant, father, 46; Marie, wife, 48; Joseph, son, 15; William, son, 13; Daniel, son, 9; Julie, daughter, 7; one house, one stable, 24 tons hay, one wagon, 1 ½ acres barley, ½ acre potatoes, one mare, one horse, 2 carts, 2 cows, 4 head young stock, one single B. Gun. (1884-TMC)

#197-202; Pierre Grant, father, male, 47; Marie, wife, female, 49; Joseph, son, male, 16; William, son, male, 14; Daniel, son, male, 10; Julie, daughter, female, 8. (1885-TMC)

#66-71; Pierre Grant, father, male, 48; Marie, wife, female, 50; Joseph, son, male, 17; William, son, male, 15; Daniel, son, male, 11; Julia, daughter, female, 9. (1886-TMC)

#370-375; Peter Grant, father, 49; Marie, wife, 50; Joseph, son, 18; William, son, 16; Daniel, son, 12; Julia, daughter, 10. (1887-TMC)

#406-411; Peter Grant, father, 50; Marie, wife, 51; Joseph, son, 19; William, son, 18; Daniel, son, 16; Julia, daughter, 14. (1888-TMC)

#476-481; Pierre Grant, male, father, 50; Marie, female, wife, 52; Joseph, male, son, 20; William, male, son, 18; Daniel, male, son, 14; Julia, female, daughter, 12. (1889-TMC)

#508-512; Peter Grant, male, father, 51; Marie, female, mother, 53; William, male, son, 19; Daniel, male, son, 15; Juli, female, daughter, 13. (1890-TMC)

Family 113; #488-492; Pierre Grant, male, father, 53, mixed bloods on reservation; Marie, female, wife, 56; William, male, son, 21; Daniel, male, son, 17; Juli, female, daughter, 15. (1892-TMC)

Grant, Susan

#451; Susan Grant [Is this Susan Gourneau?], female, widow, 75. (1889-TMC)

Hamlin, Celina

#135-136; Celina Hamlin, mother, female, 18; Leonard, son, male, 3. (1885-TMC)

#479-480; Celina Hamlin, mother, female, 18; Leandre, son, male, 2. (1885-TMC)

#475-479; Celina Hamlin, mother, 29, deserted by husband; Leonard, son, 5; Rebecca, daughter, 3; Patrice, son, 1-6. (1888-TMC)

Hamlin, Janot

Janot Amelin (x), 1 man, 1 woman, 2 children, 4 total, $5.00 a share, $20.00 paid. (1870 TM annuity)

Jonace Hamlin (x), 1 man, 1 total, $10.50 a share, $10.50 paid. (1872 TM annuity)

Hamlin, Julia

    #429, Julia Hamlin, widow, female, 40. (1886-TMC)

Hamlin, Marie

    #359-361, Marie Hamlin, mother, female, 87 (or 67?); Severe, son, male, 32; Norbert, grandson, male, 15. (1885-TMC)

Hamlin, Sevu

    #742-743; Sevu Hamlin, father, male, 32; Norbert, son [nephew ?], male, 16. (1886-TMC)

Hamlin, Solomon

    #738-741; Solemon Hamlin, father, male, 24; Selina, wife, female, 20; Lenoide, son, male, 4; Rebecca, daughter, female, 2. (1886-TMC)

    #531-535; Solomon Hamlin, male, father, 26; Celina, female, wife, 26; Leonard, male, son, 7; Rebbeca, female, daughter, 5; Patrice, male, son, 3. (1889-TMC)

    #578-582; Salomon Hamlin, male, father, 26; Celina, female, mother, 26; Leonard, male, son, 7; Rebecca, female, daughter, 5; Patrice, male, son, 4. (1890-TMC)

Hayes, John

    #453-455; John Hayes, father, 24; Harriette, wife, 21; Charles, son, 5. (1888-TMC)

    #501-502; John Hayes, male, father, 24; Veronic, female, wife, 18. (1889-TMC)

    #547-549; John Hayes, male, father, 26; Veronic, female, mother, 20; Francois, male, son, 7 months. (1890-TMC)

    Family 118; #510-512; Veronic Hayes, female, wife, 22, mixed bloods on reservation; John, male, husband, 26; Mary Jane, female, daughter, 6 months. (1892-TMC)

Henry, Michael [See Michel Allery]

Henry, Pierre [See Pierre Allery]

Herman, Edward

    #409-414; Edward Herman, father, 85; Margaret, wife, 60; Henry, son, 28; Alexandre, son, 18; Benisa, daughter, 17; Louise, daughter, 12. (1887-TMC)

    #456-460; Edward Herman, father, 86; Margaret, wife, 65; Alexander, son, 22; Tereace, daughter, 18; Louise Delorme, granddaughter, 12. (1888-TMC)

    #489-493; Edward Herman, male, father, 87; Margarett, female, wife, 66; Alexander, male, son, 23; Theresa, female, daughter, 19; Louis, male, grandson, 13. (1889-TMC)

    #537-540; Edward Herman, male, father, 88; Margaret, female, mother, 66; Alex, male, son, 25; Louis Delorme, male, son [?], 13. (1890-TMC)

Herman, Henry

    #473-474; Henry Herman, father, 28; Mary, wife, 20. (1888-TMC)

    #488; Henry Herman, male, 33. (1889-TMC)

    #535-536; Henry Herman, male, father, 39; Celia, female, mother, 20. (1890-TMC)

    Family 120; #517-519; Henry Herman, male, father, 36, mixed bloods on reservation; Cecil, female, wife, 24; Henry, male, son, 1-1/2. (1892-TMC)

Herman, Peter

    #218-219; Peter Herman, father, male, 27; Nelley, wife, _, _. (1885-TMC)

Herman, St.Pierre

#609-612; St.Pierre Herman, father, male, 27; Nancy, wife, female, 40; Baptiste Racette, nephew, male, 18; Matilda Laverdure, stepdaughter, female, 12. (1885-TMC)

#193-195; St.Pierre Herman, father, male, 27; Nancy, wife, female, 42; Matilda, stepdaughter, female, 13. (1886-TMC)

#480-482; Pierre Herman, father, 29; Nancy, wife, 42; Matilda, daughter, 14. (1888-TMC)

#480-482; Pierre Herman, father, 29; Nancy, wife, 42; Matilda, daughter, 14. (1888-TMC)

Houle, Abraham

#356-358; Abraham Hool, father, male, 25; Marguerite, wife, female, 20; Virginie, daughter, female, 2 months. (1885-TMC)

#363-365; Ambroise [?] Hoole, father, male, 26; Marguerite, wife, female, 19; Virginia, daughter, female, 1. (1886-TMC)

#394-396; Abraham Houle, father, 27; Margueritt, wife, 23; Virginia, daughter, 2. (1887-TMC)

#437-440; Abraham Houle, father, 26; Margerette, wife, 23; Virginia, daughter, 3; Israel, son, 7 months. (1888-TMC)

#524-527; Abraham Houle, male, father, 27; Margarette, female, wife, 24; Virginie, female, daughter, 4; Israel, male, son, 2. (1889-TMC)

#571-577; Abraham Houle, male, father, 27; Margaret, female, mother, 24; Virginie, female, daughter, 4; Celina, female, _, _; Joseph, male, _, 7; Norbert, male, _, _; Roger, male, _, _. (1890-TMC)

Family 124; #536-539; Abraham Houle, male, father, 29, mixed bloods on reservation; Margaret, female, wife, 20; Virginie, female, daughter, 7; Rosin, female, daughter, 10 months. (1892-TMC)

Houle, Alexandre

#229-237; Alex Houle, male, father, 42; Margaret, female, wife, 42; Baptist, male, son, 14; Marie Rose, female, daughter, 13; Eliza, female, daughter, 12; Isabel, female, daughter, 10; Napoleon, male, son, 8; Frederick, male, son, 6; Isadore, male, son, 1. (1889-TMC-off)

Family 38; #164-172, Alexander Henle, male, father, 44, mixed bloods in vicinity of reservation; Margaret, female, wife, 44; Baptist, male, son, 17; Marie Rose, female, daughter, 15; Eliza, female, daughter, 13; Isabel, female, daughter, 10; Napoleon, male, son, 8; Frederick, male, son, 7; John, male, son, 8. (1892-TMC)

Houle, Antoine

Antoine Houlle (x), 1 man, 1 woman, 8 children, 10 total, $3.00 a share, $30.00 paid. (1868 TM annuity)

Antoine Houle, father, 59; Genevieve, wife, 60; Antoine, son, 34; Bernard, son, 27; Charles, son, 22, (married June 1886); Napoleon, son, 18; Francois, son, 15; one house, one stable, 6 tons hay, one acre wheat, ½ acre potatoes, one horse, one cart, one gun. (1884-TMC)

#86-92; Antoine Hool, father, male, 60; Genevieve, wife, female, 61; Antoine, son, male, 35; Bernard, son, male, 28; Charles, son, male, 23; Napoleon, son, male, 19; Francois, male, 16. (1885-TMC)

#54-59; Antoine Hoole, father, male, 61; Genevieve, wife, female, 62; Antoine, son, male, 36; Bernard, son, male, 29; Napoleon, son, male, 20; Francois, son, male, 17. (1886-TMC)

#397-402; Antoine Houle, father, 62; Geneoie, wife, 63; Antoine, son, 37; Barnard, son, 29; Napoleon, son, 21; Francois, son, 18. (1887-TMC)

#441-446; Antoine Houle, father, 62; Genevia, wife, 63; Antoine, son, 37; Barnard, son, 30, Napoleon, son, 22; Francois, son, 19. (1888-TMC)

#508-512; Antoine Houle, male, father, 63; Genieve, female, wife, 64; Antoine, male, son, 39; Bernard, male, son, 37; Napoleon, male, son, 22. (1889-TMC)

Family 121; #520-524; Antoine Houle, male, father, 65, mixed bloods on reservation; Genevieve, female, wife, 67; Antoine, male, son, 40; Bernard, male, son, 36; Napoleon, male, son, 23. (1892-TMC)

Houle, Catherine

#583; Catherine Houle, Widow, female, 81. (1890-TMC)

Houle, Charles

#483-484; Chas. Houle, father, 26; Henrietta, wife, 19. (1888-TMC)

#503-505; Chas. Houle, male, father, 26; Harriett, female, wife, 20; Louis, male, son, 10 months. (1889-TMC)

#550-552; Chas. Houle, male, father, 29; Harriett, female, mother, 21; Louis, male, son, 3. (1890-TMC)

Family 122; #525-528; Charles Houle, male, father, 37, mixed bloods on reservation; Henrietta, female, wife, 23; Louis, male, son, 3; Frederick, male, son, 2. (1892-TMC)

Houle, Cuthbert

#584-585; Corbett Houle, male, father, 19; Clemence Female, mother, 17. (1890-TMC)

Family 125; #540-541, Culbert Houle, male, father, 22, mixed bloods on reservation; Mary Rose, female, daughter, 2. (1892-TMC)

Houle, John

#506-507; John Houle, male, father, 25; Helen, female, wife, 19. (1889-TMC)

#569-570; John Hole [Houle], male, father, 25; Helen, female, mother, 19. (1890-TMC)

Houle, Joseph Sr.

Joseph Hool, father, 54; Sophie, wife, 60; Louisa, daughter, 24; Johny, son, 20; Cuthbert, son, 14; Philomene, daughter, 10; Elie, son, 3; Marie, daugher, 8 months, (June 1886); one house, one stable, 20 tons hay, one acre vegetables, 1/4 acre potatoes, one mare, one light wagon, one plough B, one cook stove. (1884-TMC)

#669-675; Joseph Hool, father, male, 55; Sophie, wife, female, 61; Louise, [step] daughter, female, 25; John, son, male, 21; Cuthbert, son, male, 15; Philomene, daughter, female, 11; Elie, grandson, male, [..]. (1885-TMC)

#614-621; Joseph Hoole, father, male, 56; Sophia, wife, female, 62; Louisa, [step] daughter, female, 26; John, son, male, 22; Cuthbert, son, male, 16; Philomene, daughter, female, 12; Eli, [grand] son, male, 5; Marie, [grand] daughter, female, 8 months. (1886-TMC)

#415-420; Joseph Houle, father, 60; Sophia, wife, 60; Louisa, daughter, 30; Corbert, son, 17, John, son, 23; Manadan, daughter, 3 [?]. (1887-TMC)

#461-468; Joseph Houle, father, 60; Sophia, wife, 62; Louisa, daughter, 40; Corbet, son, 18; John, son, 25; Philomene, daughter, 15; Eli, son, 7; Eliza, daughter, 2. (1888-TMC)

#513-519; Joseph Houl, Joseph, male, father, 56; Sophia, female, wife, 60; Louise, female, daughter, 26; Corbert, male, son. 19; Elie, male, nephew, 3; Elize, female, granddaughter, 4; Francois Delorme, male, 98. (1889-TMC)

#558-561; Joseph Houle Sr., male, father, 60; Sophia, female, mother, 70; Ambroise Lafrisse [?], male, grandson, 8; Elize Peltier, female, granddaughter, 5. (1890-TMC)

Family 126; #542-545; Joseph Houle, sr., male, father, 61, mixed blood on reservation; Sophie, female, wife, 64; Elie, male, grandson, 10; Elise Pettier, female, granddaughter. (1892-TMC)

Houle, Joseph Jr.

#520-523; Joseph Houle Jr., male, father, 30; Veronic, female, wife, 25; Marie, female, daughter, 2; Chas. Trottier, male, stepson, 5. (1889-TMC)

#562-567; Joseph Houle Jr., male, father, 40; Veronica, female, mother, 26; Chas. Trottier, male, stepson, 6; Marie, female, daughter, 8; Bronal [?], male, son 1 month; Joseph, male, _, 7. (1890-TMC)

Houle, Joseph Jr.

Family #124; #529-535, Joseph Houle, jr., male, father, 33, mixed bloods on reservation; Sabra, female, wife, 28; Rosin, female, daughter, 12; Joseph, male, son, 11; Charles, male, son, 7; Marie Jane, female, daughter, 6;   Biann, female, daughter, 3. (1892-TMC)

Houle, Louis

Louis Houle, father, 26; Marie, wife, 19; Flachine, daughter, 2; Albert, son, 1. (July 1886-TMC)

Houle, Norbert

#396-397; Norbert Hool, father, male, 25; Caroline, wife, female, 17. (1885-TMC)

#499-500; Norbert Hool, father, male, 25; Caroline, wife, female, 17. (1885-TMC)

#417-418; Norbert Hoole, father, male, 26; Carolina, wife, female, 18. (1886-TMC)

#421-423; Norbert Houle, father, 27; Caroline, wife, 21; St.Ann, daughter, 9 months. (1887-TMC)

#469-471; Norbert Houle, father, 27; Caroline, wife, 21; St.Ann, daughter, 2. (1888-TMC)

#528-530; Norbert Houle, male, father, 29; Caroline, female, wife, 23; St.Ann, female, daughter, 2. (1889-TMC)

Houle, Onizime

Onisime Houle, father, 28; Louise, wife, 26; Louis, son, 4; Anney, daughter 2; Catherine mother, 70; Napoleon, son, born June 1885; one house, 2 horses, one colt, one cart, on gun, single barrel shot gun. (1884-TMC)

#507-511; Onizime Hool, father, male, _; Louise, wife, female, _; Louis, son, male, _; Anny, daughter, female, _; Catherine, mother, female, _. (1885-TMC)

#60-65; Onezeme Hoole, father, male, 30; Louise, wife, female, 28; Louis, son, male, 6; Anny, daughter, female, 4; Napoleon, son, male, 1; Catherine, mother, female, 72. (1886-TMC)

#403-408; Onizem Houle, father, 31; Louisa, wife, 29; Louis, son, 7; St.Ann, daughter, 5; Napoleon, son, 6; Maxim, son, 6 months. (1887-TMC)

#447-452; Onezim Houle, father, 31; Louisa wife, 28; Louis, son, 8; St.Ann, 6, girl; Napoleon, son, 4; Catharine Houle, mother, 86. (1888-TMC)

#494-500; Onezim Houle, male, father, 32; Elize, female, wife, 30; Louis, male, son, 9; Napoleon, male, son, 5; Baptist, male, son, 9 months; Mary St.Ann, female, daughter, 7; Catharine, female, mother, 81. (1889-TMC)

#541-546; Onizeme Houle, male, father, 32; Elize, female, mother, 32; Louise [sic], Napoleon, male, son, 6; Baptist, male, son, 2; Mary St.Anne, female, daughter, 7. (1890-TMC)

Family 39; #173-178; Ouizen Henle, male, father, 35, mixed bloods in vicinity of reservation; Louise, female, wife, 27; Louis, male, son, 11; Mary St.Ann, female, daughter, 9; Napoleon, male, son, 6; Baptist, male, son, 3. (1892-TMC)

Hubber, Frederick
#586-587; Fredk Hubber, white man, male, father, 35; Mary, Chippewa, female, mother, 26. (1890-TMC)

Jeannott, Alex
#273-278; Alex Jeannott, male, father, 50; Leon, male, son, 22; Alex, male, son, 17; Maria, female, daughter, 14; Joseph, male, son, 10; Marcial, female, dau [?], 8. (1889-TMC-off)

Jeannott, Corbert
#257-259; Corbert Jeannott, male, father, 20; Marie Rose, female, wife, 21; Gaspar, male, son, 2 months. (1889-TMC-off)

Jeannott, Francois
#244-247; Francois Jeannott, male, father, 81; Madalain Bouvier, female, daughter, 45; Malina, female, granddaughter, 16; Madalaine, female, granddaughter, 10. (1889-TMC-off)

Jeannot, Frederick
#540-541; Frederick Jeannot, male, father, 29; La Rose, female, wife, 23. (1889-TMC)
#593-595; Fredk Jeannott, male, father, 30; La Rose, female, wife 24; Joseph, male, son, 4 months. (1890-TMC)
Family 129; #557-559; La Rose Jeannott, female, wife, 25, mixed bloods on reservation; Frederick, male, husband, 30; Not named, female, daughter, 11 months. (1892-TMC)

Jeannott, Gaspar
#238-243; Gaspar Jeannott, male, father, 38; Amelia, daughter, 19; Madalain, female, daughter, 16; Gaspar, male, son, 14; Placide, female, daughter, 11; Alexander, male, son, 10. (1889-TMC-off)

Jeannott, Gaspar Jr.
#269-272; Gaspar Jeannott Jr., male, father, 23; Malina, female, wife, 27; San Souci, male, son, 4; Pauline, female, daughter, 10 months. (1889-TMC-off)

Jeannott, Jean Baptiste
#248-256; J. B. Jeannott, male, father, 36; Mona, female, wife, 40; George, male, son, 15; Madalain, female, daughter, 12; Rosine, female, daughter, 10; Flaragi, female, daughter, 8; Amelia, female, daughter, 5; Vitaline, female, daughter, 2; Albert, male, son, 9 months. (1889-TMC-off)

Jeannott, Pierre
#260-268; Pierre Jeannott, male, father, 58; Louisa, female, wife, 43; John, male, son, 15; Asidia, female, daughter, 13; Marie Rose, female, daughter, 12; Rafel, male, son, 10; Patrice, male, son, 7; Louis, male, son, 5; Virginie, female, daughter, 4. (1889-TMC-off)
Family 42; #188-196, Louise Jeannott, female, wife, 47, mixed bloods in vicinity of reservation; Pierre, male, husband, 62; Marie Rose, female, daughter, 13; Raphael, male, son, 12;

Batrie, male, son, 10; Leon, male, son, 9; Virginie, female, daughter, 6; Marie Louise, female, daughter, 3; Joseph, male, son, 26. (1892-TMC)

Jeannott, William John

Family 45; #209-210, John Jeanott, male, father, 19, mixed bloods in vicinity of reservation; Demetel, female, wife, 17. (1892-TMC)

Jerome, Alexander

Family 43; #197, Alexander Jerome, male, single, 25, mixed bloods in vicinity of reservation. (1892-TMC)

Jerome, Andre

Andre Jerome (x), 1 man, 1 woman, 4 children, 6 total, $4.00 a share, $24.00 paid. (1868 TM annuity)

Andrew Jerome (x), 1 man, 1 woman, 1 child, 3 total, $8.50 a share, $25.50 paid. (1871 TM annuity)

Jerome, Angele

Angelle Jerome (x), 1 man, 1 woman, 2 total, $8.50 a share, $17.00 paid. (1871 TM annuity)

Jerome, Daniel

Daniel Jerome (x), 1 man, 1 woman, 2 children, 4 total, $5.00 a share, $20.00 paid. (1870 TM annuity)

Daniel Jerome (x), 1 man, 1 woman, 2 total, $8.50 a share, $17.00 paid. (1871 TM annuity)

Family 44; #198-206, Daniel Jerome sr., male, father, 53, mixed bloods in vicinity of reservation; Mary, female, wife, 45; Frederick, male, son, 16; Virginie, female, daughter, 18; Edmond, male, (son), 13; Deline, female, daughter, 10; Julian, female, daughter, 8; Ferdinand, male, son, 5;, Betsy, female, daughter, 1. (1892-TMC)

Jerome, Daniel Jr.

Family 47; #219, Daniel Jerome jr., male, single, 23, mixed bloods in vicinity of reservation. (1892-TMC)

Jerome, David

David Jerome (x), 1 man, 1 woman, 3 children, 5 total, $4.00 a share, $20.00 paid. (1868 TM annuity)

David Jerome (x), 1 man, 1 woman, 1 boy, 2 girls, 5 total, $5.00 a share, $25.00 paid. (1869 TM annuity)

David Jerome (x), 1 man, 1 woman, 1 child, 3 total, $5.00 a share, $15.00 paid. (1870 TM annuity)

David Jerome (x), 1 man, 1 woman, 1 child, 3 total, $8.50 a share, $25.50 paid. (1871 TM annuity)

Jerome, Eliza

Eliza Jerome (x), 1 woman, 1 total, $5.00 a share, $5.00 paid. (1869 TM annuity)

Jerome, Jerome

Jerom Jerome (x), 1 man, 1 woman, 2 children, 4 total, $5.00 a share, $20.00 paid. (1870 TM annuity)

Jerome Jerome (x), 1 man, 1 woman, 2 total, $8.50 a share, $17.00 paid. (1871 TM annuity)

Jerome, Joseph

Joseph Jerome (x), 1 man, 1 woman, 5 children, 7 total, $4.00 a share, $28.00 paid. (1868 TM annuity)

Joseph Jerome (x), 1 man, 1 woman, 3 boys, 2 girls, 7 total, $5.00 a share, $35.00 paid. (1869 TM annuity)

Joseph Jerome (x), 1 man, 1 woman, 2 children, 4 total, $5.00 a share, $20.00 paid. (1870 TM annuity)

Jerome, Julian

Family 40; #179, Julian Jerome, male, single, 27, mixed bloods in vicinity of reservation. (1892-TMC)

Jerome, Louis

Louis Jerome (x), 1 man, 1 woman, 4 children, 6 total, $4.00 a share, $24.00 paid. (1868 TM annuity)

Louis Jerome (x), 1 man, 2 women, 2 boys, 2 girls, 7 total, $5.00 a share, $35.00 paid. (1869 TM annuity)

Louis Jerome (x), 1 man, 1 woman, 5 children, 7 total, $5.00 a share, $35.00 paid. (1870 TM annuity)

Louis Jerome (x), 1 man, 1 woman, 1 child, 3 total, $8.50 a share, $25.50 paid. (1871 TM annuity)

Jerome, Margaret

Margaret Jerome (x), 1 man, 1 woman, 2 children, 4 total, $8.50 a share, $34.00 paid. (1871 TM annuity)

Jerome, Martin

Martin Jerome (x), 1 man, 1 woman, 4 children, 6 total, $4.00 a share, $24.00 paid. (1868 TM annuity)

Martin Jerome (x), 1 man, 1 woman, 2 boys, 2 girls, 6 total, $5.00 a share, $30.00 paid. (1869 TM annuity)

Martin Jerome (x), 1 man, 1 woman, 4 children, 6 total, $5.00 a share, $30.00 paid. (1870 TM annuity)

Martin Jerome (x), 1 man, 1 woman, 1 child, 3 total, $8.50 a share, $25.50 paid. (1871 TM annuity)

Jerome, Martin

Family 128; #550-556, Martin Jerome, male, father, 34, mixed bloods on reservation; Mary, female, wife, 32; Betsy, female, daughter, 11; Emily, female, daughter, 9; Virginie, female, daughter, 6; Alphonsin, female, daughter, 4; Angelique, female, daughter, 16. (1892-TMC)

Jerome, Roger

Family 130; #500, Roger Jerome, male, single, 46, mixed bloods on reservation. (1892-TMC)

Jerome, St.Mathew

#596-597; St.Mathe Jerome, male, father, 22; La Rose, female, mother, 18. (1890-TMC)

Family 127; #546-549, St.Matthew Jerome, male, father, 35, mixed bloods on reservation; Mary Rose, female, wife, 20; Joseph, male, son, 1-1/2; Albert, male, son, 5 months. (1892-TMC)

Johnson, Josette

Josette Johnson (x), 1 woman, 1 boy, 2 girls, 4 total, $5.00 a share, $20.00 total. (1869 TM annuity)

Josette Johnson (x), 1 woman, 1 child, 2 total, $8.50 a share, $17.00 paid. (1871 TM annuity)

Jolibois, Baptist

Family 41; #180-187, Marie Jollibois, female, wife, 38, mixed bloods in vicinity of reservation; Baptist, male, husband, 42; Marie Matilde, female, daughter, 18; Mary Jane, female, daughter, 16; Mary Rose, female, daughter, 13; Delina, female, daughter, 10; Zilda, female, daughter, 8; Albert, male, son, 5. (1892-TMC)

Jollie, James J.

Family 46; #211-218, Mary Jollie, female, wife, 35, mixed bloods in vicinity of reservation; James J. (white), male, husband, 35; William, male, son, 11; George, male, son, 9; James, male, son, 7; John, male, son, 15; Margaret, female, daughter, 7; David, male, son, 9 months. (1892-TMC)

Keplin, Gilbert

#320-322; Gilbert Quiplain [Keplin], father, male, 34; Elise, wife, female, 23; Jean Baptiste, son, male, 2. (1885-TMC)

#332-335; Gilbert Quiplain, father, male, 35; Eliza, wife, female, 24; Jean Baptist, son, male, 3; Antoine, son, male, 10 months. (1886-TMC)

#429-432; Gilbert Kiplin, father, 34; Eliza, wife, 23; John Baptist, son, 6; Jean, son, 3. (1887-TMC)

#494-498; Gilbert Kiplin, father, 35; Eliza, wife, 28; John Baptist, son, 4; Antoine, son, 3; Clemenia, daughter, 6 months. (1888-TMC)

#547-551; Gilbert Kiplin, male, father, 34; Elise, female, wife, 29; John B., male, son, 6; Antoine, male, son, 4; Clemence, female, daughter, 1-1/2. (1889-TMC)

#602-608; Gilbert Kiplin, male, father, 37; Elise, female, mother, 30; J. B., male, son, 6; Antoin, male, son, 4; Clemence, female, daughter, 2; Joseph, male, son, 8 months. (1890-TMC)

Family 133; #567-572; Gilbert Keplin, male, father, 43, mixed bloods on reservation; Elise, female, wife, 26; J. Baptist, male, son, 7; Antoine, male, son, 6; Clemence, female, daughter, 4; Joseph, male, son, 6. (1892-TMC)

Keplin, Joseph

#309-310; Joseph Quiplain [Keplin], father, male, 27; Marguerite, wife, female, 17. (1885-TMC)

#336-338; Joseph Quiplain, father, male, 28; Marguerite, wife, female, 18; Marguerite, mother, female, 70. (TMC-1886)

#433-435; Joseph Kiplin, father, 26; Sahra, wife, 17; Margueritte, daughter, 9 months. (1887-TMC)

#491-493; Joseph Keplin, father, 27; Sahrah, wife, 19; Margaret, daughter, 2. (1888-TMC)

#542-545; Joseph Kiplin, male, father, 34; Margerette, female, wife, 19; Alex, male, son, 3 months; Sahra, female, daughter, 3 years. (1889-TMC)

#598-601; Joseph Keplin, male, father, 34; Margarett, female, mother, 20; Elizabeth, female, daughter, 4; Joseph, male, son, 2. (1890-TMC)

Family 132; #562-566; Joseph Keplin, male, father, 36, mixed bloods on reservation; Margaret, female, wife, 23; Sabra, female, daughter, 6; Alexander, male, son, 3; Betsy, female, daughter, 1. (1892-TMC)

Keplin, Marguerite

#323; Marguerite Quiplain [Keplin nee Grenon], _, female, 67. (1885-TMC)

#499; Margaret Kipin, widow, 60. (1888-TMC)

#546; Margaret Kiplin, female, widow, 62. (1889-TMC)

#602; Kepin, Margaret Widow; Female, 66. (1890-TMC)

Family 131, #561; Margaret Keplin, female, widow, 63, mixed bloods on reservation. (1892-TMC)

Keplin, Paul

Pauline Keplin (x), 1 man, 1 woman, 4 children, 6 total, $3.00 a share, $24.00 paid. (1868 TM annuity)

Paulette Kieplin (x), 1 man, 1 woman, 3 boys, 2 girls, 7 total, $5.00 a share, $35.00 paid. (1869 TM annuity)

Palette Keplin (x), 3 men, 3 women, 6 total, $5.00 a share, $30.00 paid. (1870 TM annuity)

Labombard, Baptiste

Battiste Labombard (x), 1 man, 1 woman, 1 child, 3 total, $3.00 a share, $9.00 paid. (1868 TM annuity)

Babtiste Labombard (x), 1 man, 1 woman, 1 boy, 3 total, $5.00 a share, $15.00 total. (1869 TM annuity)

Lacerte, Maria

Maria Lasarte (x), 1 woman, 1 total, $3.00 a share, $3.00 paid. (1868 TM annuity)

Mrs. Lasarte (x), 1 woman, 1 total, $5.00 a share, $5.00 total. (1869 TM annuity)

Lacerte, Peter

#503-505; Peter Lasard, father, 51; Juliet, wife, 47; Marie, daughter, 3. (1888 TMC)

#635-637; Pierre Laserte, male, father, 56; Juliet, female, wife, 48; Marie, female, daughter, 4. (1889-TMC)

#690-692; Pierre La Certe, male, father, _; Juliet, female, mother, _; Marie, female, daughter, _. (1890-TMC)

Family 159; #675-677; Pierre Lacerte, male, father, 54, mixed bloods on reservation; Judith, female, wife, 52; Marie Pauline, female, adopted daughter, 7. (1892-TMC)

Ladue/Ladeau/Ladux/Ledoux

Ledoux, Antoine

Family 161, #682, Antoine Ledeux, male, orphan (single), 17, mixed bloods on reservation. (1892-TMC)

Ladeau, Chrysostome

#734-739; Chym. Widow Ladeau, female, mother, 40; Antoine, male, son, 16; Joseph, male, son, 11; Marie, female, daughter, 4; Julia, female, daughter, 11; Demiano, male, son, 5 months. (1890-TMC)

Ladux, Francois

Family 10; #40-44; Ursule Azure, female, daughter, 11, mixed bloods on reservation; Moses, male, son, 10; #42, William, male, son, 8; Alexander, male, son, 3; Francois Ladux No. 1; male, father, 37. (1892-TMC) (See Ursule Azure)

Ladeau, Jeremiah

#284-285; Jeremiah Ladeau, male, father, 23; Meline, female, wife, 16. (1889-TMC)

Ladeux, Joseph

#345-347; Joseph Ladeux, male, father, 26; Adel, female, wife, 22; Alex, male, son, 3. (1889-TMC-off)

Family 52, #259-263, Joseph Ladeux, male, father, 29, mixed bloods in vicinity of reservation; Adel, female, wife, 27; Alexander, male, son, 6; Francois, male, son, 3; Mary Louise, female, daughter, 1-1/2. (1892-TMC)

Ladeux, Madaline

Family 53, #264-265, Madaline Ladeux, female, widow, 75, mixed bloods in vicinity of reservation; Louis, male, grandson, 13. (1892-TMC)

Ladue, Thomas

#601-606; Thomas Ladue, father, 38; Cecile, wife, 39; Antoine, son, 14; Joseph, son, 10; Julia, daughter, 8; Mary, daughter, 2. (1888-TMC)

#678-682; Ths. Ladeau, male, father, 39; Cecile, female, wife, 34; Antoine, male, son, 15; Joseph, male, son, 13; Marie, female, daughter, 3. (1889-TMC)

Lafette, Marcus

Marcus Lafette (x), 1 man, 2 women, 1 child, 4 total, $5.00 a share, $20.00 paid. (1870 TM annuity)

Lafond, Benjamin

Benj. La Font (x), 1 man, 1 woman, 11 children, 13 total, $10.00 a share, $130.00 paid. (1873 TM annuity)

Benj. Lafond (x), 1 man, 1 total, $5.00 a share, $5.00 paid. (1874 TM annuity)

Lafond [?], Marguerite

Marguerite Lafond [?] (x), 2 men, 3 women, 7 children, 12 total, $5.00 a share, $60.00 paid. (1874 TM annuity)

Lafontusne [?], Owisom

#510-519; Owisom Lafontusne, father, 47; Madalaine, wife, 44; Pierre, son, 20; Benjamin, son, 18; Louis, son, 16; Marie Rose, dau 14; Owisom, son, 12; Marian, daughter, 9; Mary Delonica, 7; Virgnia, daughter, 3. (1888-TMC)

Lafore, Francois

#562-567; Francois Lafore, father, 63; Eliza, wife, 50; Virginie, daughter, 16; Julien, son, 13; Alexander, son, 12; Pauline, daughter, 10. (1888-TMC)

Lafore, Maxim

#528-531; Maxim Lafore, father, 24; Rosalie, wife, 21; Adele, daughter, 4; Baptiste, son, 2. (1887-TMC)

#584-587; Maxim Lafore, father, 24; Rosalie, wife, 21; Adele, daughter, 5; Joseph, son, 1. (1888-TMC)

Lafountain, Antoine

#388-396; Antoine Lafountain, father, male, 35; Madeline, wife, female, 33; Isior, son, male, 13; St.Pierre, son, male, 11; Marie, daughter, female, 9; Ambroise, son, male, 7; Joseph, son, male, 5; Louis, son, male, 3; Zachery, son, male, 1. (1886-TMC) One D.B. shot gun (1884-TMC-added information)

#529-537; Antoine Lafontaine, father, 38; Madalaine, wife, 38; Ezear, son, 16; St.Pierre, son, 14; Justina, daughter, 11; Ambrois, son, 9; Joseph, son, 6; Louis, son, 4; Philomene, daughter, 6 months. (1888-TMC)

#600-607; Madalaine Lafontain, female, mother, 40; Elzeard, male, son, 17; Pierre, male, son, 15; Ambroise, male, son, 10; Louis, male, son, 6; Justine, female, daughter, 12; Philomene, female, daughter, 2, Joseph, male, son, 8. (1889-TMC)

Lafountain, Charlotte

#954-958; Charlotte Lafountain, mother, female, 58; Elsard, son, male, 23; Culbert, son, male, 22; Marie Rose, daughter, female, 18; Julien Dalernnai, granddaughter, female, 6. (1886-TMC)

#538-541; Charlotte Lafontaine, mother, 59; Elzard, son, 24; Culbert, son, 22; Julie Delamaris, stepdaughter, 10. (1888-TMC)

#644-646; Charlotte Lafontaine, female, mother, 60; Elizar, male, son, 24; Corbet, male, son, 22. (1889-TMC)

#701-703; Charlotte Widow Lafontaine, female, mother, _; Ezear, male, son, _; Corbet, male, son, _. (1890-TMC)

Family 163; #690-692; Charlotte Lafontaine, female, widow, 63, mixed bloods on reservation; Elzeard, male, son, 23; Cuthbert, male, son, 25. (1892-TMC)

Lafountaine, Isidore

Isadore Lefontaine (x), 2 men, 2 women, 4 total, $5.00 a share, $20.00 paid. (1870 TM annuity)

Lafontaine, Jean Baptiste

Baptiste Lefontaine (x), 1 man, 1 woman, 2 total, $5.00 a share, $10.00 paid. (1870 TM annuity)

#352-354; Baptist Lafountain, father, male, 41; Clemone, wife, female, 39; Marie Eliza, daughter, female, 9. (1886-TMC)

#520-522; Baptist Lafontaine, father, 30; Clemons, wife 20; Marie Elise, daughter, 8. (1888-TMC)

#597-599; J. B. Lafontaine, male, father, 39; Clemence, female, wife, 36; Elize, female, daughter, 10. (1889-TMC)

#652-654; J. B. Lafontaine, male, father, 40; Clemence, female, mother, 36; Eliza, female, daughter, 11. (1890-TMC)

Lafontaine, Louis

Louis Lafountaine, father, 39; Madelain, wife, 38; Pierre, son, 20; Benjaman, son, 18; Marierose, daughter, 15; Jeuone, son, 10; Louis, son, 8; Maryann, daughter, 7; Flilaman, daughter, 4; Virginie, daughter, 3; Patrice, son, 2. (July 1886-TMC)

#608-616; Louis Lafontaine, male, father, 48; Pierre, male, son, 21; Benjamin, male, son, 19; Eugene, male, son, 17; Marie Rose, female, daughter, 15; Louis, male, son, 13; Marian, female, daughter, 13; Philomene, female, daughter, 10; Virginie, female, daughter, 4. (1889-TMC)

#663-671; Louis Lafontaine, male, father, 49; Emily, female, mother, 40; Eugene, male, son, 19; Marie Rose, female, daughter, 15; Louis, male, son, 14; Marian, female, daughter, 12; Philomene, female, daughter, 11; Virginie, female, daughter, 9; Eliza, female, daughter, 5 months. (1890-TMC)

Family 145; #610-617; Louis Lafontaine, male, father, 49, mixed bloods on reservation; Emily, female, wife, 39; Mary Philomene, female, daughter, 13; Louis, male, son, 17; Mary Ann, female, daughter, 11; Virginie, female, daughter, 11; Eliza, female, daughter, 1-1/2; Isanor, male, son, 19. (1892-TMC)

Lafontain, Madeline

#655-662; Madalaine Widow Lafontaine, female, mother, 41; Elizeard, male, son, 18; Pierre, male, son, 16; Ambroise, male, son, 13; Joseph, male, son, 10; Louis, male, son, 2; Justine, female, daughter, 15; Philomene, female, daughter, 3. (1890-TMC)

Family 149; #631-637; Madeline Lafontain, female, widow, 43, mixed bloods on reservation; Pierre, male, son, 19; Ambroise, male, son, 18; Joseph, male, son, 17; Louis, male, son, 9; Philomene, female, daughter, 5; Ezear, male, son, 21. (1892-TMC)

Lafountain, Octave

#941-946; Octave Lafountain, father, male, 31; Josephine, wife, female, 31; Virginie, daughter, female, 9; Joseph, son, male, 5; Selina, daughter, female, 3; Marie, daughter, female, 7 months. (1886-TMC)

#539-544; Octave Lafontaine, father, 32; Josephine, wife, 32; Virginia, daughter, 10; Joseph, son, 6; Celina, daughter, 4; Sahra, daughter, 1-7 months. (1887-TMC)

#594-600; Octave Lafontaine, father, 34; Josephine, wife, 38; Virginia, daughter, 13; Joseph, daughter, 7; Celina, daughter, 5; Sahra, daughter, 3; Francois, son, 2 months. (1888-TMC)

#650-656; Octave Lafontaine, male, father, 33; Josephine, female, wife, 33; Virginie, female, daughter, 15; Joseph, male, son, 8; Celina, female, daughter, 5; Sahra, female, daughter, 3; Alexander, male, son, 1. (1889-TMC)

#704-710; Octave Lafontaine, male, father, 34; Josephine, female, mother, 34; Virginia, female, daughter, 15; Joseph, female, daughter, 9; Celina, female, daughter, 6; Sahra, female, daughter, 4; Augustine, male, son, 2 months. (1890-TMC)

Family 162; #683-689, Octave Lafontaine, male, father, 37, mixed bloods on reservation; Josephine, female, wife, 36; Virginie, female, daughter, 16; Joseph, male, son, 10; Celina, female, daughter, 8; Sabrah, female, daughter, 9; Mary L., female, daughter, 6 months. (1892-TMC)

Lafontaine, Pierre

#754-755; Pierre Lafontaine, male, father, 22; Isabel, female, mother, 16. (1890-TMC)

Family 144; #606-609; Isabel Lafontain, female, wife, 18, mixed bloods on reservation; Pierre, male, husband, 22; Pierre Arthur, male, son, 1; Moses, male, son, 8 months. (1892-TMC)

Lafournaise, Joseph Jr.

#1-3, Joseph Lafournaise Jr., father, male, 24; Marguerite, wife, female, 22; Moise, son, male, 1 month. (1885-TMC)

#430-432; Joseph Lafournais Jr., father, male, 25; Marguerite, wife, female, 21; Moise, son, male, 1. (1886-TMC)

#542-545; Joseph Lafournais Jr., father, 25; Marguerette, wife, 25; Moise, son, 3; Patrice, son, 2. (1888-TMC)

#673-677; Joseph Lafournaise, male, father, 27; Margaret, female, wife, 26; Moses, male, son, 4; Patrice, male, son, 2; Domitil, female, daughter, 10 months. (1889-TMC)

#729-733; Joseph Lafournaise, male, father, 28; Margarett, female, mother, 26; Moses, male, son, 4; Elise, female, daughter, 2. (1890-TMC)

Family 164; #693-698; Joseph Lafournaise, male, father, 30, mixed blood on reservation; Margaret, female, wife, 30; Moses, male, son, 7; Patrice, male, son, 5; Dometil Elise, female, daughter, 5; Mary Ann, female, daughter, 2. (1892-TMC)

Lafournaise, Joseph Sr.

#4-10, Joseph Lafournais Sr., father, male, 61; Susanne, Wife, female, _; Patrice, son, male, 21; Justine, daughter, female, 16; Marie Rose, daughter, female, 14; Liza, daughter, female, 12; Marcil, son, male, 8. (1885-TMC)

#422-428; Joseph Lafournais Sr., father, male, 62; Susanna, wife, female, 55; Patrice, son, male, 22; Justine, daughter, female, 17; Maria Rose, daughter, female, 15; Eliza, daughter, female, 13; Marcel, son, male, 9. (1886-TMC)

#310-315; Susan Lafouranise, female, mother, 52; Patrice, male, son, 23; Justine, female, daughter, 16; Marie Rose, female, daughter, 14; Marcel, male, son, 11; Eliza, female, daughter, 15. (1889-TMC-off)

Family 51; #244-250, Susan Lafournaise, female, widow, 60, mixed bloods in vicinity of reservation; Batric, male, son, 28; Justine, female, daughter, 23; Mary Rose, female, daughter, 22; Eliza, female, daughter, 20; Marcelle, male, son, 15; Joseph, male, grandson, 10. (1892-TMC)

Laframbois, Gabriel

#501, Gabriel Laframbois, man, 42. (1887-TMC)
#556; Gabriel Laframbois, man, 42. (1888-TMC)

Lafrombois, Gabriel

#752-753; Gabriel Laframbois, male, father, 22; Marie C., female, mother, 17. (1890-TMC)

Family 135; #576-577, Margaret Lafromboise, female, wife, 23, mixed bloods on reservation; Gabriel, male, husband 30. (1892-TMC)

Lafrombois, J. B.

#635-637; J. B. Lafrombois, father, 35; Margaret, wife, 25; Marie, daughter, 6. (1888-TMC)

#617-619; J. B. Laframboise, male, father, 35; Margaret, female, wife, 32; Marie, female, daughter, 7. (1889-TMC)

#672-673; J. B. Lafrombois, male, father, 36; Margaret, female, mother, 38. (1890-TMC)

Family 146; #618-619; J. B. Lafrombois, male, father, 39, mixed bloods on reservation; #619, Margaret, female, wife, 35. (1892-TMC)

Laframbois, Joseph

Joseph La Frombois (x), 2 men, 2 women, 1 child, 5 total, $5.00 a share, $25.00 paid. (1870 TM annuity)

Laframbois, Joseph Jr.

#916-919; Joseph Laframbois, father, male, 27; Adelphin, wife, female, 22; Victoria, daughter, female, 3; Mary, daughter, female, 3 months. (1886-TMC)

#625-629; Joseph Laframboise Jr., father, 23; Isabell, wife, 28; Napoleon, son, 7; Joseph, son, 6; Marie, daughter, 3 months. (1888-TMC)

#762-766; Joseph Lafrombois, male, father, 33; Elizabeth, female, mother, 30; Napoleon, male, son, 8; Mary, female, daughter, 4; Baptist, male, son, 7 months. (1890-TMC)

Family 142; #596-601; Joseph Lafrombois, male, father, 34, mixed bloods on reservation; Isabel, female, wife, 29; Napoleon, male, son, 11; Mary, female, daughter, 7; Baptist, male, son, 3; Elizabeth, female, daughter, 9 months. (1892-TMC)

Lafromboise, Joseph

Family 168; #710-711, Joseph Lafromboise, male, father, 25, mixed bloods on reservation; Mary Rose, female, wife, 19. (1892-TMC)

Laframbois, Louis

Louis Le Frombois (x), 2 men, 2 women, 2 children, 6 total, $5.00 a share, $30.00 paid. (1870 TM annuity)

Louis Lafranboise (x), 1 man, 1 woman, 2 total, $10.50 a share, $21.00 paid. (1872 TM annuity)

Laframbois, Marian

Marian Lafranboise (x), 1 woman, 1 total, $10.50 a share, $10.50 paid. (1872 TM annuity)

Lafrombois, Michael

Family 139, #586-590, Michael, Lafrombois, male, father, 28, mixed bloods on reservation; Margaret, female, wife, 28; Celina, female, daughter, 8; Louis, male, son, 4; Jerome, male, son, 1-1/2. (1892-TMC)

Laframbois, Narcisse

Narpis Lafranboise (x), 1 man, 1 woman, 2 total, $8.50 a share, $17.00 paid. (1871 TM annuity)

Narcises [?] (x), 1 woman, 1 total, $10.50 a share, $10.50 paid. (1872 TM annuity)

#589-596; Narcisse Lafrombois, male, father, 60; Susset, female, wife, 57; Mathew, male, son, 23; Patrice, male, son, 16; Cecil, female, daughter, 20; Elize, female, daughter, 14; Marie, female, daughter, 11; Francois, male, son, 4. (1889-TMC)

#642-648; Narciss Lafrombois, male, father, 60; Sussett, female, mother, 52; Mathias, male, son, 23; Patrice, male, son, 18; Eliza, female, daughter, 16; Marie, female, daughter, 13; Francois, male, son, 5. (1890-TMC)

Family 140; #501-505; Narcisse, Lafrombois, male, father, 64, mixed bloods on reservation; Jossett, female, wife, 61; Mathias, male, son, 24; Patrice, male, son, 21; Elise, female, daughter, 18; Mary, female, daughter, 15. (1892-TMC)

Lafreniere, Leon

Leon Lafreniere, father, 27; Sara, wife, 25; Josephine, daughter, 3; Elie, 1, (Marie born 1886). (1884-TMC)

#203-206; Leon Lafreniere, father, male, 28; Sara, wife, female, 26; Josephine, daughter, female, 4; Elie, son, male, 2. (1885-TMC)

#112-116; Leon Lafrienier, father, male, 29; Sarah, wife, female, 27; Josephine, daughter, female, 5; Eli, son, male, 3; Marie, daughter, female, 7 months. (1886-TMC)

#523-527; Leon Lafranier, father, 30; Sahra, wife, 27; Josephine, daughter, 6; Eliza, daughter, [Elie, son], 3; Lennie, daughter, [Leandre, son], 1. (1887-TMC)

#578-583; Leon Lafanier, father, 30; Sahra, wife, 28; Josephine, daughter, 7; Eliza, daughter, 4; Lenora, daughter, 3; Joseph, son, 1. (1888-TMC)

#667-672; Leon, Lafranier, male, father, 30; Sahra, female, wife, 28; Josephine, female, daughter, 8; Elie, male, son, 5; Leonie, female, daughter, 4; Joseph, male, son, 2. (1889-TMC)

#722-728; Leon Lafrenier, male, father, 32; Sahra, female, mother, 30; Josephine, female, daughter, 9; Elie, male, son, 6; Joseph, male, son, 3; Louise, female, daughter, 5; Florestine, female, daughter, 5 months. (1890-TMC)

Lagemoniere, Joseph

#552-553; Joseph Lagemoniere, male, father, 20; Eliza, female, wife, 20. (1889-TMC)

#609-611; Joseph Lagemonaire, male, father, 22; Eliza, female, mother, 22; Marie, female, daughter, 7 months. (1890-TMC)

Family 155; #662-664; Eliza Lagemonier, female, wife, 21, mixed bloods on reservation; Joseph, male, husband, 26; St.Ann, female, daughter, 8. (1892-TMC)

Lambert, Augustin

Augustin Lambert, father, 35; Philomene, wife, 26; Esral, son, 8; Napoleon, son, 6; St.Pierre, son, 4; Francois, son, 2; one single B gun. (1884-TMC)

#533-538; Augustin Lambert, father, male, 36; Philomene, wife, female, 27; Esral, son, male, 9; Napoleon, son, male, 7; St.Pierre, son, male, 5; Francois, son, male, 3. (1885-TMC)

#744-749; Augustin Lambert, father, male, 27; Philomene, wife, female, 28; Israel, son, male, 10; Napoleon, son, male, 8; St.Pierre, son, male, 6; Francois, son, male, 4. (1886-TMC)

Family 50, #235-243, Augustine Lambert, male, father, 43, mixed bloods in vicinity of reservation; Philomene, female, wife, 38; Israel, male, son, 15; Napoleon, male, son, 13; Peter,male, son, 11; Francois, male, son, 9; Joseph, male, son, 6; William, male, son, 4; Mary, female, daughter, 1½. (1892-TMC)

Landry, Maxime

#714-717; Maxime Landry, father, male, 27; Marguerite, wife, female, 20; Alexandre, son, male, 2; Norbert, son, male, 2 months. (1885-TMC)

#656-659; Maxime Landry, father, male, 28; Marguerite, wife, female, 21; Alexandre, son, male, 3; Norbert, son, male, 1. (1886-TMC)

#608-611; Maxime Landry, father, 30; Margaritte, wife, 23; Alexander, son, 5; Norbert, son, 2. (1888-TMC)

#622-626; Maxime Landry, male, father, 28; Margarett, female, wife, 26; Alexander, male, son, 6; Norbert, male, son, 3; Caroline, female, daughter, 9 months. (1889-TMC)

#676-680; Maxime Landry, male, father, _; Margarette, female, wife, _; Alexander, male, son, _; Norbert, male, son, _; Caroline, female, daughter, _. (1890-TMC)

Family 156; #665-670; Margarett Landry, female, wife, 27, mixed bloods on reservation; #666, Maxim, male, husband, 38; Alexander, male, son, 9; #668, Norbert, male, son, 7; Caroline, female, daughter, 4; St.Ann, female, daughter, 1-1/2. (1892-TMC)

Landry, Napoleon

#620-621; Napoleon Landry, male, brother, 22; Bernard, male, brother, 15. (1889-TMC)

#674-675; Napoleon Landry, male, orphan, 22; Bernard, male, orphan, 15. (1890-TMC)

Family 158; #673-674; Napoleon Landry, male, single, 24, mixed bloods on reservation; Bemharot, male, brother, 18. (1892-TMC)

Landry, Norbert

#633-634; Norbert Landry, male, father, 20; Frances, female, wife, 24. (1889-TMC)

#687-689; Norbert Landry, male, father, _; Francis, female, mother, _; Patrice, male, son, _. (1890-TMC)

Family 157; #671-672; Frances Landry, female, wife, 27, mixed bloods on reservation; Norbert, male, husband, 23. (1892-TMC)

Landry, Pierre

Pierre Landry, father, 45; Madeleine, wife, 40; Napoleon, son, 18; Pauline, son [daughter], 18; Norbert, son, 14; Bernard, son, 12; Joseph, son, 5. (1884-TMC)

#656-662; Pierre Landry, father, male, 46; Madeleine, wife, female, 44; Napoleon, son, male, 19; Pauline, daughter, female, 19; Norbert, son, male, 15; Bernard, son, male, 13; Joseph, son, male, 6. (1885-TMC)

#633-639; Pierre Landry, father, male, 47; Madeline, wife, female, 42; Napoleon, son, male, 20 (twin); Pauline, [dau], [F], 20 (twin); Norbert, son, male, 16; Burnard, son, male, 12; Joseph, son, male, 7. (1886-TMC)

#532-538; Pierre Landry, father, 48; Madeleine, wife, 43; Napoleon, son, 21; Paul, son, 21, [Pauline?]; Norbert, son, 18; Bernard, son, 15; Joseph, son, 8. (1887-TMC)

#588-593; Pierre Landry, father, 49; Madalin, wife, 44; Napoleon, son, 22; Norbert, son, 19; Bernard, son, 16; Joseph, son, 9. (1888-TMC)

Langan, Dionne

#360-364; Dionne Langan, male, father, 30; Angelic, female, dau [wife ?], 41; Eugene, male, son, 4; Madalain, female, daughter, 3; Virginie, female, daughter, 8 months. (1889-TMC-off)

Langan, Francois

#290-298; Francois Langan, male, father, 45; Philomene, female, wife, 40; Francois, male, son, 18; Joshua, male, son, 12; La Rose, female, daughter, 10; Ezear, male, son, 8; Elize, female, daughter, 6; Rose, female, daughter, 4; Isidore, male, son, 2. (1889-TMC-off)

Langan, Jean Baptiste

#369-375; J. B. Langan, male, father, 42; Angelic, female, wife, 39; Louisa, female, daughter, 13; Vivian, male, son, 10; J. Baptist, male, son, 8; Patrice, male, son, 5; Alex, male, son, 2. (1889-TMC-off)

Langan, Joseph

#279-283; Joseph Langan, male, father, 32; Marie, female, wife, 30; Marie, female, daughter, 9; Veronic, female, daughter, 6; Joseph, male, son, 4. (1889-TMC-off)

Langan, Margaret

#367-368; Margaret Langan, female, widow, 60; Edward, male, son, 20. (1889-TMC-off)

Langan, Michel

#376-384; Michel Langan, male, father, 36; Marie, female, wife, 30; Victoria, female, daughter, 13; Vital, male, son, 11; Marie Rose, female, daughter, 9; Pauline, female, daughter, 7; Joseph, male, son, 5; Gabriel, male, son, 3; Patrice, male, son, 2 months. (1889-TMC-off)

Langer, Edward

Edward Lange (x), 1 man, 1 woman, 9 children, 11 total, $3.00 a share, $33.00 paid. (1868 TM annuity)

Edward Langie (x), 1 man, 1 woman, 4 boys, 5 girls, 11 total, $5.00 a share, $55.00 total. (1869 TM annuity)

Edward Langie (x), 4 men, 4 women, 4 children, 12 total, $5.00 a share, $60.00 paid. (1870 TM annuity)

Ed. Langer (x), 1 man, 1 total, $8.50 a share, $8.50 paid. (1871 TM annuity)

Edward Langer (x), 1 man, 1 woman, 2 total, $10.50 a share, $21.00 paid. (1872 TM annuity)

Langer, Francois

#607; Francois Lange, man, 28. (1888-TMC)

#638-639; Francois Langer, male, father, 26; Frances, female, wife, 19. (1889-TMC)

#693-695; Francois Langer, male, father, _; Francis, female, mother, _; Francois, male, son, _. (1890-TMC)

Family 160; #678-681; Frank Langer, male, father, 31, mixed bloods on reservation; Frances, female, wife, 23; Francois, male, son, 3; Angelic, female, daughter, 1. (1892-TMC)

Langer, Jean

Jean Lange (x), 1 man, 1 woman, 6 children, 8 total, $3.00 a share, $24.00 paid. (1868 TM annuity)

John Lanige (x), 3 men, 3 women, 3 children, 9 total, $5.00 a share, $45.00 paid. (1870 TM annuity)

Langer, Jean Baptiste

#598-602; Jean Baptiste Langis, father, male, 31; Justine, wife, female, 26; Jean Baptiste, son, male, 7; Marie, daughter, female, 5; Ernestine, daughter, female, 2. (1885-TMC)

#627-632; Jean Baptist Langis, father, male, 32; Justine, wife, female, 27; Jean Baptist, son, male, 8; Marie, daughter, female, 6; Ernestine, daughter, female, 3; Louis, son, male, 5 months. (1886-TMC)

#612-617; J. B. Langer, father, 37; Justine, wife, 30; Jean Baptist, son, 12; Marie, daughter, 10; Ernestine, daughter, 8; Louis, son, 3. (1888-TMC)

#567-572; J. B. Langer, male, father, 37; Justine, female, wife, 32; John B., male, son, 11; Louis, male, son, 4; Marie Justine, female, daughter, 8; Marie, female, daughter, 1. (1889-TMC)

#625-630; J. B. Langer, male, father, 38; Justine, female, mother, 34; J. B., male, son, 12; Louis, male, son, 5; Marie J., female, daughter, 9; Mary D., female, daughter, 2. (1890-TMC)

Family 136; #578-583; J. Baptist Langer, male, father, 37, mixed bloods on reservation; Justine, female, wife, 35; John B., male, son, 14; Mary, female, daughter, 11; Louis, male, son, 7; Mary Desange, female, daughter, 4. (1892-TMC)

Langer, Joseph

Joseph Langie (x), 2 men, 4 women, 3 boys, 2 girls, 11 total, $5.00 a share, $55.00 paid. (1869 TM annuity)

Joseph Lange (x), 2 men, 2 women, 2 children, 6 total, $5.00 a share, $30.00 paid. (1870 TM annuity)

Langer, Joseph

#823-828; Joseph Langis, father, male, 38; Genevieve, wife, female, 38, James [Chartrand], [stepson], male, 18; Marie, daughter, female, 12; Israel, son, male, 8; Joseph, son, male, 6. (1886-TMC)

#523-526; Joseph Langer, father, 40; Genevieve, wife, 52; Marie, daughter, 16; Joseph, son, 11. (1888-TMC)

#585-588; Joseph Langer, male, father, 42; Genevieve, female, wife, 45; Joe, male, son, 12; Maria Cecil, female, daughter, 15. (1889-TMC)

#649-651; Joseph Langer, male, father, 45; Genevieve, female, mother, 65 [sic]; Joseph, male, son, 13. (1890-TMC)

Langer, Josephte

Joseph [Josephte] Lange (x), 1 woman, 6 children, 7 total, $3.00 a share, $21.00 paid. (1868 TM annuity)

Lapierre, Gabriel

#623-624; Gabriel LaPierre, father, 20; Marie, wife, 15. (1888-TMC)

Lapierre, Moise

Moise Lapierre, father, 45; Angelic, wife, 50; Joseph, son, 19; Gabriel, son, 17; Marie Louise, daughter, 19; (November 1885), William Pereantau, step-son, 23; one house, one stable, 6 tons hay, 9 acres borken, one DB gun. (1884-TMC)

#187-192; Moise Lapierre, father, male, 47; Angelic, wife, female, 52; Joseph, son, male, 21; Gabriel, son, male, 19; Mary Louise, daughter, female, 16; William Pearenteau, stepson, male, 23. (1886-TMC)

#500-502; Moses LaPierre, father, 45; Angelic, wife, 56; Joseph, son, 22. (1888-TMC)

#580-584; Moses LaPierre, male, father, 45; Angelic, female, wife, 57; Joseph, male, son, 22; Gabriel, male, son, 20; Rosalie, female, stepdaughter [?], 5. (1889-TMC)

#638-641; Moses La Pierre, male, father, 48; Angelic, female, mother, 58; Joseph, male, son, 23; Rosalie, niece, 5. (1890-TMC)

Family 134, #573-575; Moses La Pierre, male, father, 50, mixed bloods on reservation; Angelique, female, wife, 61; La Rose, female, orphan niece, 9. (1892-TMC)

Laplante, Olivier

Olivar Leplant (x), 1 man, 1 woman, 4 boys, 2 girls, 8 total, $5.00 a share, $40.00 total. (1869 TM annuity)

Laquete, Frezine

Family #154; #660-661, Frezine Laquete, female, widow, 70, mixed bloods on reservation; Riel, male, son, 6. (1892-TMC)

La Rat, Zachary

#638-641; Zachary La Rat, father, 30; Marie, wife, 30; Josephine, daughter, 3; Ellen, daughter, 1. (1888-TMC)

Larat, Pierre

#618-622; Pierre Larat, son, 20; Rosalie, mother, 53; Frances, daughter, 23; Lizzet, daughter, 15; Ellen, daughter, 13. (1888-TMC)

#750-751; Pierre La Rat, male, father, 22; Cecilia, female, mother, 19. (1890-TMC)

Family 165; #699-700; Pierre Le Rat, male, father, 23, mixed bloods on reservation; Cecilia, female, wife, 20. (1892-TMC)

La Rat, Rosalie

#627-632; Rosalie La Rat, female, mother, 48; Pierre, male, son, 22; Lizet, female, daughter, 16; Ambroise, male, nephew, 14; Genevieve, female, niece, 12; Emmanuel, male, nephew, 10. (1889-TMC)

#681-686; Rosalie La Rat, female, mother, _; Lizet, female, daughter, _; Ambroise, male, son, _; Genevieve, female, daughter, _; Emanuel, male, son, _; Helen, female, daughter, _. (1890-TMC)

LaRoque, A.

#365-366; A. LaRoque,, male, father, 27; Virginie, female, wife, 25. (1889-TMC-off)

Laroque, Baptiste

Batiste Laroque (x), 1 man, 1 woman, 8 children, 10 total, $3.00 a share, $30.00 paid. (1868 TM annuity)

Laroque, James

#343-344; James Laroque, male, father, 19; Deliahed, female, wife, 40 [?]. (1889-TMC-off)

Laroque, Joseph

Joseph Laroque (x), 1 man, 1 woman, 1 child, 3 total, $8.50 a share, $25.50 paid. (1871 TM annuity)

Laroque, Josette

Josette Laroque (x), 1 woman, 2 children, 3 total, $8.50 a share, $25.50 paid. (1871 TM annuity)

Larocque, Michael

#647-649; Michael Larocque, male, father, 48; La Rose, female, wife, 44; Michael, male, son, 19. (1889-TMC)

Laroque, Oliver

#339-342; Oliver Laroque, male, father, 28; Marie Rose, female, wife, 23; Andre, male, son, 3; Vital, male, son, 2. (1889-TMC-off)

Latnie [?], Joseph

Joseph Latnie, father, 25; Nancy, wife, 25. (July 1886-TMC)

Latreille/Latraille

Latraille, Alexander

Family 166; #701-704, Alexander Latraille, male, father, 46, mixed bloods on reservation; Clemence, female, wife, 36; Simon (Godden) male, adopted son, 12; Frederick, male, adopted son, 5. (1892-TMC)

Latreille, Mrs.

Mrs. Latraile (x), 1 woman, 1 total, $8.50 a share, $8.50 paid. (1871 TM annuity)

Latreille, Moise

Moise Latraile (x), 1 man, 1 total, $8.50 a share, $8.50 paid. (1871 TM annuity)

Laterregrass, Jean Baptist

Babtiste Le Terr Gras (x), 1 man, 1 woman, 2 total, $5.00 a share, $10.00 total. (1869 TM annuity)

#960-963; Jean Baptist Laterregrass, father, male, 35; Marie, wife, female, 29; Jean Baptist, son, male, 10; Rosellie, daughter, female, 8. (1886-TMC)

#502-506; J. B. Lattergrass, father, 37; Marie, wife, 32; Mary, daughter, 11; John Baptist, son, 12; Joseph, son, 4 months. (1887-TMC)

#557-561; J. B. Lattergrass, father, 38; Marie, wife, 32; Rosalie, daughter, 12; John B., son, 14; Joseph, son, 2. (1888-TMC)

#640-643; J. B. Lattergrass, male, father, 41; Mary, female, wife, 36; John, male, son, 15; Joseph, male, son, 3. (1889-TMC)

#696-700; J. B. Lattergrass, male, father, _; Marie, female, mother, _; John, male, son, _; Joseph, male, son, _; Justine, female, daughter, _. (1890-TMC)

Family 84; #264-268; A-ke-wenen, John B. Latteregrass, male, father, 45, full bloods on reservation; Mary, female; wife; 39; John Baptist, male, son, 18; __ female, daughter, 2; __ female, daughter, 9 months. (1892-TMC)

Lavallee, Pierre

Pierre Lavale, father, 35; Josepht, wife, _; Antoine, son, 12; Francoise, daughter, 8; Rosine, daughter, 6; Marie Terese, daughter, 9; Virginie, daughter, 2. (Jul 1886)

#573-579; Pierre La Vallee, male, father, 39; Suzett, female, wife, 35; Antoine, male, son, 14; Francois, male, son, 12; Rosin, female, daughter, 11; Marie Therese, female, daughter, 8; Virginie, female, daughter, 6. (1889-TMC)

#631-637; Pierre Lavallee, male, father, 40; Suzzett, female, mother, 36; Antoin, male, son, 15; Francois, male, son, 13; Rosine, female, daughter, 11; Theresa, female, daughter, 9; Virginie, female, daughter, 7. (1890-TMC)

Family 147; #620-627; Josett Lavallie, female, wife, 34, mixed blood on reservation; Pierre, male, husband, 45; Antoine, male, son, 10; Frances, female, daughter, 14; Theresa, female, daughter, 12; Mary Rose, female, daughter, 10; Virginie, female, daughter, 8; John B., male, son, 2 months. (1892-TMC)

Laverdure, Angelique

Angelique Lavardure (x), 1 woman, 1 total, $3.00 a share, $3.00 paid. (1868 TM annuity)

Laverdure, Baptist

#929-936; Baptist Laverdure, father, male, 37; Mary Anne, wife, female, 30; Frances, daughter, female, 14; Nancy, daughter, female, 10; Phillip, son, male, 8; Daniel, son, male, 6; Solemon, son, male, 4; George, son, male, 2. (1886-TMC)

Laverdure, David

#271, David Laverdure, father, male, 25; Elize, wife, female, 22; Jean, son, male, 7; Tousaint, son, male, 4; Clemence, daughter, female, 1. (1885-TMC)

#146-150; David Laverdure, father, male, 26; Eliza, wife, female, 23; Jean, son, male, 8; Toussaint, son, male, 5; Clemence, daughter, female, 3. (1886-TMC)

#546-547; David Laverdure, father, 27; Elize, wife, 26. (1888-TMC)

#562-564; David Laverdure, male, father, 26; Eliza, female, wife, 23; Marie, female, daughter, 1. (1889-TMC)

#622-624; David Laverdure, male, father, 31; Eliza, female, mother, 30; Clara, female, daughter, 2. (1890-TMC)

Family 143; #602-605; David Laverdure, male, father, 31, mixed bloods on reservation; Elise, female, wife, 27; Florence, female, daughter, 4; Elise, female, daughter, 2. (1892-TMC)

Laverdure, Elizabeth

Elizabeth La Verdure (x), 1 woman, 4 children, 5 total, $5.00 a share, $25.00 paid. (1870 TM annuity)

Laverdure, Francois

#911-915; Francois Laverdure, father, male, 35; Mary, wife, female, 25; Francois, son, male, 6; John, son, male, 4; Eleha [Elie], son, male, 4 months. (1886-TMC)

Laverdure, Joseph Jr.

Joseph Laverdure, father, 50; Marie, wife, 42; Justine, daughter, 19; William, son, 17; Ellen, daughter, 14; Josephine, daughter, 12; Adele, daughter, 10; Napoleon, son, 6; one flintlock gun. (1884-TMC)

#263-278; Joseph Laverdure Jr., father, male, 51; Marie, wife, female, 43; Justine, daughter, female, 20; William, son, male, 18; Ellen, daughter, female, 16; Josephine, daughter, female, 13; Adele, daughter, female, 11; Napoleon, son, male, 7. (1885-TMC)

#196-203; Joseph Laverdure Jr., father, male, 52; Marie, wife, female, 44; Justine, daughter, female, 21; William, son, male, 19; Ellen, daughter, female, 16; Josephine, daughter, female, 14; Adella, daughter, female, 12; Napoleon, son, male, 8. (1886-TMC)

#548-555; Joseph Laverdure Jr., father, 51; Mary, wife, 48; William, son, 21; Adele, daughter, 13; Josephine, daughter, 16; Napoleon, son, 12; Frances Vivier, nephew, 21; Alexis, brother, 30. (1888-TMC)

#554-561; Joseph Laverdure, male, father, 52; Mary, female, wife, 46; William, male, son, 23; Napoleon, male, son, 12; Josephine, female, daughter, 15; Adelle, female, daughter, 13; Frank Vivier, male, nephew, 22; Alexis, male, brother, 35. (1889-TMC)

#612-619; Joseph Laverdure, male, father, 56; Marie, female, wife, 50; William, male, son, 24; Napoleon, male, son, 12; Adelle, female, daughter, 18; Alexis, male, brother, 36; Simson Charrette, male, nephew, 19. (1890-TMC)

Family 152; #652-656; Joseph Laverdure, male, father, 65, mixed bloods on reservatino; Mary, female, wife, 55; Adele, female, daughter, 17; Napoleon, male, son, 14; Alexis, male, brother, 40. (1892-TMC)

Laverdure, Joseph Sr.

Joseph Laverdure, father, 71; Alexis, 25; Francois, grandson, 16; Marie, granddaughter, 14; wife, Madeline, 66, (June 1885); Marie Charette, granddaughter, 16; Clemance, granddaughter, 14; Simion, granddaughter, 13. (1884-TMC)

#650-655; Joseph Laverdure Sr., father, male, 72; Madeleine, wife, female, 66; Alexis, son, male, 26; Marie Charette, granddaughter, female, 16; Clamance, granddaughter, female, 14; Simion, granddaughter, F, 12. (1885-TMC)

#812-818; Joseph Laverdure, father, male, 73; Madeline, wife, female, 67; Alexis, son, male, 27; Francois, grandson, male, 18; Marie, granddaughter, female, 16; Clemence Charette, granddaughter, female, 16; Simon, granddaughter [?], F [?], 14. (TMC-1886)

#506-509; Joseph Laverdure Sr., father, 75; Madalain, wife, 68; Simmon, son, 16; Angelic, g.d., 9. (1888-TMC)

Laverdure, Pierre

#276-277; Pierre Laverdure, father, male, 23; Veronique, wife, female, 25. (1885-TMC)

#355-356; St.Pierre Laverdure, father, male, 24; Virginia, wife, female, 26. (1886-TMC)

#527-528; Pierre Laverdure No. 1, father, 25; Veronica, wife, 29. (1888-TMC)

#565-566; Pierre Laverdure 2d, male, father, 26; Veronica, female, wife, 27. (1889-TMC)

#620-621; Pierre Laverdure, male, father, 28; Veronica, female, mother, 28. (1890-TMC)

Family 137; #584-585; Pierre Laverdure, male, father, 27, mixed bloods on reservation; Veronic, female, wife, 27. (1892-TMC)

Laverdure, Pierre No. 2

Pierre Laverdure, father, 46; Agnes, wife, 35; Eliza, daughter, 14; Secil, daughter, 14, (twins); Leon, son, 12; Isidore, son, 9; Armayil, son, 7; Margarete, daughter, 4; Eesbel, daughter, 1; (June 1886) one winchester. (Oct 1885-TMC)

#439-447; Pierre Laverdure, father, male, 47; Agnes, wife, female, 36; Eliza, daughter, female, 15; Secil, daughter, female, 15; Leon, son, male, 13; Isidore, son, male, 10; Armyil, son, male, 8; Marguerite, daughter, female, 5; Isabelle, daughter, female, 2. (1886-TMC)

#507-516; Peter Laverdure No. 2, father, 43; Annell, wife, 42; Eliza, daughter, (twin), 14; Cecilia, daughter, (twin), 14; Leon, son, 13; Isidore, son, 10; Armagil, son, 8; Isabel, [daughter], 4; Marguerett, daughter, 2; Adell, daughter, 1 month. (1887-TMC)

#568-577, Peter Laverdure No.2, father, 46; Annett, wife, 37; Eliza, daughter, 15; Cecilia, daughter, 15; Leon, son, 12; Isidore, son, 10; Amagil, son, 8; Isabel, daughter, 6; Margaret, daughter, 4; Adell, daughter, 1. (1888-TMC)

#683-691; Pierre Laverdure No. 2, male, father, 48; Angel, female, wife, 37; Cecilia, female, daughter, 16; Leon, male, son, 15; Theodore, male, son, 12; Amagil, male, son, 10; Isabelle, female, daughter, 7; Margaret, female, daughter, 4; Adel, female, daughter, 2. (1889-TMC)

#740-749; Pierre Laverdure No. 2, male, father 49; Angel, female, mother, 38; Cecilia, female, daughter, 19; Leon, male, son, 16; Theodore, male, son, 13; Armagil, male, son, 10; Isabel, female, daughter, 8; Margaret, female, daughter, 4; Adel, female, daughter, 3; Pauline, female, daughter, 10 months. (1890-TMC)

Family 150; #638-646; Pierre Laverdure, male, father, 53, mixed bloods on reservation; Angelic, female, wife, 45; Stanislas, male, son, 17; Isadore, male, son, 15; Michael, male, son, 13; Margaret, female, daughter, 11; Adele, female, daughter, 6; Pauline, female, daughter, 4. (1892-TMC)

Laverdure, Xavier

Xavier Laverdure (x), 1 man, 1 woman, 3 children, 5 total, $3.00 a share, $15.00 paid. (1868 TM annuity)

Laverdure, William

Family 158; #657-659, William Laverdure, male, father, 24, mixed bloods on reservation; Matilda, female, wife, 24; Joseph, male, son, 4 months. (1892-TMC)

Laviolet, Albert

#316-317; Albert Laviolet, male, father, 28; Florestine, female, wife, 21. (1889-TMC-off)

Laviolet, Charles

#352-359; Chas. Laviolet, male, father, 35; Clemence, female, wife, 33; Mili, female, daughter, 13; Napoleon, male, son, 11; Tobias, male, son, 9; Emeris, female, daughter, 7; Mary Jane, female, daughter, 2; Joseph, male, son, 4 months. (1889-TMC-off)

Laviolet, Jean Baptiste

#328-331; J. B. Laviolet, male, father, 70; Nancy, female, wife, 70; Jacob, male, son, 19; Rosin, female, adopted daughter, 9. (1889-TMC-off)

La Zone [?], Francois

#517-522; Francois La Zone, father, 62; Eliza, wife, 49; Virginie, daughter, 14; Pauline, daughter, 8; Julian, son, 12; Alexander, son, 10. (1887-TMC)

Lebrun, Adolph

Family 247; #1100-1103, Marie Louis Le Brun, female, wife, 26, mixed bloods on reservation; Adolph (white), male, husband, 39; Oscar, male, son, 3; Joseph, male, son, 1. (1892-TMC)

Lecuyer, Francois

Francois Lecuyer (x), 1 man, 1 woman, 3 children, 5 total, $4.00 a share, $20.00 paid. (1868 TM annuity)

Francis Le Cyer (x), 1 man, 1 woman, 1 boy, 2 girls, 5 total, $5.00 a share, $25.00 paid. (1869 TM annuity)

Francis Lecoiyer (x), 1 man, 1 woman, 4 children, 6 total, $5.00 a share, $30.00 paid. (1870 TM annuity)

Lecuyer, Michael

Michael Lecuyer (x), 1 man, 1 woman, 2 children, 4 total, $4.00 a share, $16.00 paid. (1868 TM annuity)

Michael Le Cyer (x), 2 men, 2 women, 3 boys, 3 girls, 10 total, $5.00 a share, $50.00 paid. (1869 TM annuity)

Michael Lecheyea (x), 1 man, 2 women, 7 children, 10 total, $5.00 a share, $50.00 paid. (1870 TM annuity)

Lecuyer, Xavier

Exevie Lecheyea (x), 1 man, 1 woman, 7 children, 9 total, $5.00 a share, $45.00 paid. (1870 TM annuity)

Lefloe, Jean

#630-634; Jean Lefloe, father, 37; Angelic, wife, 32; Joseph, son, 9; Sahra, daughter, 5; Maria Louise, daughter, 7 months. (1888-TMC)

Lefort, Augustin

#286-289 (288 missing); Augustin Lefort, male, father, 21; Harriet, female, wife, 21; Leon, male, son, 2. (1889-TMC-off)

Lefort, Francois

#657-662; Francois Lefort, male, father, 64; Elise, female, wife, 60; Virginie, female, daughter, 17; Julian, male, son, 15; Alexander, male, son, 13; Pauline, female, daughter, 11. (1889-TMC)

#711-716; Francois Lefort, male, father, 65; Elise, female, mother, 52; Virginie, female, daughter, 18; Julian, male, son, 16; Alexander, male, son, 14; Pauline, female, daughter, 12. (1890-TMC)

Lefort, Maxime

#663-666; Maxim Lefort, male, father, 25; Rosalie, female, wife, 22; Adele, female, daughter, 6; Joseph, male, son, 2. (1889-TMC)

#717-721; Maxim Lefort, male, father, 26; Rosalie, female, mother, 23; Adelle, female, daughter, 7; Joseph, male, son, 3; M. R., female, daughter, 10 months. (1890-TMC)

Family 151; #647-651; Rosalie Lefort, female, wife, 24, mixed bloods on reservation; Maxim, male, husband, 29; Adele, female, daughter, 8; Joseph, male, son, 5; Marie Rose, female, daughter, 3. (1892-TMC)

Lenoir, Eliza

Eliza Lenoir (x), 1 woman, 1 child, 2 total, $5.00 a share, $10.00 paid. (1874 TM annuity)

Lenoir, Jean Baptiste

Babtiste Lenoir (x), 1 man, 2 women, 2 boys, 2 girls, 7 total, $5.00 a share, $35.00 paid. (1869 TM annuity)

Baptiste Lenoir (x), 1 man, 3 women, 7 children, 11 total, $5.00 a share, $55.00 paid. (1870 TM annuity)

J. Bte. Le Noire (x), 2 men, 3 women, 9 children, 14 total, $8.50 a share, $119.00 paid. (1871 TM annuity)

Baptiste Le Noir (x), 3 men, 4 women, 7 children, 14 total, $10.50 a share, $147.00 paid. (1872 TM annuity)

Batiste Lanoire (x), 1 man, 1 woman, 12 children, 14 total, $10.00 a share, $140.00 paid. (1873 TM annuity)

Baptiste Lenoir (x), 1 man, 1 woman, 5 children, 7 total, $5.00 a share, $35.00 paid. (1874 TM annuity)

#407-417; Baptiste Lenoir, father, male, 69; Marie, wife, female, 67; Louis, son, male, 23; Antoine, son, male, 15; Liset McDonald, granddaughter, female, 15; Eliza, granddaughter, female, 15; William grandson, male, 13; Michael, grandson, male, 12; Marie, granddaughter, female, 10; Agat, granddaughter, female, 8; Lizie Warren [?], granddaughter, female, 12. (1885-TMC)

#318-327; Mary Lenoir, female, mother, 60; Louis, male, son, 28; Antoine, male, son, 20; William, male, son, 19; Michael, male, son, 17; Elize, female, daughter, 19; Liset, female, daughter, 19; Agathe, female, daughter, 16; Elize, female, daughter, 15; Mary, female, daughter, 14. (1889-TMC-off)

Family 86 and 87; #277-283; Marie Lenoir, female, widow, 67, full bloods on reservation; Lewis, male, son, 31; William, male, son, 22; Michael, male, son, 21; Agasha, female, daughter, 19; Eliza, female, grand daughter, 19; Lisett, female, grand daughter, 21. (1892-TMC)

Lenoir, John

John Lenoir (x), 1 man, 1 child, 2 total, $5.00 a share, $10.00 paid. (1874 TM annuity)

Lenoir, Joseph A-ki-chi-ta

#391-395; Joseph Lenoir, father, male, 28; Camille, wife, female, 22; Joseph, son, male, 4; Josephine, daughter, female, 2; Jean Baptiste, son, male, 3 months. (1885-TMC)

#405-409; Joseph Lenoir, father, male, 29; Camille, wife, female, 23; Joseph, son, male, 5; Josephine, daughter, female, 3; Jean Baptist, son, male, 1. (1886-TMC)

Family 85; #269-276, A-ki-chi-ta, Joseph Lenoir, male, father, 37, full bloods on reservation; Cenoille, female, wife, 29; Joseph, male, son, 10; John Baptist, male, son, 6; Norbert, male, son, 5; Marie, female, daughter, 3; St.Pierre, male son, 1-1/2; Josephine, female, daughter, 8. (1892-TMC)

Lenoir, Josette

Josette Lanoire (x), 1 woman, 2 children, 3 total, $10.00 a share, $30.00 paid. (1873 TM annuity)

Turtle Mountain Chippewa Pembina Band 1865-1892

Lenoir, Maria

Maria Lenoir (x), 1 woman, 1 child, 2 total, $5.00 a share, $10.00 paid. (1874 TM annuity)

Lenoir, Mary

#642-649; Mary Lenior, widow, 64; Eliza McDonald, granddaughter, 18; Wm. McDonald, 16, grandson, Michael, grandson, 15; Marie, granddaughter, 12; Joseph Lenoir, grandson, 7; Josephine granddaughter, 6; John Baptist, grandson, 3. (1888-TMC)

#756-761; Mary Widow Lenoir, female, mother, 62; Louis, male, son, 29; Antoine, male, son, 21; William, male, son, 18; Michael, male, son, 17; Mary, female, daughter, 15. (1890-TMC)

Levellie, Joseph

#516-518; Joseph Levellie, father, male, _; Sophie, mother, female, _; Joseph, son, male, _. (1885-TMC)

#652-655; Joseph Laveillie, father, male, 51; Sophie, wife, female, 52; Joseph, son, male, 24; Sophie [?], mother, female, 72. (1886-TMC)

#299-304; Joseph Lavaia, male, father, 54; Sophia, female, wife, 60; Joseph, male, son, 25; Fraciene Belgarde, female, daughter, 23; Nelly, female, granddaughter, 5; Mary, female, granddaughter, 3. (1889-TMC-off)

Levellie, Pierre

#519-521; Pierre Levellie, father, male, _; Elize, wife, female, _; Joseph, son, male, _. (1885-TMC)

#648-651; Pierre Laviellie, father, male, 27; Eliza, wife, female, 22; Joseph, son, male, 2; Sariphine, daughter, female, 2 months. (1886-TMC)

#305-309; Pierre Lavaia, male, father, 27; Elise, female, wife, 24; Joseph, male, son, 5; Seraphine, female, daughter, 3; Patrice, male, son, 1-1/2. (1889-TMC-off)

Family 49; #228-234, Peter Lavais, male, father, 36, mixed bloods in vicinity of reservation; Elise, female, wife, 30; Joseph, male, son, 9; Zeraplinned, female, daughter, 7; Batrice, male, son, 5; Louise, female, daughter, 2-1/2; Mary, female, daughter, 6 months. (1892-TMC)

Lizotte, Pierre

#348-351, 351); Pierre Lissott, male, father, 60; Catherine, female, wife, 49; Joseph, male, son, 22; Adel, female, daughter, 15; Napoleon, male, son, 11. (1889-TMC-off)

Family 76; #364-372; Julia Lissott, female, wife, 47, mixed bloods in vicinity of reservation; Pierre, male, husband, 49; Joseph, male, son, 11; Etiene, male, son, 7; Rosina, female, daughter, 4; #369, Rosali, female, daughter, 3; Alfred, male, son, 2; Betsy Ledault, female, mother, 50; John B. Ledault, male, son, 24; Le Mary Margaret, female, wife, 23; Le Mary (no name), female, daughter, 6 months. (1892-TMC)

Lucier, Alexandre

#332-338; Alex Lucier, male, father, 45; Jossett, female, wife, 37; Mary, female, daughter, 19; Caroline, female, daughter, 17; Eliza, female, daughter, 14; Robert, male, son, 12; Rosina, female, daughter, 6. (1889-TMC-off)

Family 167; #705-709, Josett Lucier, female, wife, 41, mixed bloods on reservation; Alexander, male, husband, 52; Eliza, female, daughter, 13; Rosina, female, daughter, 8; Robert, male, son, 12. (1892-TMC)

Lucier, Antoine

#834-840; Antoine Lucier, father, male, 37; Liza, wife, female, 30; Tusant, son, male, 13; Alexandre, son, male, 9; David, son, male, 7; Mary, daughter, female, 3; Albert, son, male, 2 months. (1886-TMC)

Macaron, Paul

Paul Macaron (x), 1 man, 1 total, $5.00 a share, $5.00 paid. (1870 TM annuity)

Malaterre, Alexis (See also Marguerite Malaterre)

Alexis Malaterre, father, 61, (died); Margarete, wife, 55; Alexis, son, 21; Napoleon, son, 19; Adele, daughter, 14; Margurete, daughter, 8; Cleophie, daughter, 6; one DB shot gun. (1884-TMC)

Malaterre, Jeremiah

#741-747; Jerimiah Malaterre, father, 34; Alphonzine, wife, 28; Louis Phillip, son, 9; Joseph, son, 6; Edward, son, 4; Marie, daughter, 2; Caroline, daughter, 1 month. (1888-TMC)

#703-709; Jeremiah Malaterre, male, father, 30; Alphonsine, female, wife, 28; Louis Phillip, male, son, 10; Joseph, male, son, 8; Edward, male, son, 5; Mary, female, daughter, 3; Caroline, female, daughter, 1. (1889-TMC)

#777-782; Jeremiah Malaterre, male, father, 31; Alphonsin, female, mother, 27; Louis P., male, son, 11; Joseph, male, son, 8; Edward, male, son, 5; Mary, female, daughter, 4. (1890-TMC)

Family 175; #734-740; Alphonsine Malaterre, female, wife, 36, mixed bloods on reservation; Jeremiah, male, husband, 40; Phillip, male, son, 13; Joseph, male, son, 10; Edward, male, son, 8; Mary, female, daughter, 6; John, male, son, 2. (1892-TMC)

Malaterre, Louis

Family 172; #726, Cecil Malaterre, female, wife, 19, mixed bloods on reservation; #727, Louis Malaterre, male, husband, 25; #726, Veronic, female, daughter, 6 months. (1892-TMC)

Malaterre, Marguerite (See also Alexis Malaterre)

#603-608; Marguerite Malaterre, mother, female, 56; Alexis, son, male, 22; Napleon, son, male, 20; Adele, daughter, female, 15; Marguerite, daughter, female, 9; Cleophie, daughter, female, 7. (1885-TMC)

#759-764; Marguerite Malaterre, mother, female, 57; Alexis, son, male, 23; Napoleon, son, male, 21; Adelle, daughter, female, 16; Marguerite, daughter, female, 10; Clophine, daughter, female, 8. (1886-TMC)

#707-712; Margarett Mallaterre, widow, 59; Alexis, son, 23; Louis, son, 21; Margarette, daughter, 12; Adell, daughter, 17; Cleophinie, daughter, 13. 1888-TMC)

#733-737; Margaret Malaterre, female, mother, 60; Alexis, male, son, 25; Louis, male, son, 22; Adelle, female, daughter, 18; Margarette, female, daughter, 13; Sophie, female, daughter, 13. (1889-TMC)

#797-802; Margaret Malaterre, Widow, female, mother, 61; Alexis, male, son, 26; Louis, male, son, 22; Adell, female, daughter, 19; Maragarett, female, daughter, 13; Sophia, female, daughter, 14. (1890-TMC)

Malaterre, Zachary

#594-597; Zachary Malaterre, father, male, 27; Rebecca, wife, female, 27; Zachary, son, male, 4; Napoleon, son, male, 2. (1885-TMC)

#770-774; Zachery Malaterre, father, male, 28; Rebecca, wife, female, 28; Zachery, son, male, 5; Napoleon, son, male, 3; Fredrick, son, male, 1 month. (1886-TMC)

#393-398; Zachary Malater, male, father, 30; Rebecca, female, wife, 29; Zachary, male, son, 8; Napoleon, male, son, 6; Gill, male, son, 4; Zilda, female, daughter, 1-1/2. (1889-TMC-off)

Family 171; #721-725; Rebecca Malaterre, female, wife, 35, mixed blood on reservation; Zachary, male, husband, 35; Zachary, male, son, 11; Napoleon, male, son, are 8; Julius, male, son, 7. (1892-TMC)

Malbeuf, Peter

#408-416; Peter Malbeuf, male, father, 48; Marie, female, wife, 38; Pierre Male, son, 15; Marie Rose, female, daughter, 14; Ambroise, male, son, 13; Joseph, male, son, 12; William, male, son, 11; John Baptist, male, son, 10; Dometil, female, daughter, 9. (1889-TMC-off)

Marcellais, Pierre

Pierre Marcellais, father, 23; Virginie, wife, 18. (1884-TMC)

#207-208; Pierre Marcilais, father, male, 24; Virginie, wife, female, 19. (1885-TMC)

#101-102; Peter Marcellais, father, male, 25; Virginia, wife, female, 20. (1886-TMC)

#692-693; Peter Marcallais, father, 26; Virginie, wife, 21. (1888-TMC)

#801-802; Peter Marcallais, male, father, 27; Virginie, female, wife, 23. (1889-TMC)

#867-868; Peter Marcellais, male, father, 28; Virginie, female, mother, 24. (1890-TMC)

Marion, Ann

#713-716; Ann Marion, mother, 37, widow; Roderic, son, 15; Elize, daughter, 14; Mary, daughter, 6. (1888-TMC)

#795-796; Annie Marion, Widow, female, mother, 44; Lize, female, daughter, 16. (1890-TMC)

Family 169; #712-713; Ann Marion, female, widow, 45, mixed bloods on reservation; Roderick, male, son, 20. (1892-TMC)

Marion, Joseph Edward

#385-388; J. E. Marion, male, father, 27; Justine, female, wife, 23; Elizar, male, son [?], 3; Roger, male, son, 1. (1889-TMC-off)

Family 55, #269-273, __ Marion, jr., male, father, 30, mixed bloods in vicinity of reservation; Justin, femle, wife, 27; Mary Eliza, female, daughter, 7; Roger, male, son, 4; Baptist, male, son, 1. (1892-TMC)

Marion, Maxim

#717-726; Maxim Marion, father, 59; Eliza, wife, 44; Maxim, son, 23; Joseph, son, 20; Louis, son, 18; Rosalie, daughter, 16; Amable, son, 9; Elie, son, 6; Beatrice, daughter, 3; Juliana, daughter, 9 months. (1888-TMC)

#692-699; Maxim Marion, male, father, 60; Eliz, female, wife, 45; Maxim, male, son, 24; Joseph, male, son, 21; Elie, male, son, 7; Louis, male, son, 19; Rosalie, female, daughter, 17; Beatrice, female, daughter, 4. (1889-TMC)

#771-776; Maxime, Marion, male, father, 58; Elize, female, mother, 47; Joseph, male, son, 22; Elie, male, son, 7; Rosalie, female, daughter, 18; Batrice, female, daughter, 4. (1890-TMC)

Family 1770; #714-720; Elise Marion, female, wife, 49, mixed bloods on reservation; Maxim, sr. male, husband, 55; Joseph, male, son, 25; Louis, male, son, 22; Elie, male, son, 10; Beatrice, female, daughter 7; Mary, female, daughter, 1-1/2. (1892-TMC)

Martel, Alexandre

#419-421; Alexandre Martel, father, male, 34; Arseline, wife, female, 28; Maxime, son, male, 11 months. (1886-TMC)

#657-661; Alex Martell, father, 36; Mary, wife, 21; Maxim, son, 3; Joseph, son, 1; Jossett Martell, mother, 80. (1888-TMC)

#717-721; Alex Martel, male, father, 34; Marcolain, female, wife, 25; Maxim, male, son, 5; Joseph, male, son, 2; Susan Martel, female, widow, 81. (1889-TMC)

#788-791; Alex Martel, male, father, 35; Mary, female, mother, 30; Maxim, male, son, 5; Joseph, male, son, 2. (1890-TMC)

Family 177; #750-753; Alexander Martel, male, father, 38, mixed bloods on reservation; Masalina, female, wife, 36; Maxim, male, son, 7; Armidas, male, son, 2 months. (1892-TMC)

Martel, Jean Baptiste Jr.

Baptiste Martel (x), 1 man, 1 woman, 3 children, 5 total, $3.00 a share, $15.00 paid. (1868 TM annuity)

Jean Baptiste Martel Jr., father, 38; Rosalie, wife, 34; Jean Baptiste, son, 17, (to prison June 1886); Joseph, son, 15; Gregorie, son, 13; Arthur, son, 5; Marierose, daughter, 3; Jerome, son, 1; Francois son, 1 month, (June 1885); Josephte Parenteau, mother-in-law, 70. (1884-TMC)

#278-286; Jean Baptiste Martel Jr., father, male, 39; Rosalie, wife, female, 35; Jean Baptiste, son, male, 18; Joseph, son, male, 16; Gregoire, son, male, 14; Arthur, son, male, 6; Marie Rose, daughter, female, 4; Jerome, son, male, 2; Francois, son, male, 1 month. (1885-TMC)

#204-212; Jean Baptiste Martel Jr., father, male, 40; Rosalie, wife, female, 36; Joseph, son, male, 17; Eugene, son, male, 15; Arthur, son, male, 7; Mary Rose, daughter, female, 5; Jerome, son, male, 3; Francois, son, male, 1, Josepht Perrnteau, mother-in-law, female, 70. (1886-TMC)

#662-669; J. B. Martell, father, 42; Rosalie, wife, 38; Gregory, son, 17; Arthur, son, 9; Marie Rose, daughter, 7; Jerome, son, 5; Francis, son, 3; Celina, daughter, 4 months. (1888-TMC)

#710-716; J. B. Martel, male, father, 43; Rosalie, female, wife, 39; Alex, male, son, 17; Arthur, male, son, 10; Jerome, male, son, 6; Francois, male, son, 4; Mary Jane, female, daughter, 8. (1889-TMC)

#783-787; J. B. Martel, widower, male, father, 43; Gregory, male, son, 18; Jerome, male, son, 6; Francois, male, son, 5; Joseph, male, son, 20. (1890-TMC)

Family 178; #754-758; J. B. Martel, male, widower, 46, mixed bloods on reservation; Alex, male, son, 20; Mary Rose, female, daughter, 11; Jerome, male, son, 9; Francois, male, son, 7. (1892-TMC)

Martel, Jean Baptiste Jr.

#694-695; J. B. Martell Jr., father, 20; Marie Rose, wife, 20. (1888-TMC)

#442-444; J. B. Martel Jr., male, father, 22; Mary Rose, female, wife, 21; Dalianne [?], female, daughter, 5 months. (1889-TMC-off)

Family 54; #266-268, J. Baptist Martel, jr., male, father, 25, mixed bloods in vicinity of reservation; Marie Rose, female, wife, 24; Donat, male, son, 1-1/2. (1892-TMC)

Martel, Jean Baptiste Sr.

Battiste Martell (x), 1 man, 1 woman, 5 children, 7 total, $3.00 a share, $21.00 paid. (1868 TM annuity)

Babtiste Martel (x), 1 man, 2 women, 1 boy, 4 girls, 8 total, $5.00 a share, $40.00 total. (1869 TM annuity)

Jean Baptiste Martel, father, 79; Josephte, wife, 70; Domitile, ...daughter, 16, (married) (...); June 1886 not here. (1884-TMC)

#98-101; Jean Baptiste Martel Sr., father, male, 80; Josephte, wife, female, 71; Alexandre, son, male, 33; Anseline, daughter, female, 27. (1885-TMC)

Martin, Joseph

#679-681; Joseph Martin, man, 20; Mary, sister, 15; George, brother, 10. (1888-TMC)

#775-778; Joseph Martin, male, brother, 22; Marie, female, sister, 15; Geo, male, brother, 11; Frezine Martin, female, grandmother, 85. (TMC-1889)

#847-848; Joseph Martin, male, father, 22; Mary, female, mother, 17. (1890-TMC)

Family 188; #799-800; Joseph Martel, male, father, 22, mixed bloods on reservation; Mary Jane, female, wife, 17. (1892-TMC)

Martin, Mary

Family 181; #765-767, Mary Martin, female, wife, 19, mixed bloods on reservation; Joseph Martin, male, husband, 24; Patrice, male, son, 1. (1892-TMC)

Martin, Theofile

#779-785; Theofile Martin, male, father, 40; Elise, female, wife 28; Elise, female, daughter, 11; Rafel, male, son, 7; Angelic, female, daughter, 5; Joseph, male, son, 3; Francois, male, son, 2. (TMC-1889)

#849-855; Theofile, male, female, 41; Elise, female, mother, 32; Elise, female, daughter, 13; Rafel, male, son, 8; Angelic, female, daughter, 5; Joseph, male, son, 5; William, male, son, 4. (1890-TMC)

McCloud, Frank

#699-701; Frank McCloud, father, 45; Margaret, wife, 45; Elzard, son, 16. (1888-TMC)

#722-724; Frank McCloud, male, father, 49; Margaret, female, wife, 49; Elziard, male, son, 17. (1889-TMC)

#792-794; Frank McCloud, male, father, 49; Margaret, female, mother, 49; Elzeard, male, son, 17. (1890-TMC)

McCloud, Magloire

#389-392; La Glore McCloud, male, father, 21; Margaret, female, wife, 28; Joseph, male, son, 4; Elize, female, daughter, 9 [months]. (1889-TMC)

#873-876; La Gloire McCloud, male, father, 22; Margarett, female, mother, 29; Elise, female, daughter, 2; Louis, male, son, 2 months. (1890-TMC)

Family 182; #768-768-1/2; Margaret McCould, female, wife, 31, mixed bloods on reservation; La Glowe, male, husband, 26; two minor sons; 1 minor daughter. (1892-TMC)

McCloud, Moses

#696-698; Moses McCloud, father, 40; Jane, wife, 40; Liza, daughter, 23. (1888-TMC)

#700-702; Moses McCloud, male, father, 37; Jane, female, wife, 37; Eliza, female, daughter, 13. (1889-TMC)

#803-805; Moses McCloud, male, father, 38; Jane, female, mother, 45; Eliza, female, daughter, 14. (1890-TMC)

McCloud, Pierre

#702-706; Pierre McCloud, father, 38; Madalain, wife, 21; Sahra Jane, daughter, 12; Mary, daughter, 10; Adalaine, daughter, 8. (1888-TMC)

#728-731; Peter McCloud, male, father, 40; Marie, female, wife, 22; Sahra Jane, female, daughter, 13; Mary, female, daughter, 12. (1889-TMC)

#806-810; Peter McCloud, male, father, 41; Marie, female, mother, 24; Sahra J., female, daughter, 14; Mary, female, daughter, 13; Pierre A., male, son, 8 months. (1890-TMC)

Family 186; #792-796; Marie McCloud, female, wife, 26, mixed bloods on reservation; Peter, male, husband, 43; Sarah Jane, female, daughter, 16; Mary, female, daughter, 14; Rosin, female, daughter, 1-1/2. (1892-TMC)

McGillis, Starr

#422-431; Starr McGillis, male, father, 40; Elise, female, wife, 30; St.Pierre, male, son, 14; Melina, female, daughter, 13; Madalain, female, daughter, 12; William, male, son, 9; Solomon, male, son, 7; Josephine, female, daughter, 4; John, male, son, 10 months, Angelic McGillis, female, mother, 60. (1889-TMC-off)

McKay, Leonard

Leon McKay, father, 36; Sara, wife, 38; Celina, daughter, 15, (married Antoine Canada, June 1886); Joseph, son, 13; Philomene, daughter, 11; William, son, 9; Domitile, daughter, 7; Louise, daughter, 5; Napoleon, son, 3; Marie, daughter, 10 months, (June 1886); 2 horses, 2 carts, 1 light wagon, 5 tons hay. (1884-TMC)

#311-319; Leanor McKay, father, male, 37; Celina, wife, female, 39; Sara, daughter, female, 16; Joseph, son, male, 14; Philomene, daughter, female, 12; William, son, male, 10; Domitile, daughter, female, 8; Larose, daughter, female, 6; Napoleon, son, male, 4. (1885-TMC)

#292-300; Lenoard, McKay, father, male, 38; Sarah, wife, female, 40; Joseph, son, male, 15; Philomene, daughter, female, 13; William, son, male, 11; Domitile, daughter, female, 9; Louise, daughter, female, 7; Napoleon, son, male, 5; Marie, daughter, female, 10 months. (1886-TMC)

#432-441; Leonard McKay, male, father, 42; Sahrah, female, wife 44; Joseph, male, son, 18; Philomene, female, daughter, 16; William, male, son, 15; Dometil, female, daughter, 13; Mary Rose, female, daughter, 11; Napoleon, male, son, 8; Henry Joseph, male, son, 2 months; Bruno, male, son, 2 months. (1889-TMC-off)

Merchand, Felix

#383-390; Felix Merchand, father, male, 45; Marie, wife, female, 38; Marie Ricard (widow), daughter, female, 23; Alexandre Merchand, son, male, 15; Adele, daughter, female, 10; Alfred, son, male, 7; Elinore, daughter, female, 4; Gregory, son, male, 1. (1885-TMC)

#397-404; Felix Merchant, father, male, 47; Marie, wife, female, 40; Mary Ricard, stepdaughter, female, 25; Alexandre Merchant, son, male, 17; Adelle, daughter, female, 12; Alfred, son, male, 9; Elinor, daughter, female, 6; Gregry, son, male, 1. (1886-TMC)

Merchant, Mary

#650-656; Mary Merchant, mother, 39; Marie, step daughter, 25; Alexander, son, 17; Adele, daughter, 12; Alfred, son, 9; Gregory, son, 2; Nancy, daughter, 7 months. (1888-TMC)

#793-798; Mary Mercant, female, mother, 41; Alexander, male, son, 18; Adele, female, daughter, 13; Alfred, male, son, 9; Gregory, male, son, 3; Emily, female, daughter, 2. (1889-TMC)

Monette, Gregory

#829-833; Gregory Monette, father, male, 32; Philomene, wife, female, 28; Marie, daughter, female, 7; Rosellie, daughter, female, 5; Alfred, son, male, 1. (1886-TMC)

#755-759; Gregory Monnette, father, 31; Philomene, wife, 25; Rosalie, daughter, 7; Alfred, son, 3; Marie Clara, daughter, 7 months. (1888-TMC)

Montour, Abraham

Abraham Monteaur (x), 3 men, 3 women, 2 children, 8 total, $5.00 a share, $40.00 paid. (1870 TM annuity)

Montour, Pascal

#727-732; Pascall Montour, father, 36; Judith, wife, 33; Simmon, son, 9; Josin, son, 5; Albert, son, 3; Marie, daughter, 7 months. (1888-TMC)

Montreiulle, Alexis

Alexis Montrulle (x), 1 man, 1 woman, 5 children, 7 total, $4.00 a share, $28.00 paid. (1868 TM annuity)

Alex Montreille (x), 1 man, 1 woman, 2 boys, 3 girls, 7 total, $5.00 a share, $35.00 total. (1869 TM annuity)

Alexandre Montreuille (x), 1 man, 3 women, 3 children, 7 total, $5.00 a share, $35.00 paid. (1870 TM annuity)

Alex. Montreuile (x), 1 man, 1 woman, 6 children, 8 total, $10.00 a share, $80.00 paid. (1873 TM annuity)

Alexis Montreille, father, 53; Isabelle, wife, 46; Josephine, daughter, 10; Christine Hufman, adopted daughter (June 1886); one horse, one stable, 10 tons hay, one acre potatoes, one horse, one cart. (1884-TMC)

#93-95; Alexis Montreille, father, male, 54; Marguerite, wife, female, 49; Josephine, daughter, female, 9. (1885-TMC)

#72-74; Alexis Montreille, father, male, 45; Isabelle [?], wife, female, 48; Josephine, daughter, female, 10. (1886-TMC)

#673-676; Alex Montreal, father, 56; Isabell, wife, 50; Josephine, daughter, 12; Chrt-Huffman, adopted son, 12. (1888-TMC)

#747-749; Alexis Montrail, male, father, 57; Margaret, female, wife, 40; Josephine, female, daughter, 13. (1889-TMC)

#819-822; Alexis Montreil, male, father, 58; Margaret, female, mother, 50; Josephine, female, daughter, 15; Christine, female, daughter, 12. (1890-TMC)

Family 173; #729-732; Alexis Montrieal, male, father, 50, mixed bloods on reservation; Margaret, female, wife, 51; Josephine, female, daughter, 16; Christine, female, adopted daughter, 13. (1892-TMC)

Montreuille, Francois

Francis Montreuille (x), 1 man, 4 children, 5 total, $5.00 a share, $25.00 paid. (1870 TM annuity)

Montreuille, Francois

#96-97; Francois Montreille, father, male, 24; Adele, wife, female, 17. (1885-TMC)

#99-100; Francois Montreille, father, male, 25; Adelle, wife, female, 18. (1886-TMC)

#670-672; Francois Montreal, father, 27; Adele, wife, 20; Frank, son, 6 months. (1888-TMC)

#799-800; Francois Montreail, male, father, 28; Adel, female, wife, 28. (1889-TMC)

#864-866; Francois Montreal, male, father, 29; Adele, female, mother, 32; Margaret, female, dau. 9 months. (1890-TMC)

Family 179; #759-762, Francois Montreal; male, father, 23, mixed bloods on reservation; Adele, female, wife, 23; Margaret, female, daughter, 3; Xavier, male, son, 1-1/2. (1892-TMC)

Montreuille, Isabelle

Isabelle Montrulle (x), 1 woman, 1 child, 2 total, $4.00 a share, $8.00 paid. (1868 TM annuity)

Isabelle Montrielle (x), 1 woman, 1 daughter, 2 total, $5.00 a share, $10.00 total. (1869 TM annuity)

Montreuille, Joseph

Joseph Montrille (x), 1 man, 1 woman, 4 children, 6 total, $4.00 a share, $24.00 paid. (1868 TM annuity)

Joseph Montrielle (x), 1 man, 1 woman, 2 boys, 1 daughter, 5 total, $5.00 a share, $25.00 total. (1869 TM annuity)

Joseph Montreuille (x), 1 man, 1 woman, 4 children, 6 total, $5.00 a share, $30.00 paid. (1870 TM annuity)

Montreuille, William

William Montreuille (x), 1 man, 1 woman, 2 children, 4 total, $5.00 a share, $20.00 paid. (1870 TM annuity)

Morin, Alex No. 1

#750-757; Alex Morin No. 1, male, father, 55; Eliz, female, wife, 49; Elise, female, daughter, 18; Sarha, female, daughter, 16; Patrice, male, son, 12; Julia, female, daughter, 10; Helena, female, daughter, 8; Louis, male, son, 5. (1889-TMC)

Morin, Alexandre

Alex Morin, father, 38; Angelic, wife, 28; Alexander, son, 13; Terese, daughter, 11; Josephine, daughter, 9; Mary, daughter, 7; Sara, daughter, 5; Roger, son, 2; Celina, daughter, 1 month. (1884-TMC)

#78-85; Alexandre Morin, father, male, 39; Angelic, wife, female, 31; Alexandre, son, male, 19; Josephte, daughter, female, 10; Marie, daughter, female, 8; Sara, daughter, female, 6; Roger, son, male, 3; Celina, daughter, female, 8 months. (1885-TMC)

#75-81; Alexandre Morin, father, male, 40; Angelic, wife, female, 30; Alexandre, son, male, 15; Josephine, daughter, female, 11; Mary, daughter, female, 9; Roger, son, male, 4; Selina, daughter, female, 2. (1886-TMC)

#682-687; Alexander Morin, father, 40; Angelic, wife, 36; Alex, son, 19; Mary, daughter, 10; Sahra, daughter, 8; Joseph, son, 1. (1888-TMC)

#786-792; Alexander Morin, male, father, 40; Angelique, female, wife, 35; Alex, male, son, 19; Marie, female, daughter, 11; Dora, female, daughter, 9; Joseph, male, son, 2; Alfred, male, son, 11. (1889-TMC)

#823-830; Alexandre Morin, No. 4; Male, father, 56; Elise, female, mother, 49; Elise, female, daughter, 19; Sahra, female, daughter, 17; Patrice, male, son, 18; Julia, female, daughter, 12; Helena, female, daughter, 10; Louis, male, son, 6. (1890-TMC)

#856-863; Alexander Morin, male, female, 41; Angelic, female, mother, 40; Mary, female, daughter, 12; Sahra, female, daughter, 9; Joseph, male, son, 3; Alfred, male, Nephew, 12; Philip, male, son, 8 months, Alex, male, son, 20. (1890-TMC)

Family 183; #772-778; Alexander Morin, male, father, 46, mixed bloods on reservation; Angelic, female, wife, 46; Marie, female, daughter, 15; Sarah, female, daughter, 13; Joseph, male, son, 4; Phillip, male, son, 3; Alfred, male, adopted nephew, 12. (1892-TMC)

Morin, Alexander Jr.

Family 187; #797-798, Alex Morin, jr., male, father, 22, mixed bloods on reservation; Philomene, female, wife, 18. (1892-TMC)

Morin, Andre

#763-773, Andre Morin, male, father, 41; Adelaid, female, wife, 39; Andre, male, son, 20; Isidor, male, son, 18; Baptist, male, son, 16; Alfred, male, son, 11; Pierre, male, son 9; Sahra, female, daughter, 8; Louis, male, son, 6; Roderick, male, son, 4; Christine, female, daughter, 1-1/2. (1889-TMC)

#837-845; Andre Morin, male, father, 42; Adelaid, female, mother, 40; Isidore, male, son, 19; Baptist, male, son, 16; Pierre, male, son, 10; Sahra, female, daughter, 9; Roderick, male, son, 5; Christine, female, daughter, 2; Michael, male, son, 2. (1890-TMC)

Family 184; #779-789; Adele Morin, female, wife, 42, mixed bloods on reservation; Andrew, male, husband, 45; John B. male, son, 20;Alfred, male, son, 17; Peter, male, son, 13; Sarah, female, daughter, 11; Louis, male, son, 9 ; Patrick male, son, 8; #787, Christine, female, daughter, 6; Michael, male, son, 2; Marie Louise, female, daughter, 4 months. (1892-TMC)

Morin, Andre Jr.

#871-872; Andre Morin Jr., male, father, 21; Sahra, female, mother, 19. (1890-TMC)

Family 180; #763-764; Andre Morin, jr., male, father, 23, mixed bloods on reservation; Sarah, female, wife, 22. (1892-TMC)

Morin, Anna

#725-726; Anna Morin, female, mother, 39; Roderic, male, son, 17; Lize, female, daughter, 15. (1889-TMC)

Morin, Baptiste

Batiste Morin (x), 1 man, 4 women, 2 children, 7 total, $3.00 a share, $21.00 paid. (1868 TM annuity)

Babtiste Morin (x), 1 man, 1 woman, 2 boys, 4 total, $5.00 a share, $20.00 total. (1869 TM annuity)

Morin, Francois

#417-421; Francois Morin, male, father, 53; Margaret, female, wife, 55; Sahra, female, daughter, 21; Flora, female, daughter, 18; Toby, male, son, 16. (1889-TMC-off)

Morin, Isidore

Family 185; #790-791, Isidore Morin, male, father, 23, mixed bloods on reservation; Rachel, female, wife, 17. (1892-TMC)

Morin, Josette [nee Langer]

Josette Morin (x), 1 woman, 2 boys, 4 girls, 7 total, $5.00 a share, $35.00 total. (1869 TM annuity)

Josette Moran (x), 1 woman, 1 child, 2 total, $5.00 a share, $10.00 paid. (1870 TM annuity)

Morin, Louis

Louis Morin, father, 47; Margurete, (died 1885), wife, 42; Alfred, son, 21; Margurete, daughter, 19; Virginie, daughter, 17; Louis, son, 15; Joseph, (died June 1885), son, 13; Fredrick, son, 11; Edward, son, 4; Zildas, daughter, 2. (1884-TMC)

#618-626; Louis Morin, father, male, 48; Marguerite, wife, female, 43; Alfred, son, male, 22; Marguerite, daughter, female, 20; Virginie, daughter, female, 18; Louis, son, male, 16; Frederick, son, male, 12; Edward, son, male, 5; Zildas, daughter, female, 3. (1885-TMC)

#516-523; Louis Morin, father, male, 49; Alfred, son, male, 23; Marguerite, daughter, female, 21; Virginia, daughter, female, 19; Louis, son, male, 17; Fredrick, son, male, 13; Edward, son, male, 6; Zildas, daughter, female, 4. (1886-TMC)

Morin, Louis

#399; Louis Morin, male, 20. (1889-TMC-off)

Family 56; #274-275, Louis Morin, jr., male, father, 23, mixed bloods in vicinity of reservation; Marie, female, wife, 20. (1892-TMC)

Morin, Marian

#677-678; Marian Morin, widow, 75; Ande, grandson, 19. (1888-TMC)

#774; Marian Morin, female, widow, 75. (1889-TMC)

#846; Marian Morin, Widow, female, 75. (1890-TMC)

Morin, Pierre

St.Pierre Morin (x), 1 man, 1 total, $5.00 a share, $5.00 paid. (1874 TM annuity)

Pierre Morin, father, 40; Liza, wife, 30; Antoine, son, 12; Philomene, daughter, 10; Josephte, daughter, 5; Marie Louise, daughter, 3; Fredrick, son, 2 months. (1884-TMC)

#627-633; Pierre Morin, father, male, 40; Liza, wife, female, 31; Antoine, son, male, 13; Philomene, daughter, female, 11; Josephte, daughter, female, 6; Marie, daughter, female, 4; Frederick, son, male, 4 months. (1885-TMC)

#467-473; Pierre Morin, father, male, 42; Liza, wife, female, 32; Antoine, son, male, 14; Philomene, daughter, female, 12; Josephte, daughter, female, 7; Marie Louise, daughter, female, 5; Fredrick, son, male, 2. (1886-TMC)

#400-407; Peter Morin, male, father, 43; Eliza, female, wife, 35; Antoine, male, son, 17; Philomene, female, daughter, 15; Joseph, male, son [?], 13; Marie Louise, female, daughter, 11; Frederick, male, son, 9; Albert, male, son, 7. (1889-TMC-off)

Family 57, #276-283; Peter Morin, male, father, 46, mixed bloods in vicinity of reservation; Eliza, female, wife, 46; Antoine, male, son, 21; Philomene, female, daughter, 18; Jossett, female, daughter, 18; Marie Rose, female, daughter, 16; Frederick, male, son, 8; Albert, male, son, 5. (1892-TMC)

Morin, Pierre

#733-740; Pierre Morin, father, 42; Margaritte, wife, 29; Adeline, daughter, 14; Pierre, son, 12; Attalie Rose, daughter, 7; Mary Jane, daughter, 6; Tobias, son, 4; Virginia, daughter, 8 months. (1888-TMC)

#738-746; Pierre Morin, male, father, 43; Margaret, female, wife, 32; Pierre, male, son, 10; Tobie, male, son, 5; Adeline, female, daughter, 15; Mary Jane, female, daughter, 7; Virginia, female, daughter, 2; St.Ann, female, daughter, 2 months. (1889-TMC)

#811-818; Pierre Morin, male, father, 43; Margaret, female, mother, 36; Pierre, male, son, 11; Tobie, male, son, 6; Adelin, female, daughter, 16; Mary J., female, daughter, 8; Virginie, female, daughter, 3; St.Ann, female, daughter, 1-1/2. (1890-TMC)

Family 176; #741-749, Margaret Morin, female, wife, 37, mixed bloods on reservation; Pierre, male, husband, 47; Adeline, female, daughter, 17; Pierre, male, son, 13; Mary Jane, female, daughter, 10; Tobey, male, son, 8; Virginie, female, daughter, 6; St.Ann, female, daughter, 3; Mary, female, daughter, 11 months. (1892-TMC)

Morin, Roger

#758-762; Roger Morin, male, father, 26; Philomene, female, wife, 21; Baptist, male, son, 5; Alexander, male, son, 3; Solomon, male, son, 1. (1889-TMC)

#831-836; Roger Morin, male, father, 28; Philomena, female, mother, 22; Baptist, male, son, 6; Alexander, male, son, 4; Solomon, male, son, 2; Mary, female, daughter, 3 months. (1890-TMC)

Morin, William

#869-870; William Morin, male, father, 26; Caroline, female, mother, 23. (1890-TMC)

Mozzeny, Bazil

Bazil Mozzeny, father, 37; Liza, wife, 26; William, son, 7; Thomas, son, 4; Virginia, daughter, 2. (July 1886-TMC)

Mozzeny, Pascall

Pascall Mozzeney, father, 23; Caroline, wife, 20; Marie, daughter, 2; Maria, daughter, 1 month. (May 15, 1887-TMC)

#688-691; Pascall Mozzeny, father, 24; Caroline, wife, 23; Mary, daughter, 3; Marie, cousin, 12. (1888-TMC)

Mozzeny, Paul

#751-754; Paul Mozzeny, father, 45; Liza, wife, 26; William, son, 9; Thomas, son, 6. (1888-TMC)

Mozzeny, Severe

Sivier Mozzney, father, 39; Margurete, wife, 30; Marie, daughter, 1. (July 1886-TMC)

#748-750; Severe Mozzeny, father, 47; Margaret, wife, 30; Charles, son, 1. (1888-TMC)

Nadeau, Joseph

#760-761; Joseph Nadeau, father, 27; Suzane, wife, 16. (1888-TMC)

#804-806; Joseph Nadeau, male, father, 28; Susane, wife, 19; Dissey [?], female, niece, 9. (1889-TMC)

#878-880; Joseph Nadeau, male, father, 29; Susan, female, mother, 20; Justine, female, daughter, 9 months. (1890-TMC)

Family 180; #801-804; Joseph Madeau [sic], male, father, 31, mixed bloods on reservation; Susan, female, wife, 20; Mary, female, daughter, 3; Virginie, female, daughter, 1. (1892-TMC)

Naquette, Allen

Allen Naquette (x), 1 woman, 3 children, 4 total, $5.00 a share, $20.00 paid. (1870 TM annuity)

Nicholas, Eliza

Family 58; #284-290, Eliza Nicholas, female, wife, 35; Alexander, male, son, 13; Claude, male, son, 11; Julien, female, daughter, 9; Joseph, male, son, 7; Ellen, female, daughter, 5; Michael, male, son, age, 3. (1892-TMC)

Nolin, Angelique

Angelique Nolin (x), 1 woman, 1 total, $5.00 share, $5.00 paid. (1865 TM annuity)

Nolin, Charlotte

Charlotte Nolin (x), 1 man, 1 woman, 6 children, 8 total, $3.00 a share, $24.00 paid. (1868 TM annuity)

Charlotte Nolan (x), 1 woman, 4 boys, 3 girls, 8 total, $5.00 a share, $40.00 total. (1869 TM annuity)

Charlotte Parisan (x), 1 woman, 1 child, 2 total, $5.00 a share, $10.00 paid. (1870 TM annuity)

#767, Charlotte Parisien, widow, 75. (1888-TMC)

#803, Charlotte Nolan, female, widow, 71. (1889-TMC)

#877; Charlotte Nolan, Widow, female, 80. (1890-TMC)

Family 190; #805; Charlotte Nolan, female, widow, 83, mixed bloods on reservation. (1892-TMC)

Page, Charles

Charles Page, _, _; Nancy, wife, 43; Elize, daughter, 16; Josephte, daughter, 14; Elzeard, son, 12; Baptiste, son, 10; Zachary, son, 7; Alexander, son, 3; Abraham, son, 1; one house, one mare, 2 colts, 8 tons hay, (June 1886) one single B shot gun. (1884-TMC)

#347-355; Charles Pager, father, male, 50; Nancy, wife, female, 44; Elise, daughter, female, 17; Josephte, daughter, female, 15; Elzard, son, male, 13; Baptiste, son, male, 11; Zachary, son, male, 8; Alexandre, son, male, 4; Abraham, son, male, 2. (1885-TMC)

#366-374, Charles Page, father, male, 51; Nancy, wife, female, 45; Eliza, daughter, female, 18; Josephte, daughter, female, 16; Elsard, son, male, 14; Baptist, son, male, 12; Zachery, son, male, 9; Alexandre, son, male, 5; Abraham, son, male, 3. (1886-TMC)

#805-814; Chas. Page, father, 53; Nancy, wife, 47; Elize, daughter, 20; Josephte, daughter, 18; Elizard, son, 15; Baptist, son, 13; Zachary, son, 10; Alexander, son, 7; Abraham, son, 5; Philion, son, 1. (1888-TMC)

#847-855; Charles Page, male, father, 56; Nancy, female, wife, 48; Elzear, male, son, 16; Baptist, male, son, 14; Zachary, male, son, 11; Alexander, male, son, 8; Abraham, male, son, 6; William, male, son, 2; Elise, female, daughter, 21; Susate, female, daughter, 17. (1889-TMC)

#915-924; Chas. Page, male, father, 56; Mary, female, mother, 49; Elzear, male, son, 17; Baptiste, male, son, 15; Zachary, male, son, 12; Alexander, male, son, 9; Abraham, male, son, 7; Louis, male, son, 3; Elise, female, daughter, 22; Sussett, female, daughter, 10. (1890-TMC)

Family 200; #851-857; Charles Page, male, father, 61, mixed bloods on reservation; Mary, female, wife, 41; Ezear, male, son, 19; Baptist, male, son, 17; Alexander, male, son, 11; Abraham, male, son, 8; Louis, male, son, 5. (1892-TMC)

Pagnant, __

#467-475; _ Pagnant [?], male, father, 45; Margaret, female, wife, 30; Marie Rose, female, daughter, 13; Isabel, female, daughter, 11; Ursil, female, daughter, 10; Margaret, female, daughter, 11; Theresa, female, daughter, 4; Josephine, female, daughter, 3; Betsy, female, daughter, 1. (1889-TMC-off)

Pagnant, F.

#476-477; F. Pagnant [?], male, father, 23; Isabel, female, wife, 19. (1889-TMC-off)

Pagnant, Samson

Family 64; #315, Lassita Pagnant, female, wife, 20, mixed bloods in vicinity of reservation; #316, Sampson, male, husband, 17. (1892-TMC)

Paquin, Antoine

Antoine Paquin (x), 1 man, 1 woman, 1 boy, 3 girls, 6 total, $5.00 a share, $30.00 total. (1869 TM annuity)

Antoine Paukeen (x), 2 men, 2 women, 3 children, 7 total, $5.00 a share, $35.00 paid. (1870 TM annuity)

Antoine Paquin (x), 1 man, 1 woman, 2 children, 4 total, $8.50 a share, $34.00 paid. (1871 TM annuity)

Paquin, Baptiste

Babtiste Paquin (x), 1 man, 1 woman, 1 boy, 3 total, $5.00 a share, $15.00 total. (1869 TM annuity)

Parenteau, Bazil

#452-459; Bazil Peranteau, father, male, 36; Madline, wife, female, 37; Marguerite, daughter, female, 14; Marie Rose, daughter, female, 12; Exivier, son, male, 10; Caroline, daughter, female, 8; Rosalie, daughter, female, 5; Arthur, son, male, 3. (1886-TMC) ; one DB shot gun (June 1886); Susan Pereanteau, mother, 80. (January 1886)

#815-820; Bazil Perronteau, father, 41; Madalain, wife, 40; Marie Rose, daughter, 15; Exavier, son, 12; Caroline, daughter, 10; Rosalie, daughter, 7. (1888-TMC)

#857-862; Bazil Perronteau, male, father, 46; Madalain, female, wife, 47; Francois X., male, son, 12; Marie Rose, female, daughter, 15; Marie Caroline, female, daughter, 11; Rosalie, female, daughter, 8. (1889-TMC)

#930-932; Bazil Parenteau, male, father, 47; Madalaine, female, mother, 48; F. X., male, son, 13. (1890-TMC)

#930-935; Bazil Parenteau, male, father, 47; Madalaine, female, mother, 48; F. X., male, son, 13; Marie R., female, daughter, 16; Marie C., female, daughter, 12; Rosalie, female, daughter, 9. (1890-TMC)

Family 191; #806-809; Madalain Perrouteau, female, widow, 49, mixed bloods on reservation; Xavier, male, son, 16; Caroline, female, daughter, 14; Rosalie, female, daughter, 11. (1892-TMC)

Parenteau, Jossan

#821; Jossan Perronteau, widow, 80. (1888-TMC)
#807, Jossan Perrenteau, female, widow, 80. (1889-TMC)

Parenteau, Susan

#822, Susan Perronteau, widow, 80. (1888-TMC)
#808, Sussan Perrenteau, female, widow, 75. (1889-TMC)
#881; Susan Parranteau, Widow, 76. (1890-TMC)

Parisien, Charlotte

[See Charlotte Nolin]

Parisien, Edward

Edward Parisien, father, 35; Blandine, wife, ..; Henry, son, 6; Edward, son, 4; Cilina, daughter, 2; Joseph, son, 6 months; one DB shot gun. (1884-TMC)

#501-506; Edward Parisien, father, male, _; Blandine, wife, female, _; Henry, son, male, _; Edward, son, male, _; Cilina, daughter, female, _; Joseph, son, male, _. (1885-TMC)

#326-331; Edward Parisien, father, male, 37; Blandine, wife, female, 32; Henry, son, male, 8; Edward, son, male, 6; Selina, daughter, female, 4; Joseph, son, male, 1. (1886-TMC)

#796-802; Edward Parisien, father, 39; Blandine, wife, 34; Henry, son, 11; Celina, daughter, 8; Edward, son, 6; Joseph, son, 4; Justine, daughter, 2. (1888-TMC)

#839-846; Edward Parisien, male, father, 38; Blandin, female, wife, 37; Henry, male, son, 12; Edward, male, son, 8; Joseph, male, son, 4; Celina, female, daughter, 10; Justine, female, daughter, 3, Ilize, female, daughter, 7 months. (1889-TMC)

#907-914; Edward Parisien, male, father, 39; Blandine, female, mother, 38; Henry, male, son, 13; Edward, male, son, 8; Joseph, male, son, 6; Celina, female, daughter, 11; Justine, female, daughter, 4; Elize Female, daughter, 1-1/2. (1890-TMC)

Family 199; #842-850; Edward Parisien, male, father, 38, mixed bloods on reservation; Blandin, female, wife, 39; Henry, male, son, 14; Celina, female, daughter, 13; Edward, male, son, 9; Joseph, male, son, 8; Justine, female, daughter, 6; Elise, female, daughter, 4; Louise [sic], male, son, 1. (1892-TMC)

Parisien, Elzear

Family 61, #295-302, Ezear Parisir, male, father, 49, mixed bloods in vicinity of reservation; Madalain, female, wife, 49; David, male, son, 19; Villanere, female, daughter, 15; Josephine, female, daughter, 12; Joseph, male, son, 8; Marie, female, daughter, 4; Adelain, female, daughter, 1-1/2. (1892-TMC)

Parisien, Hyacinth

Hyacinth Parission (x), 1 man, 1 woman, 2 total, $10.50 a share, $21.00 paid. (1872 TM annuity)

Parisien, Ignace

Ignace Parisien, father, 57; Margurete, wife, 57; David, son, 22; Justine, daughter, 16, (married Chas. Beston); Boniface, son, 13; Marirose, daughter, 11; one DB shot gun. (1884-TMC)

#493-498; Egnace Parisien, father, male, 58; Marguerite, wife, female, 58; David, son, male, 23; Justine, daughter, female, 17; Boniface, son, male, 14; Marie Rose, daughter, female, 12. (1885-TMC)

#316-320; Egnace Parisien, father, male, 59; Marguerite, wife, female, 59; David, son, male, 24; Boniface, son, male, 15; Mary Rose, daughter, female, 13. (1886-TMC)

#791-795; Egnace Parisien, father, 61; Margaret, wife, 61; David, son, 26; Boniface, son, 18; Marie Rose, daughter, 15. (1888-TMC)

#832-837; Ignas Parisien, male, father, 65; Margaret, female, wife, 62; Daniel, male, son, 30; Boniface, male, son, 18; Marie Rose, female, daughter, 16. (1889-TMC)

#903-906; Ignas Parisin, male, father, 67; Margaret, female, mother, 65; Daniel, male, son, 30; Boniface, male, son, 21. (1890-TMC)

Family 198; #839-841; Ignasus Parisien, male, father, 69, mixed bloods on reservation; Margaret, female, wife, 67; Boniface, male, son, 21. (1892-TMC)

Parisien, Jerome

#438-441; Jerome Parisien, father, male, 34; Nancy, wife, female, 29; Jerome, son, male, 4; Elize, daughter, female, 1. (1885-TMC)

#775-777; Jerome Parisien, father, male, 35; Francoise, wife, female, 18; Jerome, son, male, 5. (1886-TMC)

#489-493; Jerome Parisien, male, father, 31; Justine, female, wife, 30; Jerome, male, son, 8; Liza, female, daughter, 6; Claudia, female, daughter, 4 months. (1889-TMC-off)

Family 63; #312-314, Jerome Parisier, male, father, 34, mixed bloods in vicinity of reservation; Justian, female, wife, 23; John, male, son, 1-1/2. (1892-TMC)

Pariseur, David

Family 207; #894-895, David Pariseur, male, father, 28, mixed bloods on reservation; Jossett, female, wife, 20. (1892-TMC)

Patenaude, Gilbert [?]

Gillear Patnode (x), 1 man, 1 woman, 2 total, $3.00 a share, $6.00 paid. (1868 TM annuity)

Patenaude, Hilaire

Hilaire Patnode (x), 1 man, 1 woman, 2 total, $8.50 a share, $17.00 paid. (1871 TM annuity)

Patenaude, Josette

Josette Patnode (x), 1 man, 1 total, $8.50 a share, $8.50 paid. (1871 TM annuity)

Patenaude, Michel

Michael Patnode (x), 1 man, 1 woman, 5 children, 7 total, $5.00 a share, $35.00 paid. (1865 TM annuity)

Patnode (x), 1 man, 1 woman, 2 children, 4 total, $3.00 a share, $12.00 paid. (1868 TM annuity)

Michael Packnaud (x), 2 men, 1 woman, 1 child, 4 total, $5.00 a share, $20.00 paid. (1870 TM annuity)

Patenaude, William

Patnode (x), 1 man, 1 woman, 2 total, $3.00 a share, $6.00 paid. (1868 TM annuity)

Paul, Pierre

#829-838; Pierre Paul, father, 56; Deliahed, wife, 54; Pierre, son, 23; Samson, son, 21; Joseph, son, 19; Deliahed, daughter, 17; Olive, daughter, 15; Rose, daughter, 13; Mary, daughter, 11; Josephine, daughter, 7. (1888-TMC)

#908-916; Pierre Paul, male, father, 56; Adeline, female, wife, 53; Napoleon, male, son, 23; Joseph, male, son, 21; Adelaide, female, daughter, 19; Olive, female, daughter, 17; Rosine, female, daughter, 14; Marie, female, daughter, 12; Josephine, female, daughter, 8. (1889-TMC)

#968-975; Pierre Paul Sr., male, father, 56; Adelaid, female, mother, 54; Joseph, male, son, 21; Adelaid, female, daughter, 20; Olive, female, daughter, 18; Rosin, female, daughter, 15; Marie, female, daughter, 13; Josephine, female, daughter, 11. (1890-TMC)

Paul, Pierre Jr.

#899-900; Pierre Paul Jr., male, father, 25; Marie Mathild, female, wife, 19. (1889-TMC)

#976-977; Pierre Paul Jr., male, father, 26; Mathilde, female, mother, 20. (1890-TMC)

Paul, Salomon

#1015-1017; Salomon Paul, male, father, 23; Mary, female, mother, 20; Marie Rose, female, daughter, 1 month. (1890-TMC)

Paulet, Antoine Jr.

#483-487; Antoine Paulet Jr., male, father, 24; Frances, female, wife, 22; Joseph, male, son, 6; Placide, female, daughter, 4; Tobias, male, son, 2. [see Sr. ??] (1889-TMC-off)

#1009-1014; Antoine Paulet Jr., male, father, 32; Marie, female, mother, 30; Alfred, male, son, 11; Virginie, female, daughter, 5; Jacob, male, son, 3; Clemence, female, daughter, 8 months. (1890-TMC)

Family 209; #905-911; Marie Paulet, female, wife, 31, mixed bloods on reservation; Antoine, male, husband, 32; Alfred, male, son, 13; Virginie, female, daughter, 6; Jacob, male, son, 5; Clemence, female, daughter, 2; Marie, female, daughter, 5. (1892-TMC)

Paulet, Antoine Sr.

#478-482; Antoine Paulet Sr., male, father, 63; Frances, female, wife, 59; Joseph, male, son, 22; Placid, female, daughter, 16; Tobias, male, son [grandson ?], 6. (1889-TMC-off)

Payton, Baptiste

Babtiste Payton (x), 4 men, 2 women, 1 daughter, 7 total, $5.00 a share, $35.00 paid. (1869 TM annuity)

Peltier, Alex

#998-1001; Alex Peltier, male, father, 26; Catharine, female, mother, 25; Baptist, male, son, 3; Pauline, female, daughter, 1 month. (1890-TMC)

Peltier, Alexander

#879-884; Alexander Peltier, father, 42; Caroline, wife, 44; Marie, daughter, 12; Alfred, son, 10; Joseph, son, 5; Baptist, son, 1. (1888-TMC)

Pelka [Peltier], Baptist

#858-863; Baptist Pelka, father, 45; Caroline, daughter, 15; Virginie, daughter, 12; Joseph, son, 10; Eliza, daughter, 8; Amelia, daughter, 5. (1888-TMC)

#917-923; Baptist Peltier, male, father, 42; Pauline, female, wife, 45; Caroline, female, daughter, 17; Justine, female, daughter, 14; Joseph, [Male, son], 12; Emily, female, daughter, 8; Jerome, male, son, 6. (1889-TMC)

#978-983; Baptiste Peltier, male, father, 44; Pauline, female, mother, 48; Justine, female, daughter, 14; Joseph, male, son, 13; Emily, female, daughter, 8; Clemence, female, daughter, 10 months. (1890-TMC)

Family 204; #875-886; Baptist Pettier, male, father, 48, mixed bloods on reservation; Pauline, female, wife, 50; Cuthbert (Ladeux), male, stepson, 19; __; Joseph (Ladeux), male, stepson, 18; Eliza, female, daughter, 11; Jerome, male, son, 9; Joseph, male, son, 14; Amelia, female, daughter, 10; Rosalie, female, daughter, 11; Clemence, female, daughter, 3; Alexander, male, son, 1. (1892-TMC)

Peltier, Benjamin

Benjamin Peltier (x), 1 man, 1 woman, 2 children, 4 total, $3.00 a share, $12.00 paid. (1868 TM annuity)

Peltier, Charles

#843-847; Chas. Peltier, father, 28; Justine, wife, 25; Alexander, son, 6; Milani, daughter, 3 months. (1888-TMC)

#863-866; Chas. Peltier, male, father, 40; Justine, female, wife, 26; Alexnader, male, son, 7; Balane, female, daughter, 2. (1889-TMC)

#925-929; Chas. Peltier, male, father, 41; Justine, female, mother, 27; Alexander, male, son, 10; Mary Rose, female, daughter, 3; Monica, female, daughter, 2 months. (1890-TMC)

Peltier, Charlotte

Charlotte Peltier (x), 1 man, 1 woman, 5 children, 7 total, $3.00 a share, $21.00 paid. (1868 TM annuity)

Peltier, Chrisoloque

#1002-1008; Chrisoloque Peltier, male, father, 42; Philomene, female, mother, 42; Mary Nancy, female, daughter, 12; Mary Melanie, female, daughter, 10; Isabell, female, daughter, 8; Hellen, female, daughter, 6; Joseph, male, son, 11 months. (1890-TMC)

Peltier, Corbett

#877-878; Corbett Peltier, father, 24; Veronique, wife, 16. (1888-TMC)

#924-926; Corbet Peltier, male, father, 24; Veronique, female, [wife], 20; Helen, female, daughter, 2 months. (1889-TMC)

#957-959; Corbett Peltier, male, father, 25; Veronique, female, mother, 21; Helen, female, daughter, 1. (1890-TMC)

Peltier, Jacques

#864-876; Jacques Peltier, father, 58; Angelic, wife, 49; Marie, daughter, 25; Frances, daughter, 15; Victor, son, 15; Bartholemen, son, 12; Josephine, daughter, 7; Clement, son, 5; Petroneill Belgard, gr-daughter, 6; Frezine, granddaughter, 6; Hilliare, [grandson], 7; Michel, [grandson], 4; Jane, [granddaughter], 4. (1888-TMC)

#886-895; Jaques Peltier, male, father, 52, Angelic, female, wife, 50; Marie, female, daughter, 26; Victor, male, son, 16; Bartholemew, male, son, 14; Clemence, male, son, 4; Josephine, female, daughter, 8; Philomene, female, granddaughter, 4; Hilaire, male, grandson, 8; Rachel, female, granddaughter, 3. (1889-TMC)

#947-954; Jaques Peltier, male, father, 54; Angelic, female, mother, 51; Marie, female, daughter, 27; Victor A., male, son, 17; Bertholomen, male, son, 15; Clemence, female, daughter, 6; Josephine, female, daughter, 9; Petroline, female, daughter, 8. (1890-TMC)

Family 203; #868-874; Jacques Pettier, male, father, 55, mixed bloods on reservation; Angelic, female, wife, 53; Marie, female, daughter, 32; Alex. Victor, male, son, 20; Batholomew, male, son, 17; Josephine, female, daughter, 10; Julian, male, son, 8. (1892-TMC)

Peltier, Jacques No. 2

#992-997; Jacques Peltier No. 2, male, father, 31; Isabell, female, mother, 30; John, male, son, 10; Mary, female, daughter, 7; Josephine, female, daughter, 3; Louis, male, son, 2-1/2 months. (1890-TMC)

Peltier, Joseph

Joseph Peltier (x), 1 man, 1 woman, 5 children, 7 total, $3.00 a share, $21.00 paid. (1868 TM annuity)

Peltier, Judith

Judick Peltier (x), 1 man, 1 woman, 1 child, 3 total, $3.00 a share, $9.00 paid. (1868 TM annuity)

Peltier, Madalain

#927-929; Madalain Peltier, female, mother, 60; Adolphus, male, son, 21; Eliza, female, granddaughter, 10. (1889-TMC)

#984-985; Madalain Peltier, Widow, female, 61; Eliza, female, granddaughter, 11. (1890-TMC)

Peltier, Paul

#883-892; Paul Peltier, father, 49; Louisa, wife, 35; Rose, daughter, 16; Isidore, son, 14; Francis, son, 12; Jean B., son, 6; Robert, son, 4; Alfred, son, 1. (1888-TMC)

#901-907; Paul Peltier, male, father, 39; Louise, female, wife, 37; Isidore, male, son, 15; Francois, male, son, 13; Jean Baptist, male, son, 7; Robert, male, son, 4; Alfred, male, son, 2. (1889-TMC)

#960-967; Paul Peltier, male, father, 44; Louise, female, 42; Isidore, male, son, 16; Francois, male, son, 14; J. Baptiste, male, son, 8; Robert, male, son, 5; Alfred, male, son, 3; Marie, female, daughter, 9 months. (1890-TMC)

Family 208; #896-904; Paul Pettier, male, father, 47, mixed bloods on reservation; Louis [sic], female, wife, 38; Isadore, male, son, 18; Francois, male, son, 17; Robert, male, son, 9; Alfred, male, son, 7; Mary Rosin, female, daughter, 3; John Baptist, male, son, 16; Alexander male, son, 4 months. (1892-TMC)

Peltier, Pierre

Pierre Peltier, father, 27; Larose, wife, 26; Angelic, daughter, 7; Marie, daughter, 5; Mary, daughter, 3. (1884-TMC)

#488-492; Pierre Peltier, father, male, 28; Larose, wife, female, 27; Angelic, daughter, female, 8; Marie, daughter, female, 6; Mary, daughter, female, 4. (1885-TMC)

#643-647; Pierre Peltier, father, male, 29; Larose, wife, female, 24; Angelic, daughter, female, 9; Marie, daughter, female, 7; Mary, daughter, female, 5. (1886-TMC)

#762-766; Peter Peltier, father, 30; Marie Rose, wife, 31; Angelic, daughter, 13; Maria, daughter, 9; Mary, daughter, 7. (1888-TMC)

#881-885; Pierre Peltier, male, father, 35; La Rose, female, daughter, 30; Angelic, female, daughter, 13; Maria, female, daughter, 11; Napoleon, male, son, 6 months. (1889-TMC)

Peltier, Pierre

#855-857; Pierre Peltier, father, 70; Josette, wife, 70; Bernhardt, son, 32. (1888-TMC)

#896-898; Peter Peltier, male, father, 72; Jossette, female, wife, 72; Bernard, male, son, 37. (1889-TMC)

#955-956; Peter Peltier, male, father, 72, Jossette, female, mother, 72. (1890-TMC)

Family 206; #892-893, Pierre Pettier, male, father, 76, mixed bloods on reservation; Jossett, female, wife, 77. (1892-TMC)

Pepin, Etienne

#878-880; Etienne Pepin, male, father, 31; Sahra, female, wife, 25; Adele, female, daughter, 4. (1889-TMC)

#943-946; Etienne, male, father, 32; Sahra, female, mother, 25; Adel, female, daughter, 4; Mary, female, daughter, 3 months. (1890-TMC)

Pepin, Eugene

Family 205; #887-891, Eugene Pepin, male, father, 35, mixed bloods on reservation; Sarah, female, wife, 29; Mary Rose, female, daughter, 7; Mary, female, daughter, 3; Isabel, female, daughter, 4 months. (1892-TMC)

Pepin, Joseph

#839-842; Joseph Pepin, father, 24; Margaret, wife, 24; Marie, daughter, 15; Joseph, son, 5 months. (1888-TMC)

Pepin, Margaret

#875-877, Margaret Pepin, female, mother, 20; Rosalie, female, daughter, 3; Antoine, male, son, 3 months. (1889-TMC)

Pepin, Pierre

Family 73; #347-354, Ellen Pepin, female, wife, 28, mixed bloods in vicinity of reservation; Pierre, male, husband 48; Margaret, female, daughter, 13; Masael, male, son, 11; Milda, female, daughter, 9; Elisie, female, daughter, 7; Oliver, male, son, 5; Anna, female, daughter, 1. (1892-TMC)

Pepin, Salomon

Salomon Pepin, father, 29; Marie, wife, 27; Marguerete, daughter, 7; Octavie, daughter, 5; Joseph, son, 2; Salomon, son, 4 months (June 1885). (1884-TMC)

#209-214; Salomon Pepin, father, male, 30; Marie, wife, female, 28; Marguerite, daughter, female, 8; Octavie, daughter, female, 6; Joseph, son, male, 3; Salomon, son, male, 4 months. (1885-TMC)

#103-108; Solomon Pepin, father, male, 31; Marie, wife, female, 29; Marguerite, daughter, female, 9; Octavie, daughter, female, 7; Joseph, son, male, 4; Solomon, son, male, 1. (1886-TMC)

#823-828; Solomon Pepin, father, 31; Mary, wife, 28; Margaret, daughter, 10; Octavia, daughter, 7; Joseph, son, 4; Mary, daughter, 7 months. (1888-TMC)

#869-874; Solomon Pepin, male, father, 33; Margaret, female, wife, 30; Margaret, female, daughter, 11; Octavia, female, daughter, 9; Joseph, male, son, 6; Vitalie, female, daughter, 2. (1889-TMC)

#938-942; Salomon Papin, widower, male, father, 34; Margaret, female, daughter, 12; Octavia, female, daughter, 10; Joseph, male, son, 7; Vitale, female, daughter, 3. (1890-TMC)

Family 210; #912-916; Solomon Pepin, male, father, 37, mixed bloods on reservation; Margaret, female, daughter, 16; Octavie, female, daughter, 14; Joseph, female, daughter [sic], 11; Mary Vitali, female, daughter, 5. (1892-TMC)

Perrault, Joseph E.

Joseph E. Perrault (x), 1 man, 1 woman, 6 children, 8 total, $10.50 a share, $84.00 paid. (1872 TM annuity)

J. E. Perrault (x), 1 man, 1 woman, 7 children, 9 total, $10.00 a share, $90.00 paid. (1873 TM annuity)

J. E. Perreault (x), 1 man, 2 women, 6 children, 9 total, $5.00 a share, $45.00 paid. (1874 TM annuity)

Phillips, Marie

#803-804; Maria Phillips, mother, 23, deserted by her husband; Andre, 1 month. (1888-TMC)

#867-868; Marie Phillips, female, mother, 24; Solomon, male, son, 2. (1889-TMC)

#936-937; Mary Philips, female, mother, 26; Solomon, male, son, 1. (1890-TMC)

Picard, Josette

Josette Picard (x), 2 women, 2 total, $5.00 a share, $10.00 total. (1869 TM annuity)

Picard, Paulette

Paulette Picard (x), 2 men, 4 women, 2 children, 8 total, $5.00 a share, $40.00 paid. (1870 TM annuity)

Plante, David

#841-842; David Plant, Father, male, 34; Leneor, wife, female, 20. (TMC-1886)

Ploufe, Antoine Villebrun or

Nam toine Pluf (x), 1 man, 1 woman, 5 children, 7 total, $5.00 a share, $35.00 paid. (1865 TM annuity)

Antoine Pluf (x), 1 man, 1 woman, 7 children, 9 total, $3.00 a share, $27.00 paid. (1868 TM annuity)

Antoine Ploreff (x), 3 men, 3 women, 3 children, 9 total, $5.00 a share, $45.00 paid. (1870 TM annuity)

Antoine Vilbrune (x), 4 men, 1 woman, 1 child, 6 total, $10.50 a share, $63.00 paid. (1872 TM annuity)

Antoine Villebrun (x), 4 men, 1 woman, 5 total, $10.00 a share, $50.00 paid. (1873 TM annuity)

Antoine Villebrun (x), 4 men, 1 woman, 5 total, $5.00 a share, $25.00 paid. (1874 TM annuity)

Ploufe, Baptiste Villebrun or

Baptiste Vilbrune (x), 1 man, 1 total, $10.50 a share, $10.50 paid. (1872 TM annuity)

Batiste Villebrun (x), 1 man, 1 total, $10.00 a share, $10.00 paid. (1873 TM annuity)

Baptiste Villebrun (x), 1 man, 1 total, $5.00 a share, $5.00 paid. (1874 TM annuity)

Ploufe, Michel Villebrun or

Michel Villebrun (x), 1 man, 1 total, $10.00 a share, $10.00 paid. (1873 TM annuity)

Michel Villebrun (x), 1 man, 1 total, $5.00 a share, $5.00 paid. (1874 TM annuity)

Ploufe, Peter Vilbrune or

Peter Vilbrune (x), 1 man, 1 woman, 2 children, 4 total, $10.50 a share, $42.00 paid. (1872 TM annuity)

Peter Villebrun (x), 1 man, 1 total, $10.00 a share, $10.00 paid. (1873 TM annuity)

Poitras, Andrew or Henri "Chasseur"

Andrew Potraw (x), 1 man, 1 woman, 9 children, 11 total, $3.00 a share, $33.00 paid. (1868 TM annuity)

Henry Pottram (x), 4 men, 4 women, 3 children, 11 total, $5.00 a share, $55.00 paid. (1870 TM annuity)

Henry Potrah (x), 1 man, 1 woman, 2 total, $8.50 a share, $17.00 paid. (1871 TM annuity)

#848-854; Chasseur Poitra, father, 62; Catherine, wife, 58; Bastian, son, 27; Joseph, son, 25; Charles, son, 21; Napoleon, son, 17; Marie Poitra, mother, 80. (1888-TMC)

#930-934; Chausser Poitra, male, father, 63; Catherine, female, wife, 60; Joseph, male, son, 26; Napoleon, male, son, 17; Marie, female, mother, 80. (1889-TMC)

#986-988; Chasseur Poitra, male, father, 64; Catherine, female, mother, 61; Napoleon, male, son, 18. (1890-TMC)

Family 194; #814-820; Chasseur Poitra, male, father, 68, mixed bloods on reservation; Catharine, (female), wife, 64; Batian, male, son, 32; Napoleon, male, son, 23; Philomene Ladeux, female, adopted daughter, 11; Marie Ladeux, female, adopted daughter, 6; Deimi Anna Ladeux, female, adopted daughter, 3. (1892-TMC)

Poitras, Bastian

#488; Bastian Poitra, male, 30. (1889-TMC-off)

Poitras, Charles

Charles Poitras, father, 38; Marie, wife, 29; Joseph, son, 15; Zachary, son, 13; Larose, daughter, 8; Alfred, son, 6; Isabel, daughter, 4; Alexandre, son, 3; Amily, daughter, 2; Jules, son, 1; one winchester, one DB shot. (1884-TMC)

#442-450; Charles Poitras, father, male, 39; Marie, wife, female, 30; Joseph, son, male, 16; Zachary, son, male, 14; Larose, daughter, female, 9; Alfred, son, male, 7; Esabel, daughter, female, 5; Amily, daughter, female, 3; Jules, son, male, 2. (1885-TMC)

#302-311; Charles Poitras, father, male, 40; Marie, wife, female, 31; Joseph, son, male, 17; Zachery, son, male, 15; LaRose, daughter, female, 10; Alfred, son, male, 8; Isabelle, daughter, female, 6; Alexandre, son, male, 5; Emily, daughter, female, 4; Julius, son, male, 3. (1886-TMC)

#774-783; Chas. Poitra, father, 44; Marie, wife, 36; Joseph, son, 20; Zachary, son, 18; Larose, daughter, 12; Alfred, son, 10; Elizabeth, daughter, 8; Alexander, son, 7; Emily, daughter, 4; Jules, son, 2. (1888-TMC)

#817-828; Chas. Poitra, male, father, 48; Marie, female, wife, 37; Joseph, male, son, 22; Zacharie, male, son, 20; Modest, male, son, 18; Joseph Alfred, male, son, 10; Alexander, male, son, 8; Jules, male, son, 6; Norbert, male, son, 4; La Rose, female, daughter, 12; Elizabeth, female, daughter, 7; Amelia, female, daughter, 3. (1889-TMC)

#885-895; Chas. Poitra, male, father, 48; Marie, female, mother, 38; Zachary, male, son, 21; Modest, male, son, 18; Joseph Alf., male, son, 14; Alex, male, son, 10; Jules, male, son, 8; Norbert, male, son, 2; LaRose, female, daughter, 15; Elizabeth, female, daughter, 12; Amelia, female, daughter, 9. (1890-TMC)

Family 197; #827-838; Charles Poitra (No. 2), male, father, 50, mixed bloods on reservation; Marie, female, wife, 39; Zachary, male, son, 21; Modest, male, son, 19; Marie Rose, female, daughter, 16; Alfred, male, son, 14; Elizabeth, female, daughter, 12; Alexander, male, son, 10; Emily, female, daughter, 8; Jules, male, son, 6; Norbet, male, son, 3; Alfred, male, son, 10 months. (1892-TMC)

Poitras, Charles

#499; Chas. Poitra, male, 22. (1889-TMC-off)

Family 60; #293-294, Charles Portra, male, father, 22, mixed bloods in vicinity of reservation; Adele, female, wife, 20. (1892-TMC)

Poitra, Charles No. 1

Family 196; #825-826, Charles Poitra (No. 1), male, father, 25, mixed bloods on reservation; Mary, female, wife, 17. (1892-TMC)

Poitras, Gabriel Jr.

Gabriel Poitras, father, 38; Mariann, wife, 38; Agnes, daughter, 14; Alfred, son, 13; Guillimine, daughter, 6; Severe, son, 4; Monique, daughter, 1; one horse, one mare, one single B gun. (1884-TMC)

#335-341; Gabriel Poitras Jr., father, male, 39; Marie Ann, wife, female, 39; Agnes, daughter, female, 15; Alfred, son, male, 13; Guillimine, daughter, female, 7; Severe, son, male, 5; Monique, daughter, female, 2. (1885-TMC)

#458-466; Gabriel Poitra, male, father, 44; Marie Ann, female, wife, 30; Agnes, female, daughter, 19; Alfred, male, son, 17; Martin, male, son, 11; Xavier, male, son, 9; Monique, female, daughter, 6; Charles, male, son, 4; Zachary, male, son, 1. (1889-TMC-off)

Family 62; #303-311, Marie Ann Poitra, female, wife, 32, mixed bloods in vicinity of reservation; Gabriel, Jr., male, husband, 46; Alfred, male, son, 18; Martin, male, son, 12; Xavier, male, son, 10; Monique, female, daughter, 8; Charles, male, son, 6; Zachary, male, son, 4; Adalaid, female, daughter, 2. (1892-TMC)

Poitras, Gabriel Sr.

Gabriel Poitras, father, 67; Isabel, wife, 66; William, son, 21; Charles, son, 19; Marie, daughter, 17, (married Alexandre Canada); one house, one stable, 15 tons hay, one single B shot gun. (1884-TMC)

#330-334; Gabriel Poitras Sr., father, male, 68; Isabel, wife, female, 67; William, son, male, 22; Charles, son, male, 20; Marie Rose, daughter, female, 18. (1885-TMC)

#768-770; Gabriel Poitra, father, 60; Isabel, wife, 67; Charles, son, 24. (1888-TMC)

#809-811; Gabriel Poitra, male, father, 66; Isabel, female, wife, 64; Charles, male, son, 22. (1889-TMC)

#882-884; Gabriel Poitra, male, father, 68; Isabel, female, mother, 66; Chas., male, son, 23. (1890-TMC)

Family 195; #821-824; Gabriel Poitra, sr., male, father, 69, mixed bloods on reservation; Isabel, female, wife, 65; Norbert, male, grandson, 8; Laura, female, granddaughter, 7. (1892-TMC)

Poitras, Henry

#494-498; Henry Poitra, male, father, 32; Marie, female, daughter, 26; Joseph, male, son, 8; Celina, female, daughter, 6; Louis, male, son, 4. (1889-TMC-off)

Family 201; #858-864, Henry Poitra, male, father, 36, mixed bloods on reservation; Mary, female, wife, 29; Joseph, male, son, 10; Celina, female, daugher, 8; Mary, female, daughter, 7; Angel, female, daughter, 2; John, male, son, 10 months. (1892-TMC)

Poitras, Joseph Jr.

Joseph Poitras, father, 21; Josephine, wife, 20; Joseph, son, 2; Belmay, son, 8 months (June 1886); one Winchester. (1884-TMC)

#451-454; Joseph Poitras Jr., father, male, 28; Josephine, wife, female, 21; Joseph, son, male, 3; Belmay, son, male, 1. (1885-TMC)

#312-315; Joseph Poitras Jr., father, male, 29; Josephine, wife, female, 22; Joseph, son, male, 4; Belmay, son, male, 2. (1886-TMC)

#786-790; Joseph Poitra Jr., father, 31; Josephine, wife, 26; Joseph, son, 6; Belmay, son, 4; no name, son, 2. (1888-TMC)

#813-816; Joseph Poitra Jr., male, father, 30; Josephine, female, wife, 23; Joseph, male, son, 6; Baptist, male, son, 2. (1889-TMC)

#896-899; Joseph Poitra Jr., male, father, 31; Josephine, female, mother, 27; Baptist, male, son, 7; Joseph, male, son, 3. (1890-TMC)

Family 211; #917-921; Joseph Poitra, 1st, male, father, 38, mixed bloods on reservation; Alphonsin, female, wife, 25; Joseph, male, son, 5; Charles, male, son, 7; Alphonsin, female, daughter, 3. (1892-TMC)

Poitras, Joseph Sr.

Joseph Poitras, father, 75; Susan, wife, 78; Alexandre Akins, grandson, 21; Modeste Poitras, grandson, 11; DB shot gun. (1884-TMC)

#188-191; Joseph Poitras Sr., father, male, 76; Susanne, wife, female, 77; Alexandre Akins, grandson, male, 22; Modest Poitras, grandson, male, 12. (1885-TMC)

#274-277; Joseph Poitras, Sr., father, male, 77; Susanna, wife, female, 78; Alexandre Akins, grandson, male, 23; Modest Poitras, grandson, male, 13. (1886-TMC)

#771-773; Joseph Poitra Sr., father, 74; Susan, wife, 75; Mathew, son, 14. (1888-TMC)

#812; Joseph Poitra Sr., male, 78. (1889-TMC)

Poitra, Joseph

#990-991; Joseph Poitra, male, father, 26; La Rose, female, mother, 23. (1890-TMC)

Family 59; #291-292, Joseph Portra, male, father, 30, mixed bloods in vicinity of reservation; LaRose, female, wife, 26. (1892-TMC)

Poitra, Joseph 2d
Family 212; #922-923, Joseph Poitra 2d, male, father, 24, mixed bloods on reservation; Alphonsin, female, wife, 19. (1892-TMC)

Poitra, Mary
#989; Mary Poitra, female, 80. (1890-TMC)
Family 192; #810, Mary Poitra, female, widow, 84, mixed bloods on reservation. (1892-TMC)

Poitras, William
#784-785; Wm. Poitra, father, 26; Alphonzine, wife, 17. (1888-TMC)
#829-831; Wm. Poitra, male, father, 24; Alphonsine, female, wife, 18; Maxim, male, son, 8 months. (1889-TMC)
#900-902; Wm. Poitra, male, father, 25; Alphonsin, female, mother, 20; Maxim, male, son, 3 months. (1890-TMC)
Family 193; #811-813; William Poitras, male, father, 28, mixed bloods on reservation; Alphonsin, female, wife, 19; Julien, female, daughter, 2. (1892-TMC)

Primeau, Jeremiah
#446-457; Jeremiah Primeau, male, father, 45; Mary, female, wife, 40; Veronica, female, daughter, 21; Joseph, male, son, 19; Sahra, female, daughter, 17; Elise, female, daughter, 14; Liz, female, daughter, 12; Alex, male, son, 10; Mary, female, daughter, 8; Rosalie, female, daughter, 6; Caroline, female, daughter, 5; Helen, female, daughter, 1. (1889-TMC-off)

Primeau, Joseph
Family 202; #865-867, Jane Premeau, female, wife, 20, mixed bloods on reservation; Joseph, male, husband, 22; Jeremiah, male, son, 10 days. (1892-TMC)

Quottie, Isabella
Isabella Quottie (x), 1 woman, 1 total, $10.50 a share, $10.50 paid. (1872 TM annuity)

Racette, Marie
Marie Rasette (x), 1 woman, 1 daughter, 2 total, $5.00 a share, $10.00 paid. (1869 TM annuity)
Mary Rosette (x), 1 woman, 2 children, 3 total, $5.00 a share, $15.00 paid. (1870 TM annuity)

Rainville/Renville/Rinville

Rainville, Joseph
#512-515; Joseph Rainville, father, male, _; Angelic, wife, female, _; Marie, sister, female, _; Jean Baptiste, brother, male, _. (1885-TMC)
#804-807; Joseph Rainville, father, male, 40; Angelic, wife, female, 36; Marie, daughter, female, 13; Jean Baptist, brother, male, 24. (1886-TMC)
#1030-1032; Joseph Renville, male, father, 25; Angelic, female, mother, 38; Therese, female, daughter, 2. (1890-TMC)
#946-949; Joseph Renville, male, father, 41; Angelica, female, wife, 40; Theresa, female, daughter, 14; Sahrah, female, daughter, 4. (1889-TMC)

Rainville, Marguerite

Margurette Renville (x), 1 woman, 5 children, 7 total, $8.50 a share, $51.00 paid. (1871 TM annuity)

Renville, Napoleon

#500-507; Napoleon Renville, male, father, 30; Susan, female, wife, 45; Angelic, female, daughter, 19; Seraphine, female, daughter, 17; Mary Rose, female, daughter, 15-1/2; Israel, male, son, 10; Joseph, male, son, 3, Philomene, female, daughter, 5. (1889-TMC-off)

Renville, Octave

#941-945; Octave Renville, male, father, 35; Jossett, female, wife, 27; Alexis, male, son, 12; John Baptist, male, son, 10; Mary, female, daughter, 7. (1889-TMC)

#1024-1029; Octave Rinville, male, father, 36; Jossett, female, mother, 30; Alexis, male, son, 13; J. Baptiste, male, son, 11; Mary, female, daughter, 9; Marie C., female, daughter, 2 months. (1890-TMC)

Family 219; #958-963; Octave Renville, male, father, 37, mixed bloods on reservation; Jossett, female, wife, 32; Alexis, male, son, 16; John B., male, son, 13; Mary Rose, female, daughter, 10; Mary Cecil, female, 2. (1892-TMC)

Reno, John

Family 214; #929-934, Angelique Reno, female, wife, 30, mixed bloods on reservation; John (white), male, husband, 40; Hulford, male, son, 11; Cordelia, female, daughter, 9; St.Ann, female, daughter, 3; George, male, son, 8 months. (1892-TMC)

Richard, Hyacinthe

Family 65; #317-320, Jossett, female, wife, 24, mixed bloods in vicinity of reservation; Hyacinth, male, husband, 24; Justine, female, daughter, 4; Clemence, female, daughter, 8 months. (1892-TMC)

Richard, Eliza

Eliza Richard, mother, _, Nancy, daughter, 8; Victora, daughter, 6; Presela, daughter, 6; William, son, 4; Alfred Desmarais, nephew, 13. (November 1886-TMC)

Richard, Louis

#514-520; Louis Richard, male, father, 55; Sophia, female, wife, 48; William, male, son, 18; Adel, female, daughter, 16; John, male, son, 14; Joseph, male, son, 12; Roger, male, son, 10. (1889-TMC-off)

Ritchot, Joseph

Joseph Richot (x), 1 man, 1 woman, 2 children, 4 total, $3.00 a share, $12.00 paid. (1868 TM annuity)

Joseph Ritchot (x), 1 man, 1 total, $10.50 a share, $10.50 paid. (1872 TM annuity)

Ritchot, Pierre

Pierre Ritchot (x), 1 man, 1 woman, 1 boy, 4 girls, 7 total, $5.00 a share, $35.00 total. (1869 TM annuity)

Pierre Richotte (x), 1 man, 1 total, $10.50 a share, $10.50 paid. (1872 TM annuity)

Ritchot, Pierre Sr.
Pierre Richotte Sr. (x), 1 man, 1 woman, 2 total, $10.50 a share, $21.00 paid. (1872 TM annuity)

Rolette, Edmund
#508-510; Edmond Rolette, male, father, 27; Lucy, female, wife, 23; Delia, female, daughter, 15 months. (1889-TMC-off)
Family 216; #943-948, Edmund Rolette, male, father, 30, mixed bloods on reservation; Lucy, female, wife, 28; Delia, female, daughter, 5; Mary, female, daughter, 3; Joseph Ledeux, male, adopted son, 16; Alice, female, daughter, 10 days. (1892-TMC)

Rolette, Jerome
Family 218; #950-957, M. Jerome, male, father, 39, mixed bloods on reservation; Celina, female, wife, 34; Emily, female, daughter, 16; Jane, female, daughter, 11; Joseph, male, son, 9; Mary, female, daughter, 7; Ernestine, female, daughter, 4; Eleanor, female, daughter, 1-1/2. (1892-TMC)

Rolette, Joseph Jr.
Joseph Rolette Junr. (x), 1 man, 1 woman, 1 child, 3 total, $4.00 a share, $12.00 paid. (1868 TM annuity)
Joe Rolette Jr. (x), 1 man, 1 woman, 1 boy, 3 total, $5.00 a share, $15.00 paid. (1869 TM annuity)
#893-901; Joseph Rolette, father, 42; Sarah, wife, 39; Emily, daughter, 16; Joseph, son, 13; Ellen, daughter, 11; Frederick, son, 9; Josephine, daughter, 7; Martine, son, 5; Louis Alex, son, 7 months. (1888-TMC)
#950-956; Joseph Rolette, male, father, 43; Sahra, female, wife, 40; Emily, female, daughter, 19; Joseph, male, son, 16; Josephine, female, daughter, 9; Martin, male, son, 7; Louis Alex, male, son, 2. (1889-TMC)
#1033-1039; Joseph Rolette, male, father, 44; Sahra, female, mother, 41; Emily, female, daughter, 19; Josephine, female, daughter, 10; Martin, male, son, 7; Louis A., male, son, 3; Anna, female, daughter, 1890. (1890-TMC)
Family 215; #935-942; Joseph Rolette, male, father, 46, mixed bloods on reservation; Sarah, female, wife, 43; Emily, female, daughter, 21; Joseph, male, son, 19; Josephine, female, daughter, 11; Martin, male, son, 9; Louis Alex, male, son, 4; Anna Jane, female, daughter, 2. (1892-TMC)

Rolette, (Mrs). Joseph
Mrs. Joseph Rolette (x), 1 woman, 5 boys, 1 daughter, 7 total, $5.00 a share, $35.00 paid. (1869 TM annuity)
Family 217; #949; Mrs. Joseph Rolette, sr., female, widow, 65, mixed bloods on reservation. (1892-TMC)

Rolette, M. J.
#1040-1042, 1048-1051; M. J. Rolette, male, father, 37; Celina, female, mother, 34; Helen E., female, mother, 34; Jane D., female, daughter, 10; Frank J., male, son, 8; Mary D., female, daughter, 5; Clemence, female, daughter, 3. (1890-TMC)

Ross, Charles
#511-513; Chas. Ross, male, father, 56; Margaret, female, wife, 56; William, male, son, 18. (1889-TMC-off)

Rossignol, Jeandron

Jeandron Rossignol (x), 1 man, 1 woman, 3 children, 5 total, $3.00 a share, $15.00 paid. (1868 TM annuity)

Jeandron Rosignol (x), 1 man, 1 woman, 1 boy, 2 girls, 5 total, $5.00 a share, $25.00 paid. (1869 TM annuity)

Jean Rosinole (x), 2 men, 2 women, 2 children, 6 total, $5.00 a share, $30.00 paid. (1870 TM annuity)

Roussin, Eustache

#902-906; Eustach Rosin, father, 28; Madalaine, wife, 27; Maria Alexandra, daughter, 5; Rose, daughter, 3; Maxim, son, 1. (1888-TMC)

#935-940; Eustach Rosin, male, father, 29; Adele, female, wife, 20; Maxim, male, son, 3; Pascal, male, son, 1; Marie, female, daughter, 6; Rosina, female, daughter, 4. (1889-TMC)

#1018-1022; Eustach Rosin, male, father, 30; Adel, female, mother, 29; Maxime, male, son, 4; Pascal, male, son, 2; Marie, female, daughter, 7; Rosina, female, daughter, 5. (1890-TMC)

Family 213; #924-928; Madeline Roussin, female, wife, 32, mixed bloods on reservation; Eustash, male, husband 33; Mary, female, daughter, 20; Rosin, female, daughter, 7; Pascal, male, son, 4. (1892-TMC)

Saice, Charles

Chas. Saice (x), 1 man, 1 woman, 7 children, 9 total, $10.00 a share, $90.00 paid. (1873 TM annuity)

Charles Saice (x), 1 man, 1 woman, 8 children, 10 total, $5.00 a share, $50.00 paid. (1874 TM annuity)

Sansgrait, Alphonse

#986-990; Alphonse Sansgrait, male, father, 27; Caroline, female, wife, 42 [?]; Marie, female, daughter, 6; Celina, female, daughter, 4; Jean Baptist, male, son, 2. (1889-TMC)

#1082-1086; Alphonse San Grait, male, father, 30; Caroline, female, mother, 41; Marie, female, daughter, 7; Celina, female, daughter, 5; J. Baptist, male, son, 3. (1890-TMC)

Family 222; #972-976; Caroline San Grait, female, wife, 48, mixed bloods on reservation; Alphonse, male, husband 32; Marie, female, daughter, 8; Celina, female, daughter, 6; J. Baptist, male, son, 5. (1892-TMC)

Sayer, Joseph

#724-727; Joseph Saire, father, male, 41; Frizine, wife, female, 39; Joseph, son, male, 17; Alexandre, son, male, ... (1885-TMC)

#660-664; Joseph Saier, father, male, 42; Fresien, wife, female, 40; Joseph, son, male, 18; Alexandre, son, male, 13; Adelle, adopted daughter, female, 12. (1886-TMC)

Sayer, Joseph

#226-228; Joseph Cyre, male, father, 20; Christine, female, wife, 20; Ellen, female, daughter, 8 months. (1889-TMC)

#267-270; Joseph Cyre, male, father, 22; Christine, female, mother, 22; Ellen, female, daughter, 2; Louis, male, son, 4 months. (1890-TMC)

Family 52; #225-229, Justin Cyre, female, wife, 27, mixed bloods on reservation; Joseph, male, husband, __; Ellen, female, daughter, 4; Louis James, male, son, 2-1/2; Alexander, male, son, 1. (1892-TMC)

Sayis, John

John Saise (x), 1 man, 1 total, $5.00 a share, $5.00 paid. (1874 TM annuity)

Sayis, Joseph

Joseph Sayuse (x), 2 men, 2 children, 4 total, $5.00 a share, $20.00 paid. (1870 TM annuity)

Joseph Saise (x), 1 man, 2 women, 6 children, 9 total, $5.00 a share, $45.00 paid. (1874 TM annuity)

Sayis, Virginie

Virginie Saise (x), 1 woman, 1 total, $5.00 a share, $5.00 paid. (1874 TM annuity)

Schindler, Frederick William

Family 69; #330-332, Elise Schindler, female, wife, 19, mixed bloods in vicinity of reservation; F. W. (white), male, husband, 31; Hettie, female, daughter, 6. (1892-TMC)

Short, David

#530-531; David Short, male, father, 28; Sahra, female, wife, 17. (1889-TMC-off)

Short, Roderick

#914-917; Roderick Short, father, 29; Arzel, wife, 28; Maxim, son, 4; Justine, daughter, 1 month. (1888-TMC)

#981-985; Roderick Short, male, father, 29; Ursil, female, wife, 29; Marie, female, daughter, 5; Justine, female, daughter, 1; Marie, female, niece, 11. (1889-TMC)

#1079-1081; Roderick Short, male, father, 31; Ursil, female, mother, 30; Rosalie, female, daughter, 3 months. (1890-TMC)

Slater, James

#521-529; James Slater, male, father, 40; Marie, female, wife, 30; Rose, female, daughter, 17; John, male, son, 14; Joshua, male, son, 12; Margaret, female, daughter, 10; Isidore [?], male, son, 6; J. Baptist, male, son, 8; Louis, male, son, 1. (1889-TMC-off)

Smith, Israel

#978-980; Israel Smith, male, father, 25; Marie, female, wife, 22; Roger Thifault, male, brother in law, 8. (1889-TMC)

#1075-1078; Israel Smith, male, father, 29; Mary, female, mother, 25; Roger Thifault, male, brother-in-law, 8; Louis Thifault, male, brother-in-law, 10. (1890-TMC)

Family 224; #980-984; Israel Smith, male, father, 31, mixed bloods on reservation; Mary, female, wife, 27; Roger Thifault, male, brother-in-law, 9; Louis Thifault, male, brother-in-law, 12; Louis, male, son, 10 months. (1892-TMC)

Smith, Joseph

Joseph Smith (x), 1 man, 2 women, 2 children, 5 total, $5.00 a share, $25.00 paid. (1870 TM annuity)

Joseph Smith, father, _; Charlotte, wife, _; Israel, son, 25; Judith, daughter, 23; Matil, daughter, 12; Zachary, son, _; Charles, son, 8. (July 1886-TMC)

#918-923; Joseph Smith, father, 59; Charlotte, wife, 58; Israel, son, 27; Judith, daughter, 25; Zachary, son, 13; Charles, son, 10. (1888-TMC)

#972-977; Joseph Smith Sr., male, father, 59; Charlotte, female, wife, 58; Zachary, male, son, 17; Charles, male, son, 13; Judie, female, daughter, 31; Jacque, male, grandson, 2. (1889-TMC)

#1069-1074; Joseph Smith Sr., male, father, 59; Charlotte, female, mother, 58; Zachary, male, son, 18; Charles, male, son, 14; Judie, female, daughter, 34; Antoine, male, son [grandson ?], 3. (1890-TMC)

Family 221; #968-971; Joseph Smith sr., male, father, 61, mixed bloods on reservation; Charlotte, female, wife, 61; Zacharie, male, son, 19; Charles, male, son, 16. (1892-TMC)

Smith, Joseph Jr.

#969-971; Joseph Smith Jr., male, father, 35; Julia, female, wife, 21; Joseph, male, son, 6. (1889-TMC)

#1065-1068; Joseph Smith Jr., male, father, 37; Julia, female, mother, 28; Joseph Arthur, male, son, 4; Clara M. J., female, daughter, 7 months. (1890-TMC)

Family 220; #964-967; Joseph Smith, jr., male, father, 38, mixed bloods on reservation; Julia, female, wife, 26; Ashur, male, son, 8; #967, female, daughter, 3. (1892-TMC)

Smith, Louis

Louis Smit (x), 1 man, 1 woman, 1 child, 3 total, $5.00 a share, $15.00 paid. (1865 TM annuity)

St.Antona [St.Arnaud], Alexander

Family 67; #324-326, Philomene St.Antona, female, wife, 41, mixed bloods in vicinity of reservation; Alexander, male, husband, 50; Alexander, male, son, 19. (1892-TMC)

St.Antona [St.Arnaud], John Baptist

Family 68; #327, John B. St.Antona, male, father, 27, mixed bloods in vicinity of reservation; #328, Julia, female, wife, 23; #329, Alphonsia, female, daughter, 2. (1892-TMC)

St.Germain, Andre

#551-554; Andre St.Germain, male, father, 40; Rosin, female, wife, 34; Josephine, female, stepdaughter, 12; Elise, male, son, 8. (1889-TMC-off)

St.Germain, Francois

#555-556; Francois St.Germain, male, father, 23; Alphonsine, female, wife, 20. (1889-TMC-off)

Family 66; #321-323, Rosin St.German, female, wife, 21, mixed bloods in vicinity of reservation; Francis, male, husband, 29; Marie Theresa, female, daughter, 2. (1892-TMC)

St.Germain, Pierre

#532-533; Pierre St.Germain, male, father, 22; LaRose, female, wife, 19. (1889-TMC-off)

St.Germain, Therese

#557-561; Therese St.Germain, female, mother, 50; Dometil, female, daughter, 16; Virginia, female, daughter, 14; Caroline, female, daughter, 10; Eliza, female, daughter, 9. (1889-TMC-off)

St.Grey, Alphonse

#924-928; Alphonse St.Grey, father, 35; Caroline, wife, 37; Mary, daughter, 4; Celina, daughter, 3; Henry, son, 1. (1888-TMC)

St.Pierre, Elizabeth

Elizabeth St.Pierre (x), 1 woman, 2 children, 3 total, $5.00 a share, $15.00 paid. (1870 TM annuity)

St.Pierre, Francois

Francis St.Pierre (x), 1 man, 1 total, $3.00 a share, $3.00 paid. (1868 TM annuity)

St.Pierre, Louis

Louis St.Pierre (x), 1 man, 1 woman, 5 children, 7 total, $4.00 a share, $28.00 paid. (1868 TM annuity)

Louis St.Pierre, father, 54; Marie, wife, 46; Norbert, son, 25; Francois, son, 23; Martin, son, 19; Ellen, daughter, 14; [..]. (1884-TMC)

#108-113; Louis St.Pierre, father, male, 55; Marie, wife, female, 47; Norbert, son, male, 26; Francois, son, male, 24; Martin, son, male, 20; Ellen, daughter, female, 15. (1885-TMC)

#339-344; Louis St.Pierre, father, male, 56; Marie, wife, female, 48; Norbert, son, male, 27; Francois, son, male, 25; Martin, son, male, 21; Ellen, daughter, female, 18. (1886-TMC)

#907-913; Louis St.Pierre, father, 72; Marie, wife, 49; Francois, son, 27; Martin, son, 22; Ellen, daughter, 18; Margaret, daughter, 26; Charles, grandson, 2. (1888-TMC)

#957-961; Louis St.Pierre, male, father, 60; Marie, female, wife, 58; Martin, male, son, 21; Francois, male, son, 22; Joseph, male, grandson, 3. (1889-TMC)

#1052-1056; Louis St.Pierre, male, father, 66; Marie, female, wife, 65; Martin, male, son, 23; Francois, male, son, 22; Peter Dejarlais, male, grandson, 4. (1890-TMC)

St.Pierre, Louise Marie

Family 223; #977-979, Louise Marie St.Pierre, female, widow, 67, mixed bloods on reservation; Francois, male, son, 25; Martin, male, son, 25. (1892-TMC)

St.Pierre, Norbert

#962-968; Norbert St.Pierre, male, father, 29; Marie, female, wife, 28; Andre, male, son, 12; Napoleon, male, son, 7; Francois X., male, son, 6; Allale, female, daughter, 4; Adalain, female, daughter, 2. (1889-TMC)

#1057-1063; Norbert St.Pierre, male, father, 29; Mary, female, mother, 32; Andre, male, son, 12; Joseph, male, son, 8; F. X., male, son, 10; Alla C., female, daughter, 7; Adeline, female, daughter, 5; Mary, female, daughter, 10 months. (1890-TMC)

Swan/Swain

Swain, Francois

#543-550; Francois Swain, male, father, 30; Sahra, female, wife, 30; Francois, male, son, 11; Marie, female, daughter, 8; Roger, male, son, 6; Rosalie, female, daughter, 4; Augustine, male, son, 3; Julia, female, daughter, 2 months. (1889-TMC-off)

Swan, Frederick

#534-542; Frederick Swan, male, father, 35; Margaret, female, wife, 35; Mary, female, daughter, 13; Herman, male, son, 12; Margaret, female, daughter, 8; Chas., male, son, 4; Patrick, male, son, 3; Augustine, male, son, 3 months; John, male, son, 3 months. (1889-TMC-off)

Swain, Mrs. Joseph

Mrs. Jos. Swain (x), 1 woman, 1 child, 2 total, $5.00 a share, $10.00 paid. (1874 TM annuity)

Thibert, X.

#570-574; X. Thiber, male, father, 53; Sophia, female, wife, 50; Eliz, female, daughter, 21; Emily, female, dau [granddaughter?], 2; Jossett Slater, female, mother-in-law, 70. (1889-TMC-off)

Thifault, Louis

#423-429; Louis Thifault, father, male, 53; Thomas, son, male, 25; Marie, daughter, female, 20; Joseph, son, male, 11; David, son, male, 9; Louis, son, male, 6; Roger, son, male, 3. (1885-TMC)

#410-416; Louis Thifault, father, male, 54; Francois, son, male, 26; Joseph, son, male, 12; Marie, daughter, female, 21; David, son, male, 10; Louis, son, male, 7; Roger, son, male, 4. (1886-TMC)

#929-933; Louis Thifault, father, 56; Marie, daughter, 23; David, son, 12; Louis, son, 9; Roger, son, 6. (1888-TMC)

#991-998; Louis Thifault, male, father, 57; Susan, female, wife, 37; David, male, son, 12; Louis, male, son, 10; Moses, male, stepson, 17; Baptist, male, stepson, 3; Michael, male, stepson, 1; Betsy, female, stepdaughter, 1. (1889-TMC)

#1087-1094; Louis Thifault, male, father, 54; Susan, female, mother, 45; David, male, son, 12; Moses Delorme, male, stepson, 19; Helen, female, stepdaughter, 17; Marie, female, stepdaughter, 15; Rose LaPierre, female, stepdaughter, 6; J. B., male, stepson, 5. (1890-TMC)

Family 226; #990-993; Louis Thifault, male, father, 61, mixed bloods on reservation; Susan, female, wife, 44; Helen, female, stepdaughter, 17; John Baptist, male, grandson, 8. (1892-TMC)

Thifault, Thomas

Thomas Thifoux (x), 1 man, 1 woman, 2 total, $8.50 a share, $17.00 paid. (1871 TM annuity)

Thifault, Thomas

#958-959; Thomas Thyfault, father, 30; Margarett, wife, 17. (1888-TMC)

#1014-1016; Thomas Thifault, male, father, 30; Margarett, female, wife, 18; Helen, female, daughter, 2 months. (1889-TMC)

Family 70; #333-336, Thomas Thifault, male, father, 34, mixed bloods in vicinity of reservation; Margaret, female, wife, 22; Vitalie, female, daughter, 3; Rafael, male, son, 1. (1892-TMC)

Thomas, Joseph

Joseph Tomah (x), 1 man, 2 women, 1 child, 4 total, $5.00 a share, $20.00 paid. (1870 TM annuity)

Joseph Thomas, husband, 38; Catherine, wife, 36; Joseph, son, 18; William, son, 16; St.Pierre, son, 15; Marie, daughter, 13; Didia, daughter, 11; John, son, 7; Celina, daughter, 5; Alexander, son, 3; Adele, daughter, 4 months. (28 May 1887)

#944-953; Joseph Thomas, father, 40; Catherine, wife, 40; Joseph, son, 21; William, son, 18; Mary, daughter, 14; Diddia, daughter, 12; Selina, daughter, 8; Alexander, son, 6; Adel, daughter, 2. (1888-TMC)

#1017-1025; Joseph Thomas, male, father, 42; Catherine, female, wife, 42; William Male, son, 19; Clodia, female, daughter, 13; Marie, female, daughter, 15; Celina, female, daughter, 8; Alexander, male, son, 6; Delphine, female, daughter, 3. (1889-TMC)

Family 227; #904-909; Joseph Thomas, male, father, 44, mixed bloods on reservation; Catherine, female, wife, 44; Clodia, female, daughter, 16; John, male, son, 13; Celina, female, daughter, 10; Alexander, male, son, 8; Adele Thomas, female, daughter, 6. (1892-TMC)

Thomas, Julia

#1112-1115; Julia Thomas, female, mother, 31; John B., male, son, 11; J. Baptist, male, son, 3; Virginie, female, daughter, 10 months. (1890-TMC)

Family 225; #985-989; Julia Thomas, female, wife, 34, mixed bloods on reservation; Baptist No. 1, male, son, 14; Baptist No. 2, male, son, 5; Virginie, female, daughter, 3; Mary, female, daughter, 10 months. (1892-TMC)

Thomas, Louis Jr.

Louis Tomah Jr. (x), 2 men, 2 women, 4 total, $5.00 a share, $20.00 paid. (1870 TM annuity)

Louis Thomas junr. (x), 1 man, 1 woman, 2 total, $8.50 a share, $17.00 paid. (1870 TM annuity)

Thomas, Louis Sr.

Louis Tomah Sr. (x), 3 men, 3 women, 1 child, 7 total, $5.00 a share, $35.00 paid. (1870 TM annuity)

Mrs. Louis Thomas senr. (x), 1 woman, 2 children, 3 total, $8.50 a share, $25.50 paid. (1871 TM annuity)

#568-569; Louis Thomas, male, father, 70; Margaret, female, wife, 66. (1889-TMC-off)

Family 71; #345-346, Louis Thomas, male, father, 74, mixed bloods in vicinity of reservation; Margaret, female, wife, 60. (1892-TMC)

Thomas, Thomas

#562-567; Thomas Thomas, male, father, 32; Margaret, female, wife, 33; Clement, male, son, 10; Norman, male, son, 9; Rosa, female, daughter, 4; John, male, son, 2. (1889-TMC-off)

Family 71; #337-344, Thomas Thomas, male, father, 33, mixed bloods in vicinity of reservation; Margaret, female, wife, 36; Clemence, male, son, 12; Norman, male, son, 10; Rosa, female, daughter, 8; William John, male, son, 6; Ellen, female, daughter, 3; Mary, female, daughter, 7. (1892-TMC)

Thomas, William

Family 231; #1016, William Thomas, male, father, 23, mixed bloods on reservation; #1017, Clemence, female, wife, 20. (1892-TMC)

Trottier, Baptiste

Babtiste Trotier (x), 1 man, 1 woman, 2 boys, 3 girls, 7 total, $5.00 a share, $35.00 total. (1869 TM annuity)

Trottier, Isabella

Isabella Trotier (x), 1 woman, 4 children, 5 total, $8.50 a share, $42.50 paid. (1871 TM annuity)

#1109-1111; Isabelle Trottier, female, mother, 53; Joseph, male, son, 24; Chas., male, son, 10. (1890-TMC)

Trottier, Louise

#575-579; Louise Trottier, female, widow, 65; Moses, male, grandson, 6; Alex, male, grandson, 11; Rosin, female, granddaughter, 4; La Rose, female, granddaughter, 1. (1889-TMC-off)

Trottier, Margaret

Margaret Trotier (x), 1 woman, 1 daughter, 2 total, $5.00 a share, $10.00 total. (1869 TM annuity)

Margarette Trotier (x), 1 woman, 1 child, 2 total, $8.50 a share, $17.00 paid. (1871 TM annuity)

Turcotte, Daniel

Family 229; #1009-1011, Daniel Turcott, male, father, 20, mixed bloods on reservation; Rosin, female, wife, 18; Daniel, male, son, 8 months. (1892-TMC)

Turcotte, Jean Baptiste

Baptiste Turcotte, father, 47; Margarete, wife, 27; Susan, daughter (married June 1886), 16; Adell, daughter, 14; Rosine, step-daughter, 10, Donais, _, 12; Isabel, step-daughter, 8; Francois, step-son, 4; William, step-son, 4; Cilena, step-daughter, 1; Madeline Turcotte, mother, 11, Daniel, son, 11; (Peter, son, born June 1886); one house, one stable, 15 tons hay, 5 acres broke, one horse, one light wagon, one cart, one stove C., one stove, W. (1884-TMC)

#223-231; Baptiste Tucotte, father, male, 48; Marguerite, wife, female, 39; Susanne, daughter, female, 17; Adele, daughter, female, 15; Daniel, son, male, 13; Anastasie, daughter, female, 10; Joseph, son, male, 8; Angelic, daughter, female, 6; Celine, daughter, female, 2. (1885-TMC)

#123-131; Baptiste Turcotte, father, male, 49; Marguerite, wife, female, 29; Adelle, daughter, female, 16; Daniel, son, male, 11; Rosine Davis [?], stepdaughter, female, 12; Isabelle, stepdaughter, female, 10; William stepson [?], male, 4; Selina, stepdaughter [?], female, 2; Peter, son, male, 1. (1886-TMC)

#934-943; J. B. Turcotte, father, 51; Margaret, wife, 30; Rosine, daughter, 13; Daniel, son, 15; Peter, son, 21; Isabel, daughter, 15; Francois, son, 11; William, son, 6; Celina, daughter, 4; Angelic, daughter, 9. (1888-TMC)

#999-1009; J. B. Turcotte, male, father, 55; Margaret, female, wife, 33; Daniel, male, son, 16; Francois, male, son, 12; William, male, son, 8; St.Pierre, male, son, 4; Colin, male, son, 1; Isabel, female, daughter, 16; Rosin, female, daughter, 15; Celina, female, daughter, 6; Angelique, female, daughter, 10. (1889-TMC)

#1095-1104; J. B. Turcotte, male, father, 56; Margarett, female, mother, 34; Daniel, male, son, 18; Francois, male, son, 13; William, male, son, 9; St.Pierre, male, son, 5; Colin, male, son, 2; Rosin, female, daughter, 16; Celina, female, daughter, 7; Angelique, female, daughter, 10. (1890-TMC)

Family 228; #1000-1009; John Baptist Turcott, male, father, 53, mixed bloods on reservation; Margret, female, wife, 28; Angelique, female, daughter, 16; Francois, male, son, 14; William, male, son, 12; Celine, female, daughter, 9; Pierre, male, son, 7; Collin, male, son, 5; Mary female, daughter, 3. (1892-TMC)

Turcotte, Modest

#1125- 1129; Modest Turcotte, male, father, 30; Madalain, female, mother, 35; Louise, female, daughter, 7; Marie, female, daughter, 3; Jane, female, daughter, 2. (1890-TMC)

Turcotte, Napoleon

#954-957; Napoleon Turcott, father, 25; Madaline, wife, 24; Marie Louise, daughter, 3; Andre, son, 1. (1888-TMC)

#1010-1013; Napoleon Turcott, male, father, 28; Madalaine, female, wife, 26; Marie Louise, female, daughter, 6; Antoine, male, son, 4. (1889-TMC)

#1105-1108; Napoleon Turcotte, male, father, 29; Madalain, female, mother, 27; Marie Louise, female, daughter, 7; Antoine, male, son, 5. (1890-TMC)

Family 230; #1012-1015; Napoleon Turcotte, male, father, 34, mixed bloods on reservation; Madeline, female, wife, 30; Marie Louise, female, daughter, 18; Antoine, male, sone, 8. (1892-TMC)

Turcotte, Pascal

#819-822; Pascal Turcotte, father, male, 28; Mary, wife, female, 23; Patrick, son, male, 7; Joseph, son, male, 2. (1886-TMC)

Turcotte, Vital

Family 74; #355-362, Vital Turcott, male, father, 33, mixed bloods in vicinity of reservation; Adele, female, wife, 29; Christine, female, daughter, 14; John, male, son, 12; Charles, male, son, 10; Patrice, male, son, 8; Ceulia, female, daughter, 4; Marie, female, daughter, 6. (1892-TMC)

Vaillant, Pierre

#994-996; Pierre Vaillant, father, 52; Ursule, wife, 51; Joseph Laframbois, 19, son. (1888-TMC)

#1045-1048; Pierre Vagnant, male, father, 53; Ursule, female, wife, 51; Joseph Lafranier, male, stepson, 20. (1889-TMC)

Vallee, Baptiste (Jr.)

Baptiste Valler (Jr.) (x), 1 man, 1 woman, 1 child, 3 total, $3.00 a share, $9.00 paid. (1868 TM annuity)

Babtiste Vallee (x), 1 man, 1 woman, 1 daughter, 3 total, $5.00 a share, $15.00 total. (1869 TM annuity)

Baptiste Valley (x), 1 man, 1 woman, 2 total, $5.00 a share, $10.00 paid. (1870 TM annuity)

Baptiste Valler Jun. (x), 1 man, 1 woman, 2 total, $8.50 a share, $17.00 paid. (1871 TM annuity)

Baptiste Vallie, father, 46; Sophie, wife, 38; Norbert Belgarde, stepson, 18; Isidore, stepson, 16; Firman, stepson, 12; Larose, stepdaughter, 1; Marie Vallie, daughter, 3; Jean Baptiste, son, 1; (June 1886) flint lock gun. (1884-TMC)

#398-406; Baptiste Vallie, father, male, 46; Sophie, wife, female, 38; Norbert Belgard, stepson, male, 18; Isidore, stepson, male, 16; Firman, stepson, male, 14; Alexis, stepson, male, 12; Marie, step-daughter, female, 7; Larose Vallie, daughter, female, 3; Jean Baptiste, son, male, 1. (1885-TMC)

#375-383; Baptiste Vallie, father, male, 47; Sophia, wife, female, 39; Norbert Belgard, stepson, male, 19; Isidore, stepson, male, 17; Firman, stepson, male, 15; Alexis, stepson, male, 14; Louise, stepdaughter, female, 14; Louise, stepdaughter, female, 8; Marie Vallie, daughter, female, 4; Jean Baptist, son, male, 2. (1886-TMC)

#969-975; Baptist Valle, father, 52; Delaide, wife, 48; Firmin Belgarde, step-son, 19; B. Celena, daughter, 10; Caroline, daughter, 5; John B., son, 2; Abraham, son, 3. (1888-TMC)

#1039-1044; Baptist Vallie, male, father, 55; Sophia, female, wife, 49; Baptist, male, son, 7; Abraham, male, son, 4; Marie Caroline, female, daughter, 6; Celina, [F], daughter, 13. (1889-TMC)

#1146-1151; Baptist Vallee, male, father, 58; Sophia, female, mother, 44; J. Baptist, male son, 6; Abraham, male, son, 5; Mary C., female, daughter, 8; Marie, female, daughter, 1-1/2. (1890-TMC)

Family 234; #1030-1036; Baptist Vallie, male, father, 60, mixed bloods on reservation; Sophia, female, wife, 49; Celina, female, daughter, 15; Margaret, female, daughter, 11; John Baptist, male, son, 9; Abraham, male, son, 6; Mary, female, daughter, 4. (1892-TMC)

Vallee, Francois

Frank Vallee (x), 1 man, 1 total, $5.00 a share, $5.00 paid. (1874 TM annuity)

Francois Vallee, father, 38; Marie, wife, 38; Marie Rose, daughter, 11; Adele, daughter, 3; Amma, daughter, 6 months (June 1885). (1884-TMC)

#120-124; Francois Vallie, father, male, 39; Marie, wife, female, 39; Marie Rose, daughter, female, 12; Adele, daughter, female, 4; Amma, daughter, female, 6 months. (1885-TMC)

#214-218; Francois Vallie, father, male, 40; Marie, wife, female, 40; Marie Rose, daughter, female, 13; Adella, daughter, female, 5; Emma, daughter, female, 2. (1886-TMC)

#976-979; Francois Valle, father, 42; Marie, wife, 38; Adel, daughter, 5; Seraphine, daughter, 1 month. (1888-TMC)

#1142-1145; Francois Vallee, male, father, 44; Marie, female, mother, 39; Adel, female, daughter, 9; Seraphine, female, daughter, 3. (1890-TMC)

#1035-1038; Francois Vallie, male, father, 47; Marie, female, wife, 38; Seraphine, female, daughter, 7; Adele, female, daughter, 2. (1889-TMC)

Vallee, Jean Baptiste (Sr.)

Baptiste Valler (Sr.) (x), 1 man, 3 women, 4 children, 8 total, $3.00 a share, $24.00 paid. (1868 TM annuity)

Jean Babtiste Vallee (x), 1 man, 1 woman, 4 boys, 2 girls, 8 total, $5.00 a share, $40.00 total. (1869 TM annuity)

John Bte. Valley (x), 3 men, 3 women, 2 children, 8 total, $5.00 a share, $40.00 paid. (1870 TM annuity)

Baptiste Valler (x), 1 man, 1 total, $8.50 a share, $8.50 paid. (1871 TM annuity)

Vallie, Joseph

Joseph Vallee (x), 1 man, 3 women, 1 child, 5 total, $5.00 a share, $25.00 paid. (1874 TM annuity)

#127, Joseph Vallie, _, male, 75. (1885-TMC)

#213, Joseph Vallie, widower, male, 76. (1886-TMC)

Valle, Louis

#580-585; Louis Valle, male, father, 30; Catharine, female, wife, 40; Justine, female, daughter, 11; Agatha, female, daughter, 8; Andre, male, son, 4; Julia, female, daughter, 3. (1889-TMC-off)

Vandelle, Baptist

#474-476; Baptist Vandelle, father, male, 44; Henrietta, wife, female, 44; Maria, daughter, female, 9. (1886-TMC)

#981-983; Baptist Vandall, father, 45; Henriate, wife, 42; Marie, daughter, 10. (1888-TMC)

Vandelle, Bernard

#849-850; Burnard Vandelle, father, male, 25; Teresa, daughter, female, 4. (1886-TMC)

Vandelle, Francois

#460-466; Francois Vandelle, father, male, 33; Isabelle, wife, female, 43; Isabelle, daughter, female, 12; Marie, daughter, female, 10; Marguerite, daughter, female, 1; Jean Baptist, nephew, male, 16; Marie Plant, mother-in-law, female, 60. (1886-TMC)

Vandelle, Jean Baptist

Jean Baptiste Vandelle, father, 36; Margerete, wife, 33; Monique, daughter, 15; Marierose, daughter, 13; Francois, son, 9; Angel, daughter, 6; Silina, daughter, 5; Marie, daughter, 3; Jean Baptiste, son, 5 months. (September 1885-TMC)

#485-493; Jean Baptist Vandelle, father, male, 37; Marguerite, wife, female, 34; Monique, daughter, female, 16; Marie Rose, daughter, female, 14; Francois, son, male, 10; Angel, daughter, female, 7; Selina, daughter, female, 6; Marie, daughter, female, 4; Jean Baptist, son, male, 1. (1886-TMC)

#984-992; J. B. Vandall, father, 40; Margarett, wife, 37; Marie Rose, daughter, 16; Francois, son, 12; Angelic, daughter, 10; Celina, daughter, 8; Mary, daughter, 5; John B., son, 3; Patrice, son, 1. (1888-TMC)

#1026-1034; J. B. Vandall, male, father, 45; Margaret, female, wife, 39; Frank, male, son, 12; John B., male, son, 4; Patrick, male, son, 2; La Rose, female, daughter, 13; Angelic, female, daughter, 10; Celina, female, daughter, 8; May, female, daughter, 6. (1889-TMC)

#1130-1138; J. B. Vandall, male, father, 46; Margaret, female, mother, 40; Frank, male, son, 14; John B., male, son, 4; Patrick, male, son, 3; LaRose, female, daughter, 17; Angelique, female, daughter, 12; Celina, female, daughter, 10; Mary, female, daughter, 8. (1890-TMC)

Family 232; #1018-1026; J. Baptist Vandall, male, father, 45, mixed bloods on reservation; Margaret, female, wife, 42; Frank, male, son, 17; Angel, female, daughter, 14; Celina, female, daughter, 11; Mary, female, daughter, 9; John, male, son, 7; Patrick, male, son, 5; Joseph, male, son, 1-1/2. (1892-TMC)

Vandelle, Joseph

#448-451; Joseph Vandelle, father, male, 48; Julianne, wife, female, 33; Marie, daughter, female, 9; Betsy Brankin, mother-in-law, female, 60. (1886-TMC)

Vandelle, Pierre

#301; Pierre Vendelle, widower, male, 68. (1886-TMC)
#959; Pierre Vandelle, widower, male, 72. (1886-TMC)
#993; Pierre Vandall, father, 74. (1888-TMC)
#1164; Pierre Vandall, Widower, male, 70. (1890-TMC)

Vangriant, Pierre

#1139-1141; Pierre Vangriant, White Man, male, father, 54; Ursule, Chippewa, female, mother, 53; Joseph, male, son, 21. (1890-TMC)

Vetal, Baptiste

Baptiste Vebal (x), 1 man, 1 woman, 4 children, 6 total, $3.00 a share, $18.00 paid. (1868 TM annuity)

Babtiste Vetal (x), 1 man, 1 woman, 2 boys, 2 girls, 6 total, $5.00 a share, $30.00 total. (1869 TM annuity)

Baptiste Vetal (x), 1 man, 1 woman, 5 children, 7 total, $5.00 a share, $35.00 paid. (1870 TM annuity)

Batiste Vatal (x), 1 man, 1 woman, 2 children, 4 total, $8.50 a share, $34.00 paid. (1871 TM annuity)

Vilbrune [see Plouf]

Villeneuve, Pascal

Family 75; #363, Pascal Villneuve, male, single,19, mixed bloods in vicinity of reservation. (1892-TMC)

Vivier, Ambroise

Ambroise Vivier, father, 27; Genevieve, wife, 29; Marie, daughter, 9; Terese, daughter, 7; Napoleon, son, 2; daughter born June 1884, 2 months; one house, one stable, 18 tons hay, one mare, one cart, 2 cows, 5 head young stock, ½ acre potatoes. (1884-TMC)

#192-196; Ambroise Vivier, father, male, 28; Genevieve, wife, female, 31; Marie, daughter, female, 10; Terese, daughter, female, 8; Napoleon, son, male, 3. (1885-TMC)

#84-89; Ambroise Vivier, father, male, 29; Genevieve, wife, female, 31; Marie, daughter, female, 11; Terese, daughter, female, 9; Napoleon, son, male, 4; no name, daughter, female, 1 month. (1886-TMC)

Vivier, Ambroise

#962-968; Ambroise Vivier, father, 33; Genevive, wife, 35; Marie, daughter, 12; Terrace, daughter, 10; Napoleon, son, 6; Adell, daughter, 4; St.Ann, daughter, 2. (1888-TMC)

#1050-1056; Ambroise Vivier, male, father, 34; Genevive, female, wife, 28; Marie, female, daughter, 14; Theresa, female, daughter, 12; Napoleon, male, son, 6; Adel, female, daughter, 4; St.Ann, female, daughter, 3. (1889-TMC)

#1154-1161; Francois Vivier, male, father, 35; Genevieve, female, mother, 30; Marie, female, daughter, 15; Theresa, female, daughter, 13; Napoleon, male, son, 8; Adel, female, daughter, 6; St.Ann, female, daughter, 4; Philomene, female, daughter, 3 months. (1890-TMC)

Family 235; #1037-1044; male, father, 37, mixed bloods on reservation; Genevieve, female, wife, 37; Marie, female, daughter, 15; Theresa, female, daughter, 13; Napoleon, male, son, 10; Adele, female, daughter, 8; St.Ann, female, daughter, 6; Philomene, female, daughter, 3. (1892-TMC)

Vivier, Francois

Francois Vivier, father, 64; Josephte, wife, 63; one house, sone stable, one acre barley, 1/4 acre potatoes, 3 tons hay, one horse. (1884-TMC)

#73-74; Francois Vivier, father, male, 65; Josephte, wife, female, 66. (1885-TMC)

#82-83; Francois Vivier, father, male, 66; Joset, wife, female, 65. (1886-TMC)

#960-961; Francois Vivier, father, 68; Josett, wife, 73. (1888-TMC)

#1048-1049; Francois Vivier, male, Father, 72; Jossett, female, wife, 75. (1889-TMC)

#1152-1153; Francois Vivier, male, father, 75; Jossett, female, mother, 75. (1890-TMC)

Family 236; #1045-1046; Francois Vivier sr., male, father, 74, mixed bloods on reservation; Jossett, female, wife, 75. (1892-TMC)

Vivier, Francois 2d

#1162-1163; Francois Vivier No. 2, male, father, 23; Therese, female, mother, 20. (1890-TMC)

Family 223; #1027-1029; Francois Vivier 2d, male, father, 27, mixed bloods on reservation; Theresa, female, wife, 22; Mary Jane, female, daughter, 10 months. (1892-TMC)

Vivier, Louis

Louis Vivier (x), 1 man, 1 woman, 3 children, 5 total, $3.00 a share, $15.00 paid. (1868 TM annuity)

Louis Vivier (x), 1 man, 1 woman, 2 boys, 3 girls, 7 total, $5.00 a share, $35.00 total. (1869 TM annuity)

Louison Vivier (Jr.?) (x), 1 man, 1 total, $8.50 a share, $8.50 paid. (1871 TM annuity)

Wallet, Ambroise

#586-591; Ambroise Wallet, male, father, 34; Josephine, female, wife, 30; Josephine, female, daughter, 12; Adeline, female, daughter, 7; Rafel, male, son, 3; Louise Ann, female, daughter, 3. (1889-TMC-off)

Family 245; #1085-1091, Ambroise Wallet, male, father, 38, mixed bloods on reservation; Josephine, female, wife, 33; Josephine, female, daughter, 13; Adeline, female, daughter, 11; Joseph, male, son, 5; Mary, female, daughter, 3; Philomene, female, daughter, 1-1/2. (1892-TMC)

Wallett, Francois

Francois Wallett (x), 3 men, 3 women, 2 children, 8 total, $5.00 a share, $40.00 paid. (1870 TM annuity)

Wallett, Isidore

Isadore Wallett (x), 4 men, 4 women, 3 children, 11 total, $5.00 a share, $55.00 paid. (1870 TM annuity)

Wallet, Joseph

Joseph Willet (x), 1 man, 1 total, $3.00 a share, $3.00 paid. (1868 TM annuity)

Wallette, Joseph

Joseph Walette, father, 26; Virginie, wife, 24; Louis, son, 4; Adeline, daughter, 1; Elzard, son, 5 months (June 1885); one single B gun. (1884-TMC)

#539-543; Joseph Wallette, father, male, 27; Virginie, wife, female, 25; Louis, son, male, 5; Adeline, daughter, female, 2; Elzard, son, male, 5 months. (1885-TMC)

#252-256; Joseph Walette, father, male, 28; Virginia, wife, female, 26; Louis, son, male, 6; Adelina, daughter, female, 3; Elzard, son, male, 1. (1886-TMC)

Wallette, Moses

#1017-1020; Moses Wallette, father, 25; Milane, wife, 25; Francois, son, 3; Joseph, son, 1. (1888-TMC)

#1071-1073; Moses Walette, male, father, 25; Melanie, female, daughter, 25; Joseph, male, son, 2. (1889-TMC)

#1185-1188; Moses Wallett, male, father, 26; Melanie, female, mother, 29; Joseph, male, son, 3; J. B., male, son, 7 months. (1890-TMC)

Family 244; #1080-1084; Moses Wallet, male, father, a ge 30, mixed bloods on reservation; Melanie, female, wife, 30; John Baptist, male, son, 3; Joseph, male, son, 5; Josephine, female, daughter, 5 months. (1892-TMC)

Wilkie, Albert

#997; Albert Wilkie, man, 29. (1888-TMC)

#1070; Albert Wilkie, male, 30. (1889-TMC)

#1183-1184; Albert Wilkie, male, father, 31; Josephine, female, mother, 16. (1890-TMC)

Family 238; #1052-1054; Albert Wilkie, male, father, 33, mixed bloods on reservation; Josephine, female, wife, 19; Mary, female, daughter, 1. (1892-TMC)

Wilkie, Alexandre

Alexander Wilkey (x), 1 man, 1 woman, 6 children, 8 total, $3.00 a share, $24.00 paid. (1868 TM annuity)

Alex Wilkie (x), 1 man, 1 woman, 3 boys, 3 girls, 8 total, $5.00 a share, $40.00 total. (1869 TM annuity)

Alexander Wilkie (x), 3 men, 2 women, 2 children, 7 total, $5.00 a share, $35.00 paid. (1870 TM annuity)

#937-940; Alexandre Wilkie, father, male, 55; Louise, wife, female, 57; Marie, daughter, female, 14; Rosin Lafountain, granddaughter, female, 7. (1886-TMC)

#1013-1016; Alexander Wilkie, father, 57; Louise, wife, 60; Mary daughter, 16; Rosin Lafontaine, granddaughter, 9. (1888-TMC)

#1074-1076; Alexander Wilkie, male, father, 57; Louise, female, wife, 60; Rosine, female, granddaughter, 10. (1889-TMC)

#1189-1191; Alexander Wilkie, male, father, 59; Louise, female, mother, 59; Rosine, female, granddaugther, 11. (1890-TMC)

Family 243, #1077-1079; Alexander Wilkie, male, father, 59, mixed bloods on reservation; Louise, female, wife, 56; Rosin, female, daughter, 14. (1892-TMC)

Wilkie, Antoine

#843-848; Antoine Wilkie, father, male, 37; Esther, wife, female, 28; Antoine, son, male, 8; Ernestine, daughter, female, 3; Isiared, son, male, 2; Fredrick, son, male, 1. (1886-TMC)

Family 246; #1092-1099, Antoine Wilkie, male, father, 43, mixed bloods on reservation; Jossett, female, wife, 35; Antoine, male, son, 15; Mary, female, daughter, 10; Napoleon, male, son, 9; Moses, male, son, 5; John, male, son, 3; Mary Jane, female, daughter, 1-1/2. (1892-TMC)

Wilkie, Augustin Jr.

#1005-1009; Augustin Wilkie Jr., father, 33; Octavie, wife, 27; Larose, daughter, 4; Virginie, daughter, 1; Madalain, daughter, 3 months. (1888-TMC)

#1057-1061; Augustine Wilkie Jr., male, father, 37; Octavia, female, wife, 26; La Rose, female, daughter, 6; Virginie, female, daughter, 4; Madalain, female, daughter, 2. (1889-TMC)

#1165-1170; Augustin Wilkie Jr., male father, 39; Octavia, female, mother, 27; LaRose, female, daughter, 7; Virginie, female, daughter, 5; Madalaine, female, daughter, 3; Mary C., female, daughter, 2 months. (1890-TMC)

Family 241; #1064-1070; Augustine Wilkie, jr., male, father, 39, mixed bloods on reservation; Octavie, female, wife30; La Rose, female, daughter, 8; Virginie, female, daughter, 7; Madeline, female, daughter, 6; Mary Cecil, female, daughter, 3; John Augustine, male, son, 4 months. (1892-TMC)

Wilkie, Augustin Sr.

Augustin Wilkey (x), 1 man, 1 woman, 6 children, 8 total, $3.00 a share, $24.00 paid. (1868 TM annuity)

Augustin Wilkey (x), 1 man, 1 woman, 3 boys, 3 girls, 8 total, $5.00 a share, $40.00 total. (1869 TM annuity)

Augustin Wilkie (x), 3 men, 3 women, 3 children, 9 total, $5.00 a share, $45.00 paid. (1870 TM annuity)

Augustin Wilkie (x), 1 man, 1 woman, 2 children, 4 total, $8.50 a share, $34.00 paid. (1871 TM annuity)

Augustin Wilkie (x), 1 man, 1 total, $10.50 a share, $10.50 paid. (1872 TM annuity)

#418-422; Augustin Wilkie, father, male, 54; Angelic, daughter, female, 24; Madeline, daughter, female, 17; Jerome, son, male, 13; Justine, daughter, female, 8. (1885-TMC)

#384-387; Augustin Wilkie, father, male, 55; Angelic, daughter, female, 25; Madeline, daughter, female, 18; Joseph, son, male, 9 [?]. (1886-TMC)

#998-999; Augustin Wilkie Sr., father, 58; Joseph, son, 2 [22 ?]. (1888-TMC)

#1062-1063, Augustine Wilkie Sr., male, father, 59; Joseph, male, son, 18. (1889-TMC)

#1171-1172; Augustin Wilkie Sr., widower, male, father, 60; Joseph, male, son, 18. (1890-TMC)

Family 239; #1055-1056, Augustine Wilkie, sr., male, father, 61, mixed bloods on reservation; Joseph, male, son, 20. (1892-TMC)

Wilkie, Gabriel

#1010-1012; Gabriel Wilkie, father, 23; Marie, wife, 20; John B., son, 1. (1888-TMC)

#1067-1069; Gabriel Wilkie, male, father, 24; Marie, female, wife, 20; John Baptist, male, son, 2. (1889-TMC)

#1179-1182; Gabriel Wilkie, male, father, 25; Marie, female, mother, 21; John B., male, son, 3; Raphael, male, son, 6 months. (1890-TMC)

Family 242; #1071-1076; Gabriel Wilkie, male, father, 27, mixed bloods on reservation; Marie, female, wife, 25; John Baptist, male, son, 5; Raphael, male, son, 2; Pierre Alfred, male, son, 10 days; Simon Charrett, male, brother-in-law,19. (1892-TMC)

Wilkie, Jean Baptiste

Jean Bte. Wilkey (x), 1 man, 1 woman, 3 children, 5 total, $3.00 a share, $15.00 paid. (1868 TM annuity)

John B. Wilkie Jr. [Sr.?] (x), 1 man, 1 woman, 2 boys, 1 daughter, 5 total, $5.00 a share, $25.00 total. (1869 TM annuity)

Jean Bte. Wilkie (x), 2 men, 2 women, 1 child, 5 total, $5.00 a share, $25.00 paid. (1870 TM annuity)

Baptiste Wilkie (x), 1 man, 1 woman, 1 child, 3 total, $8.50 a share, $25.50 paid. (1871 TM annuity)

Wilkie, Jean Baptiste (Jr.)

Baptiste Wilkey (x), 1 man, 1 woman, 5 children, 7 total, $3.00 a share, $21.00 paid. (1868 TM annuity)

Babtiste Wilkie Jr. (x), 1 man, 1 woman, 3 boys, 3 girls, 8 total, $5.00 a share, $40.00 total. (1869 TM annuity)

Baptise Wilkie (x), 3 men, 3 women, 3 children, 9 total, $5.00 a share, $45.00 paid. (1870 TM annuity)

#377-382; Jean Baptiste Wilkie, father, male, 60; Marie, wife, female, 54; Albert, son, male, 25; Gabriel, son, male, 20; Berthelde, daughter, female, 17; Celine, daughter, female, 12. (1885-TMC)

#321-325; Jean Baptist Wilkie, father, male, 61; Marie, wife, female, 55; Albert, son, male, 26; Berthalda, daughter, female, 18; Selina, daughter, female, 13. (1886-TMC)

#1000-1004; John B. Wilkie, father, 63; Mary, wife, 51; Bathilda, daughter, 20; Celina, daughter, 15; Petronel Monnett, granddaughter, 9. (1888-TMC)

#1064-1066; J. B. Wilkie, male, father, 64; Marie, female, wife, 57; Bathilda, female, daughter, 2. (1889-TMC)

#1173-1176, 1178; J. B. Wilkie, male, father, 66; Marie, female, mother, 60; Badelde, female, daughter, 21; Petronill, female, granddaughter, 11; Rosalie, female, granddaughter, 10. (1890-TMC)

Family 237; #1047-1051; John Baptist Wilkie, male, father, 67, mixed bloods on reservation; Marie, female, wife, 61; Philomene, female, granddaughter, 14; Rosalie, female, granddaughter, 11; Clara, female, granddaughter, 9. (1892-TMC)

Wilkie, Jean Baptiste

#1192-1197; J. B. Welkie Jr., male, father, 37; Sahra, female, daughter, 36; J. B. male, son, 14; Albert, male, son, 11; Virginie, female, daughter, 7; Josephine, female, daughter, 2. (1890-TMC)

Family 240; #1057-1063; J. Baptist Wilkie, 2d, male, father, 36, mixed bloods on reservation; Sarah, female, wife, 46; John B., male, son, 16; Albert, male, son, 13; Virginie, female, daughter, 8; Joseph, male, son, 4; William, male, son, 2. (1892-TMC)

[Zaste] Jast, Alexis

#639-643; Alexis Jast [Zaste], father, male, 49; Angelic, wife, female, 39; Elise, daughter, female, 12; Matilda, daughter, female, 9; Elzard, son, male, 3. (1885-TMC)

#622-626; Alexis Jast, father, male, 50; Angelic, wife, female, 38; Eliza, daughter, female, 13; Matilda, daughter, female, 10; Patrice, son, male, 4. (1886-TMC)

#422-428; Alexis Jast, father, 57; Angelic, wife, 39; Elise, daughter, 14; Milet, daughter, 11; Patrice, son, 5. (1887-TMC)

#485-490; Alexis Jast, father, 46; Angelic, wife, 45; Elise, daughter, 16; Milet, daughter, 13; Patrice, son, 6; John Baptist, son, 2. (1888-TMC)

#536-539; Alexis Jast, male, father, 49; Angelic, female, wife, 47; Elise, female, daughter, 17; Mathild, female, daughter, 14; Elzear, male, son, 7; Jean Baptist, male, son, 3. (1889-TMC)

#588-592; Alexis Jast, male, father, 50; Angelic, female, wife, 48; Matilde, female, daughter, 15; Elzear, male, son, 8; J. B., male, son, 4. (1890-TMC)